# RUSSIAN
## PHRASEBOOK

Russian phrasebook
3rd edition – March 2000

Published by
Lonely Planet Publications Pty Ltd ABN 36 005 607 983
90 Maribyrnong St, Footscray, Victoria 3011, Australia

Lonely Planet Offices
Australia Locked Bag 1, Footscray, Victoria 3011
USA 150 Linden St, Oakland CA 94607
UK 10a Spring Place, London NW5 3BH
France 1 rue du Dahomey, 75011 Paris

Cover illustration
*Don't Look Now, Natascha!* by Patrick Marris

ISBN 1 86450 106 5

Printed through Colorcraft Ltd, Hong Kong
Printed in China

## About the Authors

Jim Jenkin wrote the 1st and 2nd editions of Lonely Planet's *Russian Phrasebook*. After completing his Honours thesis on a semantic comparison of Russian and Latvian verb prefixes and a period of research in St Petersburg, he returned to Melbourne to recommence his PhD on a semantic-functional organisation for an English-Russian dictionary. He also co-authored *English, Have A Go* (OUP), and wrote the German chapter of Lonely Planet's *Western Europe Phrasebook*.

Before six years of teaching English as a Foreign Language at the Royal Melbourne Institute of Technology, Jim tutored in Russian at Melbourne University. He now runs RMIT's 'English in Aviation' unit, teaching technical English to pilots (roger, turn left heading 320 etc) in Australia and China, and wrote a national pilot English exam for the CAAC.

Jim dreams to one day become musical arranger for a glamorous Russian singer like Alla Pugachyova.

Inna Zaitseva is an Australian citizen of Russian background. She immigrated to Australia five years ago from the city of Vinnitsa, in the Ukraine. She worked for Vinnitsa Pirogov Memorial Medical University's Scientific and Research Center.

For seven years she lived and worked in the small town of Leninsk scattered in the lifeless deserts of Kysyl-Kum in central Kazakhstan, better known as the Russian Secret Space Centre Cosmodrome Baykonur. While there, at the beginning of Perestroyka she was lucky enough to meet Mikhail Gorbachev personally.

Once in Australia, Inna acquired an Honours Degree in Arts (History) from the University of Melbourne. She is currently doing a Masters degree comparing the politics of multiculturalism in Australia, Canada and the USA. She has published a number of articles on the subject in the *Generation Journal*, as well as a number of articles in Russian in the local Russian media. She has also taught Russian at one of the Russian ethnic schools and been an actress in the Russian Theatre Group. A number of their plays have been broadcast on SBS Radio Australia.

## From the Authors
The authors would like to express their heartfelt thanks to everyone at Lonely Planet for their constant support and insightful comments. To Sally Steward and Peter D'Onghia, for their oversight and vision; to Patrick Marris for the great cover; to Vicki Webb for her help in getting the final manuscript together; and in particular to Olivier Breton, our editor, for outstanding linguistic knowledge, sharp eye, taste, judgement and understanding. Spasiba bal'shoe!

## From the Publishers
Yet another epic chapter in the lives of those involved: Vicki Webb earnt the title of 'proofer extraordinaire'; Karin Vidstrup Monk tirelessly oversaw, tied up loose ends, helped edit and generally pulled things together; Olivier Breton was the editor and Julian Chapple took time out from free living to apply his talents to layout. Patrick Marris was wholly responsible for the cover, from the amazingly evocative illustration to the layout. Natasha Vellelely did the map. Peter D'Onghia oversaw production, and Sally Steward oversaw everything. Also thanks to Fabrice Rocher and Fleur Goding for their work.

The illustrations found in the book were reproduced courtesy of Progress Publishing Group Plo. who are based in Moscow. These illustrations originally appeared in *Russian for All* by E. Stepanova et al. published in 1972.

# CONTENTS

# RUSSIAN FEDERATION

ARCTIC OCEAN

BERING SEA

SEA OF OKHOTSK

SEA OF JAPAN

NTH KOREA
STH KOREA
YELLOW SEA

BARENTS SEA

RUSSIAN FEDERATION

MONGOLIA

CHINA

KAZAKHSTAN

NORWAY
SWEDEN
FINLAND
ESTONIA
LITHUANIA
LATVIA
BELARUS
UKRAINE
GEORGIA
AZERBAIJAN

Black Sea
Caspian Sea
Aral Sea

Sankt-Peterburg
✪ MOSKVA
Nizhniy Novgorod
Kazan'
Samara
Yekaterinburg
Chelyabinsk
Novosibirsk
Saratov
Volgograd

0    500   1000 km

# INTRODUCTION

Russian is the fourth most widely-spoken language in the world, being the first language of more than 220 million people, both in the Russian Federation and large immigrant communities in Israel, the US, Canada, Germany and Australia. Russian is also spoken by most people in the former republics of the USSR, and understood throughout Eastern Europe, but you need some sensitivity in using Russian in these areas.

Despite the distribution of Russian speakers, the standard variety used in this book is universally understood. Russian has slight regional differences, but these are not generally termed 'dialects' – the pronunciation of individual sounds or vocabulary differs only slightly, similar to variations in English across the US. One reason for this uniformity is that 'standard' Russian is strictly enforced by the Russian education system – deviations from this standard are stigmatised, implying a lack of education and culture.

Russian uses the Cyrillic alphabet, which is based on Greek. St Cyril and St Methodius, Greek missionaries in the ninth century, translated the Bible into the language now known as Old Church Slavonic, using a modified alphabet to represent non-Greek sounds. This early script developed into the alphabets used in many modern Slavic languages, including Russian. Before the dissolution of the USSR in 1991, the influence and power of Russian language and culture was widespread all over the former Soviet Union, and Russian Cyrillic was introduced to transcribe various non-Slavic and even non-Indo-European languages such as Mongolian and Kurdish.

You don't need to learn the Cyrillic alphabet to use this book, but it's not difficult, and it's very useful (especially for reading placenames). Some letters even look and sound the same as English (A, E, K, M, O, T). Also, most letters only have one or two possible pronunciations, which you can predict from context. The one trap is that some letters look like English but sound totally different – the letter H sounds like 'N', and P sounds like 'R'!

INTRODUCTION

Russian is very closely related to Belarusian and Ukrainian (all being East Slavic languages) – and politics aside, a Russian and a Ukrainian can communicate quite well, each using their own language. In fact all the Slavic languages have more in common than, for example, the Germanic languages, and so Russian makes a convenient springboard for learning Czech or Polish.

Russian and English are also related, both being members of the Indo-European language family. This means you can guess the meanings of many basic words, like kot 'cat', mat' 'mother', tri 'three', malako 'milk'. Also, Russian, like English, has borrowed a great number of words from other European languages: sigareta 'cigarette', viza 'visa', paspart 'passport', tualet 'toilet', revalyutsiya 'revolution'. Interestingly (or confusingly) such words have sometimes taken on slightly different meanings: nomer means 'hotel room' as well as 'number', and mashyna usually means 'car'.

One thing you'll notice in Russia is that there's no tradition of superficial warmth in public. You may be surprised by people's offhandedness, or even rudeness, in shops and offices. However, on a personal level, Russians are the opposite – showing immense warmth and hospitality, and openness about personal matters. This paradox is partly a legacy of the Soviet regime which drove a wedge between an individual's public and private face, and Russians talk about razgavory na kukhne, a 'kitchen conversation', a term for genuine, heartfelt communication with people you trust. It's never considered rude to ask a friend about their salary or marriage.

As there's been limited contact between Russia and the west, and it's hard to find English speakers outside the major centres, your effort to speak the local language will often be greeted with surprise and interest. Fsevo kharosheva!

**INTRODUCTION**

## ABBREVIATIONS USED IN THIS BOOK

| | | | |
|---|---|---|---|
| coll | colloquial | n | neuter |
| inf | informal | pl | plural |
| f | feminine | pol | polite |
| m | masculine | sg | singular |
| ACC | accusative case | INST | instrumental case |
| DAT | dative case | NOM | nominative case |
| GEN | genetive case | PREP | prepositional case |

## HOW TO USE THIS PHRASEBOOK
### You *Can* Speak Another Language

It's true – anyone can speak another language. Don't worry if you haven't studied languages before, or that you studied a language at school for years and can't remember any of it. It doesn't even matter if you failed English grammar. After all, that's never affected your ability to speak English! And this is the key to picking up a language in another country. You don't need to sit down and memorise endless grammatical details and you don't need to memorise long lists of vocabulary. You just need to start speaking. Once you start, you'll be amazed how many prompts you'll get to help you build on those first words. You'll hear people speaking, pick up sounds from TV, catch a word or two that you think you know from the local radio, see something on a billboard – all these things help to build your understanding.

### Plunge In

There's just one thing you need to start speaking another language – courage. Your biggest hurdle is overcoming the fear of saying aloud what may seem to you to be just a bunch of sounds.

The best way to start overcoming your fear is to memorise a few key words. These are the words you know you'll be saying again and again, like 'hello', 'thank you' and 'how much?'. Here's an important hint though: right from the beginning, learn at least one phrase that will be useful but not essential. Such as 'good morning' or 'good afternoon', 'see you later' or even a conversational

**INTRODUCTION**

piece like 'lovely day, isn't it?' or 'it's cold today' (people everywhere love to talk about the weather). Having this extra phrase (just start with one, if you like, and learn to say it really well) will enable you to move away from the basics, and when you get a reply and a smile, it'll also boost your confidence. You'll find that people you speak to will like it too, as they'll understand that at least you've tried to learn more of the language than just the usual essential words.

## Ways to Remember

There are several ways to learn a language. Most people find they learn from a variety of these, although people usually have a preferred way to remember. Some like to see the written word and remember the sound from what they see. Some like to just hear it spoken in context (if this is you, try talking to yourself in Russian, but do it in the car or somewhere private, to give yourself confidence, and so others don't wonder about your sanity!). Others, especially the more mathematically inclined, like to analyse the grammar of a language, and piece together words according to the rules of grammar. The very visually inclined like to associate the written word and even sounds with some visual stimulus, such as from illustrations, TV and general things they see in the street. As you learn, you'll discover what works best for you – be aware of what made you really remember a particular word, and if it sticks in your mind, keep using that method.

## Kicking Off

Chances are you'll want to learn some of the language before you go. The first thing to do is to memorise those essential phrases and words. Check out the basics (pg 57) ... and don't forget that extra phrase (see Plunge In!). Try the sections on making conversation or greeting people for a phrase you'd like to use. Write some of these words down on a separate piece of paper and stick them up around the place. On the fridge, by the bed, on your computer, as a bookmark – somewhere where you'll see them often. Try putting some words in context – the 'How much is it?' note, for instance, could go in your wallet.

## Building the Picture

We include a chapter on grammar in our books for two reasons.

Firstly, some people have an aptitude for grammar and find understanding it a key tool to their learning. If you're such a person, then the grammar chapter will help you build a picture of the language, as it works through all the basics.

The second reason for the grammar chapter is that it gives answers to questions you might raise as you hear or memorise some key phrases. You may find a particular word is always used when there is a question – check out the grammar heading on questions and it should explain why. This way you don't have to read the grammar chapter from start to finish, nor do you need to memorise a grammatical point. It will simply present itself to you in the course of your learning. Key grammatical points are repeated throughout the book.

## Any Questions?

Try to learn the main question words (see pg 42). As you read through different situations, you'll see these words used in the example sentences, and this will help you remember them. So if you want to hire a bicycle, turn to the Bicycles section in Getting Around (use the Contents or Index pages to find it quickly). You've already tried to memorise the word for 'where' and you'll see the word for 'bicycle'. When you come across the sentence 'Where can I hire a bicycle?', you'll recognise the key words and this will help you remember the whole phrase. If there's no category for your need, try the dictionary (the question words are repeated there too, with examples), and memorise the phrases 'Please write that down' and 'How do you say ...?' (see pg 72).

## I've Got a Flat Tyre

Doesn't seem like the phrase you're going to need? Well in fact, it could be very useful. As are all the phrases in this book, provided you have the courage to mix and match them. We have given specific examples within each section. But the key words remain the same even when the situation changes. So while you may not be planning on any cycling during your trip, the first part of the phrase 'I've got ...' could refer to anything else, and there are plenty of words in the dictionary that, we hope, will fit your needs. So whether it's 'a ticket', 'a visa' or 'a condom', you'll be able to put the words together to convey your meaning.

## Finally

Don't be concerned if you feel you can't memorise words. On the inside front and back covers are the most essential words and phrases. You could also try tagging a few pages for other key phrases, or use the notes pages to write your own reminders.

# PRONUNCIATION

Many Russian sounds are also found in English, and the others aren't difficult to master. You should have little difficulty getting your meaning across.

## VOWELS

Russian vowels are relatively simple.

a   as the 'a' in 'path'
e   as the 'ye' in 'yet' (when unstressed e can be greatly reduced, sounding like the letter и)
ё   as the 'yo' in 'yonder'
и   as the 'i' in 'litre'
o   as the 'o' in 'more' when stressed; as the 'a' in 'path' when unstressed
y   as the 'u' in 'put', not as in 'cut'
ы   as the 'y' in 'busy'
э   as the 'e' in 'ten'
ю   as the 'yu' in 'yule'
я   as the 'ya' in 'yard'

## Diphthongs

The letter й, like 'y' in English, can be added after vowels to make a diphthong.

ай   as the 'igh' in 'sigh'
ей   as the 'ya' in 'yank'
ий   as the 'ee' in 'see'
ой   as the 'oy' in 'boy' when stressed; as the 'ay' in 'pay' when unstressed
ый   a longer ы

PRONUNCIATION

## CONSONANTS

| | |
|---|---|
| б | as the 'b' in 'bit' |
| в | as the 'v' in 'vet' |
| г | as the 'g' in 'goat' |
| д | as the 'd' in 'day' |
| ж | as the 's' in 'pleasure' |
| з | as the 'z' in 'zoo' |
| й | as the 'y' in 'toy'; always follows a vowel |
| к | as the 'k' in 'king' |
| л | as the 'l' in 'lump' |
| м | as the 'm' in 'my' |
| н | as the 'n' in 'not' |
| п | as the 'p' in 'put' |
| р | as the 'r' in 'rib', but rolled |
| с | as the 's' in 'sit' |
| т | as the 't' in 'ton' |
| ф | as the 'f' in 'fun' |
| х | as the 'ch' in German 'Bach' |
| ц | as the 'ts' in 'hits' |
| ч | as the 'ch' in 'chip' |
| ш | as the 'sh' in 'shop' |
| щ | as the 'sh ch' in 'fresh chips' |
| ь | 'soft sign', represented by an apostrophe (') – this palatalises the preceding consonant (ie the consonant is pronounced as if there is a very short 'y' after it). |
| ъ | 'hard sign' – this stops a vowel from palatalising a preceding consonant. It's very rare and not shown in the transliteration system in this book. |

**DID YOU KNOW ...**  In Russia, the letter ё is usually written as е – you'll only see the dots in dictionaries and textbooks for the benefit of non-native speakers.

# TRANSLITERATION SYSTEM

The transliteration system in this phrasebook is intended to assist you in learning to pronounce Russian letters and sounds, with an emphasis on practicality. Most letters are transliterated in accordance with the sounds given in the pronunciation guides above. A few exceptions are listed below.

## Vowels

e    is written e

## Diphthongs

ай    is written as ay
ей    is written as ey
ий    is written as iy
ой    written as oy (when stressed)
       as ay (when unstressed)
ый    is written as y

## Consonants

ж    is written zh
х    is written kh

PRONUNCIATION

## RUSSIAN ALPHABETICAL ORDER

АБВГДЕЖЗИЙКЛМНОПРСТУФХЦЧШЩЪЫ ЬЭЮЯ

абвгдежзийклмнопрстуфхцчшщъыьэюя

PRONUNCIATION

## SPELLING EXCEPTIONS

You don't need to read this if you're going to use the transliteration only. However, if you want to learn the script, you should learn these rules.

### Consonant Assimilation

Occasionally you'll notice that the transliteration of a consonant doesn't appear to match its corresponding letter. The word сделал 'did' is transliterated zdelal not sdelal; водка 'vodka' is votka not vodka. This is because a consonant may affect another consonant before it, both within a word or between words. For example, the unvoiced к k in водка causes the д, which is usually pronounced as d, to be pronounced as t.

If the second consonant is voiced – produced with the vocal cords (throat) vibrating – it will make the preceding consonant voiced. Likewise, if the second consonant is unvoiced – produced without vibration of the vocal cords – it will make the preceding consonant unvoiced.

The five most important pairs of sounds are:

| Voiced | | Unvoiced | |
|---|---|---|---|
| в | v | Ф | f |
| г | g | К | k |
| б | b | П | p |
| ш | sh | Щ | shch |
| д | d | Т | t |

The one exception is that there is no assimilation before вv: 'with you' с вами is pronounced s vami, not z vami.

Assimilation occurs in English too, but is much more complicated because it can go forwards as well as backwards; compare the 's' in 'cats' and 'dogs'.

## Final Consonants

Voiced consonants at the end of a word also become unvoiced: for example гид 'guide' is pronounced git not gid снег 'snow' is snek not sneg

## Hard & Soft Consonants

The consonants ж zh, ш sh, and ц ts are described as 'hard' consonants. This means that if the vowels е ye, ё yo and и i follow them, they are pronounced е, о and у

| уже | 'already' | looks like uzhye but is pronounced uzhe |
| шёл | 'went' (m) | looks like shyol but is pronounced shol |
| живу | 'I live' | looks like zhivu but is pronounced zhyvu |

On the other hand, the consonants ч ch and щ shch are 'soft'. That means that any vowel is pronounced like it has a short 'y' before it.

| часто | 'often', | looks like chasta but is pronounced chyasta |
| щи | 'cabbage soup', | looks like shchi but is pronounced shchyi |

PRONUNCIATION

| THEY MAY SAY ... | | |
| --- | --- | --- |
| Ох! | okh! | Oh! |
| Уф! | uf! | Phew!; That's terrible! |
| Опля! | oplya! | Whoops! |
| Фу! | fu! | Yuck! |
| Ой! | oy! | Ouch! |
| Цссс! | tsss! | Shh! or 'Listen, I've got a secret'. |
| На! | na! | Take this. |
| М-да | mmm – da | Well, maybe. |
| Ай-яй-яй! | ay-yay-yay! | Shame on you! |
| Ага! | aga | I see! |

PRONUNCIATION

### Irregular 'г'

The letter г in the endings -его and -ого is pronounced like a v, not g. For example, моего 'of my ...', is pronounced maevo, not maego. This also occurs in the middle of the word сегодня 'today', pronounced sevodnya

### STRESS

In Russian, as in English, one syllable is strongly stressed in longer words. Unfortunately, it's difficult to predict which one. The stressed syllable is transliterated in bold type throughout this book.

Stress affects the quality of two vowels in particular: when unstressed, e can be greatly reduced, sounding like i; and o is reduced to the a as in 'about' (this is indicated in the transliteration).

Some Russian words sound like English words except for the stress: 'taxi' is pronounced taksi, 'telephone' is telefon

---

### STRESS SNOBS

Educated Russians look down on other Russians who misplace stress. For example, pronouncing созвонимся 'let's ring each other' as sazvonimsa instead of the standard sazvanimsa, or магазин 'shop' as magazin instead of magazin, will raise the same sort of eyebrows as a double negative does in English. Russian stress snobs often trip up by hypercorrecting; that is, applying the rules of stress to sound educated, but in the wrong places. A good example is stressing all words of French origin on the final syllable: they may pronounce фундамент 'basis/foundation' as fundament whereas, in fact, in standard Russian it's fundament

## INTONATION

Intonation is when your voice goes up and down in a sentence.
This is important in Russian because you can change a statement
into a question simply by changing the intonation.

Generally with a statement, your voice stays mid-range and level
and then drops on the stressed syllable of the last word.

This is our hotel.

eta nasha gastinitsa                    Это наша гостиница.

With a 'yes/no' question, your voice stays low and level, and rises
sharply on the stressed syllable of the last word, then drops slightly.

Is this our hotel?

eta nasha gastinitsa?                   Это наша гостиница?

PRONUNCIATION

**THEY MAY SAY ...**

| | |
|---|---|
| khuem grushy okolachivaet | He's lazy.<br>(lit: he shakes pears off the tree by hitting the tree with his dick) |
| kazhdy drochit kak on khochet | You can't change someone.<br>(lit: everyone wanks how they want) |
| obossat'sa mozhna | So what? How crappy!<br>(lit: I could piss myself - not!) |

## REGIONAL ACCENTS

Russia has three main regional accents – although the differences between them are slight. The central accent, spoken around Moscow, is the standard variety, and is used in this book. In the Volga accent (north-east and east of Moscow), o is always pronounced as o, even when unstressed; so хорошо 'good' sounds like khoroshoinstead of kharasha The southern accent (south of Moscow down to the Caspian) is most noticeable in the pronunciation of г as h instead of g; so гриб 'mushroom' sounds like hrip instead of grip (Gorbachev said 'mushroom' like this).

# GRAMMAR

You don't need to read this chapter to be able to use this phrasebook, but knowing some basic grammar will certainly enable you to be more inventive with your Russian.

## WORD ORDER

As a rule, you can use English word order, subject-verb-object, in Russian and you'll be understood.

I want US dollars.
    ya kha**chu do**lary

> Я хочу доллары.
> (lit: I want dollars)

However, a pronoun object usually comes before the verb.

I know her.
    ya eyo **zna**yu

> Я её знаю.
> (lit: I her know)

You can put a noun object before the verb for emphasis.

I forgot my **passport**!
    ya **pas**part za**byl** (m)/za**by**la (f)!

> Я паспорт забыл!
> (lit: I passport forgot)

Finally, you can forget the above rules, and do something very Russian. Start your sentence with known information (to set the context), and build up to new and important information at the end.

There's **no bread** at the bakery!
    v **bu**lachnay net **khle**ba!

> В булочной нет хлеба!
> (lit: in bakery no bread)

A **salesperson** cheated me!
    mi**nya** abma**nul** pra**da**vets

> меня обманул
> Продавец!
> (lit: me cheated salesperson)

### ARTICLES

Russian has no articles, definite (the) or indefinite (a). So **турист** for example can mean 'tourist', 'a tourist' or 'the tourist'.

### NOUNS
#### Gender

Nouns in Russian are termed masculine, feminine and neuter. These are grammatical, not logical, categories – a table is masculine, a book is feminine. Happily, you can usually tell a noun's gender by its ending.

It's important to distinguish between genders, because adjectives and verbs can change depending on the gender of the noun.

- Masculine nouns end in either a consonant or **й**.

| | | |
|---|---|---|
| sport | sport | **спорт** |
| television | televizar | **телевизор** |
| tram | tramvay | **трамвай** |

- Feminine nouns end in either **a** or **я** (but not **мя**).

| | | |
|---|---|---|
| map | karta | **карта** |
| revolution | revalyutsiya | **революция** |

- Neuter nouns end in **о**, **е** or **мя**.

| | | |
|---|---|---|
| window | akno | **окно** |
| sea | more | **море** |
| (given) name | imya | **имя** |

#### Plurals

To form the plural of masculine nouns, add **ы** to a consonant, or change **й** to **и**.

| | | |
|---|---|---|
| magazine | zhurnal | **журнал** |
| magazines | zhurnaly | **журналы** |
| kiss | patseluy | **поцелуй** |
| kisses | patselui | **поцелуи** |

Some common nouns ending in a soft sign (ь).

**MASCULINE**

| day | den' | день |
| rain | dozhd' | дождь |
| potatoes | kartofel' | картофель |
| ship | karabl' | корабль |
| the Kremlin | kreml' | кремль |
| briefcase | partfel' | портфель |
| way | put' | путь |
| rouble | rubl' | рубль |

**FEMININE**

| chest | grud' | грудь |
| door | dver' | дверь |
| queue | ochered' | очередь |
| liver | pechen' | печень |
| square | ploshchad' | площадь |
| salt | sol' | соль |
| exercise book | tetrad' | тетрадь |

Feminine nouns are made plural by replacing а with ы, and я with и.

| woman | zhenshchina | женщина |
| women | zhenhschiny | женщины |
| week | nedelya | неделя |
| weeks | nedeli | недели |

Russian has a rule that ы changes to и after г, ж, к, х, ц, ч, ш and щ, which effects some masculine and feminine plurals.

| vegetable | ovashch | овощ |
| vegetables | ovashchi | овощи |

| book | kniga | книга |
| books | knigi | книги |

To form the plural of neuter nouns, о changes to а, е to я, and мя changes to ена.

| dish | blyuda | блюдо |
| dishes | blyuda | блюда |
| building | zdanie | здание |
| buildings | zdaniya | здания |
| time | vremya | время |
| times | vremena | времена |

Nouns ending in ь (see Consonants on pg 16) can be either masculine or feminine, and unfortunately you just have to learn which are which. Luckily there aren't too many.

## CASE

Case indicates the function of a noun or pronoun in a sentence, such as subject, object, indirect object. English usually indicates case by word order – 'the dog bit the man' means the dog did the biting, while 'the man bit the dog' means the man did it. However, some English pronouns change their form according to case: 'he' is a subject and 'him' is an object, so you can say 'the dog bit him' but not 'the dog bit he'.

Russian nouns as well as pronouns change their endings according to case. There are six cases in total.

## Nominative

The nominative case indicates the subject of the sentence, and also the form you'll find listed in dictionaries.

guide git гид

The guide bought the tickets.

   git kupil bilety            Гид купил билеты.
                                     (lit: guide-NOM bought tickets)

Nominative is also used for the complement of a subject in the present tense. In English, a complement is the part of a sentence that comes after 'am/are/is'. In sentences such as the following, the verb 'to be' usually isn't necessary in Russian.

doctor vrach врач

My brother is a doctor.

   moy brat vrach             Мой брат врач.
                                       (lit: my brother doctor-NOM)

## Accusative

This is the direct object of the sentence. Masculine and neuter nouns usually stay the same, but feminine nouns change a to y, and я to ю.

fish ryba рыба

I want fish.

   ya khachu rybu            Я хочу рыбу.
                                       (lit: I want fish-ACC)

tower bashnya башня

We saw the tower.

   my videli bashnyu         Мы видели башню.
                                       (lit: we saw tower-ACC)

The accusative is also used for nouns which follow the prepositions в, v 'to/into' and на, na 'to/onto'. The preposition в is used for enclosed spaces as well as cities and countries.

| to the supermarket | v universam | в универсам |
| to Moscow | v maskvu | в Москву |

The preposition на is used for big, flat areas like streets and squares, as well as events like concerts and lectures.

to Red Square
  na krasnuyu ploshchat'    на Красную площадь
to a concert
  na kantsert    на концерт

## Genitive

This refers to possession, a bit like the English 'of' or the possessive 's' ('s), except that the possessor always comes after the possessed. The genitive is marked on the possessor.

John's passport
  paspart dzhona    паспорт Джона
  (lit: passport John-GEN)

For masculine nouns, the suffix a is added to a consonant or й is changed to я.

| restaurant | restaran | ресторан |

the manager of the restaurant
  administratar restarana    администратор ресторана
  (lit: manager restaurant-GEN)

For feminine nouns, a changes to ы, and я to и.

| fur coat | shuba | шуба |

the price of the fur coat
  tsena shuby    цена шубы
  (lit: price fur-coat-GEN)

Neuter nouns change o to a, e to я and мя to мени.

| word | slova | слово |

the word's meaning
  znachenie slova    значение слова
  (lit: meaning word-GEN)

GRAMMAR

The genitive is also used after the prepositions bez **без** 'without', okala **около** 'near', do **до** 'before' and posle **после** 'after'.

| lunch | a bet | обед |
| after lunch | posle abeda | после обеда |

Nouns which follow these expressions of quantity also take the genitive case.

| a little; few; some | nemnoga | немного |
| a lot; much; many | mnoga | много |
| How much; | | |
| How many? | skol'ka? | Сколько? |
| kilo | kilagram | килограмм |
| box | karopka | коробка |
| tin | banka | банка |
| packet | pachka | пачка |
| cup | chyashka | чашка |
| bottle | butylka | бутылка |
| glass | stakan | стакан |

## Dative

This is the indirect object, or the person to whom something is given or shown.

I gave my ticket to the conductor.

ya dala bilet pravadniku   Я дала билет проводнику.
(lit: I gave ticket conductor-DAT)

Masculine nouns add **y** to a consonant and change **й** to **ю**.

policeman       militsianer     **милиционер**
Show your papers to the policeman!

predyavite dakumenty   Предъявите документы
militsianeru!          милиционеру!
(lit: show papers policeman-DAT)

## DATIVE VERBS

| | | |
|---|---|---|
| to help | pamagat'<br>pamoch' | помогать<br>помочь |
| to promise | abeshchat'<br>paabeshchat' | обещать<br>пообещать |
| to telephone | zvanit'<br>pazvanit' | звонить<br>позвонить |
| to disturb | meshat'<br>pameshat' | мешать<br>помешать |
| to harm | vredit'<br>pavredit' | вредить<br>повредить |
| to sympathise with | sachusvavat'<br>pasachusvavat' | сочувствовать<br>посочувствовать |
| to envy; | zavidavat'<br>pazavidavat' | завидовать<br>позавидовать |

Feminine nouns change a and я to е.

girl/girlfriend    devushka    девушка
I gave sweets to my girlfriend.
    ya dal kanfety devushke    Я дал конфеты девушке.
                         (lit: I gave sweets girl-DAT)

Neuter nouns change о to у, е to ю and мя to ени. As the dative case usually requires a noun to be animate, neuter nouns won't often appear in the dative.

A number of important verbs need to be followed by an object in the dative, not accusative as you might expect.

### Instrumental

The instrumental case is used to express means or 'that with which
something is done', for example:

You need to write with a pen.
   nada pisat' ruchkay     Надо писать ручкой.
                            (lit: must write pen-INST)

Its other common use is after the preposition с 'together with; in
the company of', for example:

I went with my brother.
   ya khadil s bratam     Я ходил с братом.
                         (lit: I went with brother-INST)

Masculine nouns add -ом to a final consonant or change a final й
to ем.

texta        falamaster       фломастер

I wrote the letter with a texta.
   ya napisala pis'mo     Я написала письмо
   flamasteram          фломастером.
                        (lit: I wrote letter texta-INST)

Feminine nouns change а to ой or я to ей.

Anna        Anna       Анна
We had dinner with Anna.
   my pauzhynali s annay     Мы поужинали с Анной.
                      (lit: we had-dinner with Anna-INST)

Neuter nouns change о to ом, е to ем and мя to менем.

bread with butter
   khlep s maslam       хлеб с маслом
                      (lit: bread with butter-INST)

### Prepositional

Confusingly, the prepositional case is not used after every preposition. It got its name because its *only* function is to be used after certain prepositions, primarily в, v 'in/at' and на, na 'on/at'.

The prepositions в and на are also used with the accusative case (see pg 27), to describe motion towards something. When used in the prepositional case, however, they describe location (where something is).

GRAMMAR

He's at the shop.
  on v magazine

Он в магазине.
(lit: he v shop-PREP)

He went to the shop.
  on khadil v magazin

Он ходил в
магазин.
(lit: he went v shop-ACC)

The difference between в and на is the same as for the accusative (see pg 27).

| in Moscow | v maskve | в Москве |
| in class | na uroke | на уроке |

The prepositional case is also used after o to mean 'about'.

a book about sport
  kniga a sporte

книга о спорте
(lit: book a sport-PREP)

Masculine nouns take the ending e in the prepositional case.

house    dom  дом
I live in a house.
    ya zhyvu v dome          Я живу в доме.
                             (lit: I live in house-PREP)

Feminine nouns change a and я to e.

car    mashyna  машина
My money is in the car.
    mai den'gi v mashyne     Мои деньги в машине.
                             (lit: my money in car-PREP)

Neuter nouns change o to e and e to и.

wine    vino  вино
In vino veritas.
    istina v vine            Истина в вине.
                             (lit: truth in wine-PREP – a
                             common expression in Russia!)

## PRONOUNS
### You

Unlike English, Russian has two words for 'you':

ты    ty    familiar form which is traditionally used only with a
            child or good friend.
вы    vy    polite form used with strangers and acquaintances.

This phrasebook generally uses вы except in the Interests and Dat-
ing chapters, where you're more likely to be on friendly terms. In
post-Soviet Russia, however, the situation is changing, and young
Russians may use ты on first meeting. Even Russians can have
trouble deciding which is appropriate!

    Remember that ты is only a singular form. When addressing
two or more people, use вы whether you know them well or not.

## CAPITALS

Unlike English, Russian doesn't use a capital
letter in the word for 'I', я ya.

### Possessive Pronouns

Most possessive adjectives (my, your etc) also change according
to gender and number.

Here's my passport.
vot moy paspart

Вот мой паспорт.
(lit: here my-masc passport)

Here's my visa.
vot maya viza

Вот моя виза.
(lit: here my-fem visa)

Here's my birth certificate.
vot mayo
svidetel'stva
a razhdenii

Вот моё
свидетельство
о рождении.
(lit: here my-neuter certificate)

Here are my belongings.
vot mai veshchi

Вот мои вещи.
(lit: here my-pl belongings)

## PRONOUNS

|      | I/me          | you (sg)       | he          | she        | It          |
|------|---------------|----------------|-------------|------------|-------------|
| NOM  | я<br>ya       | ты<br>ty       | он<br>on    | она<br>ana | оно<br>ano  |
| ACC  | меня<br>menya | тебя<br>tebya  | его<br>evo  | её<br>eyo  | его<br>evo  |
| GEN  | меня<br>menya | тебя<br>tebya  | его<br>evo  | её<br>eyo  | его<br>evo  |
| DAT  | мне<br>mne    | тебе<br>tebe   | ему<br>emu  | ей<br>ey   | ему<br>em   |
| INST | мной<br>mnoy  | тобой<br>taboy | им<br>im    | ей<br>ey   | им<br>im    |
| PREP | мне<br>mne    | тебе<br>tebe   | нём<br>nyom | ней<br>ney | нём<br>nyom |

## PLURAL PRONOUNS

|      | we           | you (pl)      | they         |
|------|--------------|---------------|--------------|
| NOM  | мы<br>my     | вы<br>vy      | они<br>ani   |
| ACC  | нас<br>nas   | вас<br>vas    | их<br>ikh    |
| GEN  | нас<br>nas   | вас<br>vas    | их<br>ikh    |
| DAT  | нам<br>nam   | вам<br>vam    | им<br>im     |
| INST | нами<br>nami | вами<br>vami  | ими<br>imi   |
| PREP | нас<br>nas   | вас<br>vas    | них<br>nikh  |

GRAMMAR

## POSSESSIVE PRONOUNS

|  | m | f | n | pl |
|---|---|---|---|---|
| **MY** | мой | моя | моё | мои |
|  | moy | maya | mayo | mai |
| **YOUR** (sg) | твой | твоя | твоё | твои |
|  | tvoy | tvaya | tvayo | tvai |
| **HIS/ITS** | его | его | его | его |
|  | evo | evo | evo | evo |
| **HER** | её | её | её | её |
|  | eyo | eyo | eyo | eyo |
| **OUR** | наш | наша | наше | наши |
|  | nash | nasha | nashe | nashy |
| **YOUR** (pl) | ваш | ваша | ваше | ваши |
|  | vash | vasha | vashe | vashy |
| **THEIR** | их | их | их | их |
|  | ikh | ikh | ikh | ikh |

### Case

Like nouns, pronouns change according to case.

I know him.
ya evo znayu

Я его знаю.
(I-NOM him-ACC know)

Could you please give me a map?
dayte mne,
pazhalsta, kartu

Дайте мне,
пожалуйста, карту.
(give me-DAT please map)

Note that pronouns starting with a vowel add an initial н after a preposition.

We went with them.
my s nimi ezdili

Мы с ними ездили.
(lit: we c them-INST went)

## A WORD ABOUT CASE

In English, we're able to recognise the 'role' of a noun in a sentence (whether it's a subject, direct object or indirect object) by its position in the sentence and/or by the use of prepositions. However, like Latin, German and many other languages, Russian employs what are known as 'cases' to make these distinctions. Different 'case endings' (inflections) act like labels on the nouns to indicate their role and their relationship to other words in a sentence. The case endings of the other words in the sentence, such as the articles, adjectives, adverbs or pronouns, must agree in number and gender with the case ending of the noun to which they refer.

Russian has six cases, and their application relates to grammatical usage in English. Here's a brief explanation of each case.

**1.** The **nominative** case refers to the the subject of a verb in a sentence, and is also the form you'll find in a dictionary. It indicates what or who is performing an action:

**The thief who robbed the banker's house with a gun** gave presents to his friends on the inside. (the thief 'robbed' and the thief 'gave').

**2.** The **accusative** is the direct object of a sentence. It indicates what or whom the verb refers to. Here it indicates what was given:

The thief who robbed the banker's house with a gun gave **presents** to his friends on the inside.

## A WORD ABOUT CASE

**3.** The **genitive** case refers to possession, a bit like the English 'of' or the possessive 's' ('s). It indicates **whose** or **of what/of whom**:

The thief who robbed **the banker's** house with a gun gave presents to his friends on the inside.

**4.** The **dative** case is the indirect object, or the person to whom something is given or shown:

The thief who robbed the banker's house with a gun gave presents **to his friends** on the inside.

**5.** The **instrumental** is used to express means or 'that with which something is done':

The thief who robbed the banker's house **with a gun** gave presents to his friends on the inside.

**6.** The **prepositional** case describes location (where something is), and to give the sense of 'about/ concerning':

The thief who robbed the banker's house with a gun gave presents to his friends **on the inside**.

GRAMMAR

## ADJECTIVES

Adjectives change their endings to agree with the nouns they qualify
in gender, number and case. You can usually avoid using adjectives
in cases other than the nominative, so only gender and number
are dealt with here.

Adjectives in any dictionary will be given in the masculine form.
They always end in ый, stressed ой, or ий.

| new (m) | novy | новый |
| expensive (m) | daragoy | дорогой |
| (dark) blue (m) | siniy | синий |

You can use this form with any masculine noun, before the noun
or after 'to be'.

| computer (m) | kamp'yuter | компьютер |

This is a new computer.
| eta novy kamp'yuter | Это новый компьютер |

The computer is new.
| kamp'yuter novy | Компьютер новый |

With feminine nouns, change the endings ый and ой to ая, and
ий to яя.

| new (f) | novaya | новая |
| expensive (f) | daragaya | дорогая |
| (dark) blue (f) | sinyaya | синяя |
| book (f) | kniga | книга |

This is a new book.
| eta novaya kniga | Это новая книга. |

With neuter nouns, change the endings ый and ой to ое, and
ий to ее.

| new (n) | novae | новое |
| expensive (n) | daragoe | дорогое |
| (dark) blue (n) | sinee | синее |
| coat (n) | pal'to | пальто |

The coat's expensive.
| pal'to daragoe | Пальто дорогое. |

To form the plural for all genders, change the endings ый and ой to ые, and ий to ие.

Mushrooms are delicious.
    griby fkusnye             Грибы вкусные.

All the ties are dark blue.
    fse galstuki sinie         Все галстуки синие.

## This & That

The demonstrative pronouns etat, этот 'this' and tot, тот 'that' also change according to gender and number.
    They become:

before feminine nouns эта, eta and та, ta
before neuter nouns это, eta and то, to
before plurals эти, eti and те, te

city (m)  gorat  город
This city is beautiful.
    etat gorat krasivy       Этот город красивый.

dog (f)  sabaka  собака
That dog is dangerous.
    ta sabaka apasnaya      Та собака опасная.

Don't confuse these with the pronoun это eta, used to introduce something or someone, corresponding to 'this is' or 'these are'. The pronoun это never changes, no matter what noun follows.

This is a house.
    eta dom              Это дом.

This is a dog.
    eta sabaka          Это собака.

These are mushrooms.
    eta griby            Это грибы.

## COMPARATIVES

To form a comparative, just replace the ending of the adjective with ee. 'Than' in Russian is chem чем.

interesting interesny интересный
Music's more interesting than movies.

| | |
|---|---|
| muzyka interesnee | Музыка интереснее, |
| chem kino | чем кино. |

### Irregular Comparatives

| | | |
|---|---|---|
| better | luchshe | лучше |
| worse | khuzhe | хуже |
| bigger | bol'she | больше |
| smaller | men'she | меньше |
| older | starshe | старше |
| further | dal'she | дальше |
| cheaper | deshevle | дешевле |
| more expensive | darozhe | дороже |

## SUPERLATIVES

To form the superlative, add самый, samy, before an adjective. This is the equivalent to saying 'the most ...' or 'the -est' in English. Both самый and the adjective take normal adjective endings.

| | | |
|---|---|---|
| beautiful | krasivy | красивый |
| city (m) | gorat | город |
| river (f) | reka | река |

Moscow is the most beautiful city.

| | |
|---|---|
| maskva – samy | Москва – самый |
| krasivy gorat | красивый город. |
| | (lit: Moscow most beautiful city) |

The Volga is the most beautiful river.

| | |
|---|---|
| volga – samaya | Волга – самая |
| krasivaya reka | красивая река. |
| | (lit: Volga most beautiful river) |

GRAMMAR

## QUESTIONS
### Yes/No Questions

You don't need to change the sentence structure in Russian to form a yes/no question; only the intonation needs to be changed. (See pg 15.)

This is my room.
    eta moy nomer
                Это мой номер.
                (lit: this my room)

Is this my room?
    eta moy nomer?
                Это мой номер?
                (lit: this my room)

| Question Words | | |
| --- | --- | --- |
| How? | kak? | Как? |
| How much/many? | skol'ka? | Сколько? |
| What? | shto? | Что? |
| When? | kagda? | Когда? |
| Where? | gde? | Где? |
| Where to? | kuda? | Куда? |
| Who? | kto? | Кто? |
| Why? | pachemu? | Почему? |

Just use a question word at the start of the sentence.

He's reading.
    on chitaet
                Он читает.
                (lit: he read)

What's he reading?
    shto on chitaet?
                Что он читает?
                (lit: what he read?)

The museum's closed.
    muzey zakryt
                Музей закрыт.
                (lit: museum closed)

Why is the museum closed?
    pachemu muzey zakryt?
                Почему музей закрыт?
                (lit: why museum closed?)

GRAMMAR

## VERBS

Verbs in dictionaries almost always end in -ать or -ить. This is called the 'infinitive' or 'dictionary form'. You'll usually need to change the ending before using the verb in a sentence.

### Present

For verbs ending in -ать, drop the -ть and add endings as follows:

| to read | chita-t' | читать |
|---|---|---|
| I read | ya chita-yu | я читаю |
| you (sg, inf) read | ty chita-esh' | ты читаешь |
| he/she reads | on/ana chita-et | он/она читает |
| we read | my chita-em | мы читаем |
| you (pl) read | vy chita-ete | вы читаете |
| they read | ani chita-yut | они читают |

For verbs ending in -ить, drop all three letters and add these endings:

| to speak (inf) | gavar-it' | говорить |
|---|---|---|
| I speak | ya gavar-yu | я говорю |
| you (ty) speak | ty gavar-ish' | ты говоришь |
| he/she speaks | on/ana gavar-it | он/она говорит |
| we speak | my gavar-im | мы говорим |
| you (pl) speak | vy gavar-ite | вы говорите |
| they speak | ani gavar-yat | они говорят |

I read Russian.
  ya chitayu pa-ruski

Я читаю по-русски.
(lit: I read Russian)

Do you speak Russian?
  vy gavarite pa-ruski?

Вы говорите
по-русски?
(lit: you (pl, pol) speak Russian?)

### Past

Past-tense endings depend on the gender and number of the subject, not the person. Drop the -ть ending (not the и, unlike the present tense) and add -л after a masculine subject, -ла after a feminine subject, -ло after a neuter subject, and -ли after a plural.

to buy  kupit' **купить**
I (m) bought a dictionary.
  ya kupil slavar'

Я купил словарь.
(lit: I bought dictionary)

I (f) bought a dictionary.
  ya kupila slavar'

Я купила словарь.

My brother bought vodka.
  moy brat kupil votku

Мой брат купил водку.

We bought tickets.
  my kupili bilety

Мы купили билеты.

### Future

Russian often uses the present tense to refer to the future. You can make yourself clear by specifying the time. (See pg 50 for more details.)

to work  rabotat' **работать**

I'm working tomorrow.
  ya rabotayu zaftra

Я работаю завтра.
(lit: I work tommorow)

## KEY VERBS

| | | |
|---|---|---|
| to be able (can) | moch' smoch' | мочь смочь |
| to agree | saglashat'sa saglasit'sa | соглашаться согласиться |
| to be | byt' | быть |
| (not used in the present tense, see pg 51) | | |
| to bring | prinasit' prinesti | приносить принести |
| to come (on foot) | prikhadit' priyti | приходить прийти |
| (by vehicle) | priezhat' priekhat' | приезжать приехать |
| to cost | stoit' | стоить |
| to depart (leave) (on foot) | ukhadit' uyti | уходить уйти |
| (by vehicle) | uezhat' uekhat' | уезжать уехать |
| to do | delat' zdelat' | делать сделать |
| to go (on foot) | itti payti | идти пойти |
| (by vehicle) | ekhat paekhat' | ехать поехать |
| to have (see pg 52) | | |

GRAMMAR

## KEY VERBS

| | | |
|---|---|---|
| to know | znat' | знать |
| to like/love | lyubit' | любить |
| to make | delat'zdelat' | делать |
| | | сделать |
| to meet | fstrechat' | встречать |
| | fstretit' | встретить |
| to need (see pg 54) | | |
| to prefer | pretpachitat' | предпочитать |
| | pretpachest' | предпочесть |
| to return | vazvrashchyat'sa | возвращаться |
| | vernut'sa | вернуться |
| to say | gavarit' | говорить |
| | skazat' | сказать |
| to see | videt' | видеть |
| | uvidet' | увидеть |
| to stay | astanavlivat'sa | останавливаться |
| | astanavit'sa | остановиться |
| to take | brat' | брать |
| | vzyat' | взять |
| to understand | panimat' | понимать |
| | panyat' | понять |
| to want | khatet' | хотеть |
| | zakhatet' | захотеть |

GRAMMAR

## KEY VERBS CONJUGATED

| to be able/can | moch' | мочь |
|---|---|---|
| I can | ya magu | я могу |
| you can (sg/inf) | ty mozhesh' | ты можешь |
| he/she can | on/ana mozhet | он/она может |
| we can | my mozhem | мы можем |
| (pl/pol)you can | vy mozhete | вы можете |
| they can | ani mogut | они могут |

| to buy | pakupat' | покупать |
|---|---|---|
| I buy | ya pakupayu | я покупаю |
| you (sg/inf) buy | ty pakupaesh' | ты покупаешь |
| he/she buys | on/ana pakupaet | он/она покупает |
| we buy | my pakupaem | мы покупаем |
| you (pl/pol) buy | vy pakupaete | вы покупаете |
| they buy | ani pakupayut | они покупают |

| to eat | est' | есть |
|---|---|---|
| I eat | ya em | я ем |
| you (sg/inf) eat | ty esh' | ты ешь |
| he/she eats | on/ana est | он/она ест |
| we eat | my edim | мы едим |
| you (pl/pol) eat | vy edite | вы едите |
| they eat | ani edyat | они едят |

| to go (on foot) | itti | идти |
|---|---|---|
| I go | ya idu | я иду |
| you (sg/inf) go | ty idyosh' | ты идёшь |
| he/she goes | on/ana idyot | он/она идёт |
| we go | my idyom | мы идём |
| you (pl/pol) go | vy idyote | вы идёте |
| they go | ani idut | они идут |

GRAMMAR

## KEY VERBS CONJUGATED

| to go (by vehicle) | ekhat' | ехать |
|---|---|---|
| I go | ya edu | я еду |
| you (sg/inf) go | ty edesh' | ты едешь |
| he/she goes | on/ana edet | он/она едет |
| we go | my edem | мы едем |
| you (pl/pol) go | vy edete | вы едете |
| they go | ani edut | они едут |

| to live | zhyt' | жить |
|---|---|---|
| I live | ya zhyvu | я живу |
| you (sg/inf) live | ty zhyvyosh' | ты живёшь |
| he/she lives | on/ana zhyvyot | он/она живёт |
| we live | my zhyvyom | мы живём |
| you (pl/pol) live | vy zhyvyote | вы живёте |
| they live | ani zhyvut | они живут |

GRAMMAR

## Reflexive Verbs

These verbs bring the action back onto the subject – a bit like 'myself' or 'yourself' in English. It's formed by adding the ending -ся (-сь after a vowel) to the verb form.

He's washing the car.
on moet mashynu      Он моет машину.

He's washing (himself).
on moetsa      Он моется.

Some verbs that don't seem to have this reflexive meaning do, in fact, take the reflexive ending. The most common are:

| | | |
|---|---|---|
| to study; | | |
| to be a student | zanimat'sa | заниматься |
| go to school; | | |
| to be a school student | uchit'sa | учиться |
| to be afraid | bayat'sa | бояться |
| to hope | nadeyat'sa | надеяться |
| She goes to school. | ana uchitsa | Она учится. |
| I hope so. | nadeyus', | Надеюсь, |
| | shto da | что да. |

## ADVERBS

Adverbs are formed by replacing the adjective ending with o. The adverb usually comes before the verb.

wonderful      prekrasny      прекрасный
You play wonderfully.
vy prekrasna igraete      Вы прекрасно играете.
(lit: you wonderfully play)

You can also use the adverb form to make a whole sentence. This refers to a general state of affairs, not to a particular person or thing.

| | | |
|---|---|---|
| Wonderful! | prekrasna! | Прекрасно! |
| How interesting! | interesna! | Интересно! |
| It's hot. | zharka | Жарко. |
| Good/OK. | kharasho | Хорошо. |

## PERFECTIVE/ IMPERFECTIVE

In the dictionary at the end of this phrasebook – and in any good
dictionary – you'll notice that there are usually two Russian
infinitives given for any English verb, for example:

to read
  chitat'/prachitat'                     читать/прочитать
to do
  delat'/zdelat'                         делать/сделать
to receive
  paluchat'/paluchit'                    получать/получить

The first form is called the 'imperfective' – this is used when we're
not interested whether an action is finished or not. The activity
may be habitual (indicated in English by words like 'often' and
'every day'), or still in progress (indicated by the suffix '-ing').

I often read in Russian.
  ya **chyasta** chitayu            Я часто читаю
  pa-**ruskiy**                     по-русски.
                                    (lit: I often read-IMP Russian)

What are you doing?
  shto ty **delaesh**'?             Что ты делаешь?
                                    (what you do-IMP)

I'm reading.
  ya chitayu                        Я читаю.
                                    (I read-IMP)

Yesterday I did some reading.
  ya (f) chitala fchera             Я читала вчера.
                                    (lit: I read-IMP yesterday)

The second form is termed 'perfective' – this can emphasise that a
past action has been completed.

I finished the book yesterday.
  ya prachitala (f)                 Я прочитала
  knigu fchera                      книгу вчера.
                                    (I read-PERF book yesterday)

I got a letter.

> ya paluchil (m) pis'mo

Я получил письмо.
(I got-PERF letter)

A verb in the perfective tense can't refer to an activity in the present, because current actions are by nature unfinished. If you put present tense endings on a perfective verb, it always refers to what will be completed in the future.

I'm going to read
all the instructions.

> ya prachitayu fse
> instruktsii

Я прочитаю все
инструкции.
(I read-PERF all instructions)

**NO ARTICLES**

Russian doesn't have words for 'the' and 'a'.

## TO BE

The verb 'to be' is usually omitted in the present tense.

to be byt'                        быть

I'm a doctor.

> ya vrach

Я врач.
(lit: I doctor)

Moscow's big.

> maskva bal'shaya

Москва большая.
(lit: Moscow big)

She's in the bank.

> ana v banke

Она в банке.
(lit: she in bank)

In the past tense, быть changes like any normal verb (see pg 44). Note that the feminine ending -a is stressed.

I (m) was in Vladivostok.
ya byl va vladivastoke

Я был во
Владивостоке.

I (f) was in Novosibirsk.
ya byla v navasibirske

Я была в
Новосибирске.

They were in the bus.
ani byli v aftobuse

Они были в
автобусе.

## TO HAVE

Although Russian has a verb 'to have', Russians almost always use the formula:

у, u + genitive noun/pronoun + есть, est' (lit: near me is ...)

This is followed by the nominative (the dictionary form of the noun).

I have (a car).
u menya est' (mashyna)

У меня есть (машина).
(lit: u me-GEN est' car-NOM)

Do you have (a map)?
u vas est' (karta)?

У вас есть (карта)?
(lit: u you-GEN est' map-NOM)

## NEGATIVES

Russian negatives are easy. Just add the word не ne before the verb.

I read Russian.
ya chitayu pa-ruski

Я читаю по-русски.
(lit: I read Russian)

I don't read Russian.
ya ne chitayu pa-ruski

Я не читаю по-русски.
(lit: I ne read Russian)

GRAMMAR

## MODALS
### Can (Able To)

Russian has two equivalents to the English verb 'can'. The verb мочь, moch' implies physical capability.

I can't lift this.
ya ne magu eta padnyat'  Я не могу это поднять.
(lit: I not can this lift)

Can you help me?
vy mozhete pamoch' mne?  Вы можете помочь мне?
(lit: you can help me)

The verb уметь, umet' implies ability due to training.

I can't speak German.
ya ne umeyu gavarit'  Я не умею говорить
pa-nemetski  по-немецки.
(lit: I not can speak German)

Can you cook?
vy umeete gatovit'?  Вы умеете готовить?
(lit: you can cook?)

### Can/Cannot (Permission)

To express whether or not something is permitted, Russian uses можно, mozhna meaning 'it is permitted' and нельзя, nel'zya 'it is not permitted'. These are impersonal, meaning that they don't have a subject, and can either be used on their own or with a verb (in the infinitive).

| | | |
|---|---|---|
| May I? | mozhna? | Можно? |
| Can I come in? | mozhna vayti? | Можно войти? |
| | | (lit: mozhna enter) |
| No, you can't. | nel'zya | нельзя. |
| You're not allowed to drink here. | zdes' nel'zya pit' | Здесь нельзя пить. |
| | | (lit: here nel'zya drink) |

### MAY I?

To ask permission to do something (enter; take a photo; use the telephone...) just ask...

| | | |
|---|---|---|
| May I? | mozhna? | Можно? |

### Must/Have To

The verbs 'must' and 'have to' are expressed as a type of adjective in Russian, dolzhen должен. Endings change according to gender and number, but vary slightly from those of standard adjectives. They're followed by an infinitive.

I (m) have to ...
  ya dolzhen ...        я должен ...
I (f) have to ...
  ya dalzhna ...        я должна ...
You (pol) have to ...
  vy dalzhny ...        вы должны ...

GRAMMAR

You have to check in.
  vy dalzhny
  zaregistrirovat'sa

Вы должны
зарегистрироваться.
(lit: you dalzhny register)

Do I (m) have to give you
my passport?
  ya dolzhen dat'
  vam paspart?

Я должен дать
вам паспорт?
(lit: I-NOM dolzhen
give you passport?)

## Want/Would Like

Russian, like English, has both polite and more direct forms of
saying you would like something.

I want ... (direct)
  ya khachu

я хочу

I'd like ... (pol)
  ya by khatel (m)/
  khatela (f)

я бы хотел/
хотела

I want dollars, not roubles.
  ya khachu dolary,
  a ne rubli

Я хочу доллары,
а не рубли.
(lit: I want dollars but not roubles)

I (f) would like to buy a jumper.
  ya by khatela kupit'
  dzhemper

Я бы хотела купить
джемпер.
(lit: I would like buy jumper)

GRAMMAR

## NOW GO FORTH

Don't hold back – make up your own sentences! As we've seen, Russian word order is similar to English – you can translate word for word, and still stand a good chance of being understood. Secondly, Russian grammar is in some ways easier than English – there are no articles, and 'to be' is not used in the present tense. A sentence like 'I tourist', ya turist, is perfectly grammatical in Russian. Thirdly, if you find grammar intimidating, don't worry too much – context will get your meaning across, even if you get the verb ending wrong.

GRAMMAR

# Встреча    MEETING PEOPLE

There are two ways of saying 'you' in Russian – the polite вы, vy and the familiar ты, ty (see pg 33 of the Grammar chapter if you want to know more). This chapter is about first encounters, so all the examples have the safer vy form. However, younger people generally use ты, ty.

## YOU SHOULD KNOW

## Вам следует знать

Hello.
  zdrastvuitye!

Здравствуйте!

Goodbye.
  da svidanya!

До свидания!

Yes.
  da

Да.

No.
  niet

Нет.

Excuse me.
  izvinite, pazhalsta

Извините, пожалуйста.

Please.
  pazhalsta

Пожалуйста.

Thank you.
  spasiba

Спасибо.

Many thanks.
  bal'shoe spasiba

Большое спасибо.

## GREETINGS & GOODBYES   Приветствия

The all-purpose greeting zdravstvuitye! is appropriate for most occasions. Expressions like 'good morning' or 'good afternoon' are quite polite and are best reserved for more formal occasions. A more informal greeting – like English 'hi'– is privet! (some young women say privetik!), while Russian men will greet a group of male friends with zdarova muzhiki! (lit: hello peasants!).

Hello.
    zdrastvuitye!                     Здравствуйте!
Hi.
    privet!                           Привет!
Good morning.
    dobrae utro!                      Доброе утро!

Good afternoon.
    dobry den'!                       Добрый день!

Good evening.
    dobry vecher!                     Добрый вечер!

Hey lads! (or similar greeting)
    zdarova muzhiki!                  Здорово, мужики!
                                      (lit: hello peasants)

Goodbye.
    da svidanya!                      До свидания!
All the best.
    vsevo kharosheva!                 Всего хорошего!
Bye!
    paka!                             Пока!
See you tomorrow.
    da zavtra!                        До завтра!
See you next time.
    da vstrechi!                      До встречи!

In Russian, an exclamation mark is conventionally used after greetings and imperatives.

MEETING PEOPLE

## CIVILITIES                Будьте вежливы!

It's unusual to ask a stranger 'How are you?' – in Russian it means you really want to know. But with friends it's a different story – there's a range of expressions you can use to get them to tell you what's been happening. If you ask a friend how they are, the answer will be truthful and detailed.

How are things?
    kak dela?                  Как дела?

How's life?
    kak zhizn'?                Как жизнь?

What's new?
    shto novava?               Что нового?

Good thanks.
    spasibo, kharasho!         Спасибо, хорошо!

Great.
    atlichna!                  Отлично!

There's nothing new.
    nichevo novava netu!       Ничего нового нету!

Don't ask!
    ne sprashivayte!           Не спрашивайте!

Thank you (very much).
    (bol'shoye) spasiba        (Большое) спасибо.

You're welcome.
    pazhalsta                  Пожалуйста.

Sorry.
    izvinitye, pazhalsta       Извините,
                               пожалуйста.

Can I get through?
    mozhna praiti?             Можно пройти?

May I?; Do you mind?
    mozhna?                    Можно?

**Forms of Address**    Разрешите обратиться?

In Russian, as in English, you can always use your first name in friendly, informal situations. In fact, Russians have an extensive range of 'diminutives', or affectionate forms, for most first names. Inna, for example, can be Innusya, Innochka, Inka, Innulya, Inn, Inneska, to name a few variations.

The usual polite form of address is the person's first name together with their patronymic (a middle name derived from their father's name), as in Sergey Ivanovich, meaning 'Sergey, son of Ivan'. Therefore when you're introduced, try to remember both first name and patronymic

> ### CAPITAL LETTERS
>
> Unlike English, Russian doesn't use capital letters for languages and nationalities.

– the family name is less important. Russian does have equivalents of 'Mr' and 'Mrs', but these are only used in official contexts or with foreigners.

| | | |
|---|---|---|
| Mr | gospodin | господин |
| Mrs | gospozha | госпожа |

## BODY LANGUAGE    Язык жестов

Here are some tips on some distinctively Russian gestures:

- a movement like cutting your throat with your hand means 'I'm full!'
- flicking your throat with your index finger indicates drinking (usually 'Let's drink' or 'He's drunk').
- gesturing in one direction with your head means 'Follow me' (with various connotations, maybe to have a serious talk, or a fight, or it could be a sexual proposition)
- a hand placed on one hip means 'So what?'
- tapping your forehead with your finger means someone is stupid (so be careful before you attempt this!)

# FIRST ENCOUNTERS   Будьте знакомы!

Shaking hands is a given between men. However, a man generally doesn't extend his hand to a woman – it's up to the woman to offer first. Remember to take off your glove before you shake hands, and don't forget the superstition about not shaking hands over the threshold of a doorway.

I'd like to introduce you to ... (pol)
   paznakom'tes', eto ...      Познакомтесь, это ...

This is ... (inf)
   eta ...      Это ...

Nice to meet you.
   ochen' priyatna      Очень приятно.

What's your name?
   kak vas zavut?      Как Вас зовут?

My name is ...
   menya zavut ...      Меня зовут ...

I had a great time.
   ya provyol (m)/provela (f)      Я провёл/провела
   ochen' kharoshae vremia      очень хорошее время.

It was nice to meet you.
   byla priyatna      Было приятно
   paznakomitsa      познакомиться.

Hope to see you again
   nadeyus', uvidimsa      Надеюсь, увидимся
   yeshcho      еще.

Say hello to ...
   peredavayte privyet ...      Передавайте привет ...

## COMPLICATED COMMAS

Just as English speakers judge people on their spelling, Russians judge people on their correct or incorrect use of commas – they're the literacy litmus test.

MEETING PEOPLE

## MAKING CONVERSATION                     Поговорим?

Today's Russia is unrecognisable compared with that of the Soviet era. Previously, there was a range of taboo topics – even talking about what a certain factory produced, or how someone was given a position at work, could lead to a chat with the KGB.

Now people say what they want, wherever they want, and how loudly they want. Politics has become the most talked about topic of all. Even on your first meeting, it's quite acceptable to ask someone in detail about their work, salary and family. Just take care with issues of nationality and religion – Russia is a multiethnic society and its citizens come from a wide range of ethnic and cultural backgrounds.

Do you live here?
   vy zdes' zhyvyote ?          Вы здесь живёте?
Where are you going?
   daleko sabirayetes'?     Далеко собираетесь?
                            (lit: going far?)

What are you doing?
   chem vy zanimaetes'?    Чем вы занимаетесь?
What do you think (about) ...?
   shto vy dumaete (o) ...?  Что вы думаете (о) ...?
Can I take your photo?
   mozhno vas            Можно вас
   sfotografiravat'?       сфотографировать?
What's this called?
   kak eta nazyvaetsia?    Как это называется?
How beautiful!
   kak krasiva!           Как красиво!

Great!
zdorava!
Здорово!

It's very nice here.
zdes' tak kharasho!
Здесь так хорошо!

We love it here!
nam nravvitsa zdyes'!
Нам нравится здесь!

What a cute baby!
kakoye kharosheye dityo!
Какое хорошее дитё!

Have you been waiting long?
(in a queue)
vy davno stoitye?
Вы давно стоите?

That's strange.
stranna!
Странно!

That's funny!
smeshno!
Смешно!

Are you here on holiday?
vy zdes' v otpuske?
Вы здесь в отпуске?

I'm here ...          ya zdes' ...
Я здесь ...
 for a holiday   v otpuske
  в отпуске
 to study    uchus'
  учусь
 on business   pa biznesu
  по бизнесу
(biznes is a new concept in Russia and is usually used to refer
to foreigners or young entrepreneurs)

How long are you here for?
kak dolga vy zdes'
nakhodites'?
Как долго вы здесь
находитесь?

I'm/We're here for ... weeks/days.
ya/my zdes' ... nedel'/
dney
Я/Мы здесь ... недель/
дней

Do you like it here?
vam zdes' nravitsa?
Вам здесь нравится?

I/We like it here very much.
mne/nam zdes' ochen'
nravitsa
Мне/Нам здесь очень
нравится.

## USEFUL PHRASES

Полезные
выражения

Sure.
  nesamnena — Несомненно.

Just a minute.
  minutku — Минутку.

It's OK.
  kharasho/ladna — Хорошо/Ладно.

It's important.
  eta vazhna — Это важно.

It's not important.
  eta ne vazhna — Это не важно.

It's possible.
  eta vazmozhna — Это возможно.

It's not possible.
  eta nevazmozhna — Это невозможно.

Look!
  pasmatrite! — Посмотрите!

Listen!
  paslushayte! — Послушайте!

I'm ready.
  ya gatof (m)/gatova (f) — Я готов/Я готова.

Are you ready?
  vy gatovy ? — Вы готовы?

Good luck!
  shasliva! — Счастливо!

Just a second!
  sekundachku! — Секундочку!

MEETING PEOPLE

### TAKE YOUR SHOES OFF!

It's considered polite to take off your gloves
before shaking hands. Shoes should be removed
when entering someone's home, and you'll be
given a pair of slippers tapachki тапочки.

# NATIONALITIES        Гражданство

Nationality is defined by the United Nations Convention as 'owing allegiance to a government and being entitled to its protection'. However, in Russia, nationality is synonymous with ethnicity. In the former USSR, 'Jewish' and 'Chechen', for example, were given as nationality in internal passports. This hints at some fairly controversial attitudes you may encounter in Russia.

Many country names are similar to English.

| Where are you from? | atkuda vy? | Откуда вы? |
|---|---|---|
| I'm from ... | ya iz ... | Я из ... |
| Australia | afstralii | Австралии |
| Canada | kanady | Канады |
| England | anglii | Англии |
| Europe | evropy | Европы |
| India | indii | Индии |
| Ireland | irlandii | Ирландии |
| Japan | yaponii | Японии |
| the USA | se she a | США |

## CAUTION!

If you praise an item in someone's home – like a vase or a book – your host might offer it to you!

MEETING PEOPLE

| I come from a/the ... | ya iz ... | Я из ... |
|---|---|---|
| I live in a/the ... | ya zhyvu v ... | Я живу в ... |
| city | gorade | городе |
| countryside | sel'skay mesnasti | сельской местности |
| mountains | garakh | горах |
| village | derevne | деревне |
| I live on the seaside. | ya zhyvu na marskom paberezh'e | Я живу на морском побережье. |

## VISITING FRIENDS

When visiting a Russian home, it's customary to take a small gift. There are no strict rules – a bottle of wine or vodka, a box of chocolates, or flowers are fine. However, it's generally appreciated if you put some thought into it. If it's winter, a gift of fruit shows that you've made an effort. If you decide on flowers, take an odd number as superstition has it that even numbers are only for funerals. Children will appreciate small gifts such as chocolate bars.

## CULTURAL DIFFERENCES

How do you do this in your country?

kak eta delayut v vashey strane?

Is this a local or national custom?

eta mesny ili natianal'ny abychay?

I don't want to offend you.

ya ne khachu vas abidet'

I'm sorry, it's not the custom in my country.

izvinite, no eta ne abychay mayey strany

I'm not accustomed to this.

ya ne privyk (m)/ privykla (f) k etamu

I don't mind watching, but I'd prefer not to participate.

ya ne vazrazhayu pasmatret', no predpachitayu ne uchasvavat'

## Культурные различия

Как это делают в вашей стране?

Это местный или национальный обычай?

Я не хочу вас обидеть.

Извините, но это не обычай моей страны.

Я не привык/ привыкла к этому.

Я не возражаю посмотреть, но предпочитаю не участвовать.

**MEETING PEOPLE**

## VERY SUPERSTITIOUS

Don't shake hands or pass anything across the threshold of a door – it's believed you will have an argument!

### AGE

Возраст

| How old ...? | skol'ka ... let? | Сколько ... лет? |
|---|---|---|
| are you (to a child) | tebe | тебе |
| are you (to an adult) | vam | Вам |
| is your son/ daughter | vashemu synu/ docheri | вашему сыну/ дочери |

| I'm ... years old. | mne ... let | мне ... лет |

See Numbers & Amounts, pg 199, for your age.

### OCCUPATIONS

Профессии

You may hear the word inzhener 'engineer', in many surprising contexts. For example, inzhener-ekonomist roughly corresponds to 'accountant', and an inzhener pa tekhniki bezapasnasti i akhrane truda (lit: engineer in labour safety and protection technology), is a health and safety officer.

What work do you do?
   kem vy rabotaete?     Кем вы работаете?
I'm unemployed.
   ya bezrabotny (m)/     Я безработный/
   bezrabotnaya (f)     безработная.

MEETING PEOPLE

| I'm a/an ... | ya ... | я ... |
|---|---|---|
| artist | khudozhnik (m) | художник |
| | khudozhnitsa (f) | художница |
| businessperson | biznesmen (m) | бизнесмен |
| | zhenshchina-<br>biznesmen (f) | женщина-<br>бизнесмен |
| doctor | vrach | врач |
| engineer | inzhener | инженер |
| journalist | zhurnalist (m) | журналист |
| | zhurnalistka (f) | журналистка |
| lawyer | yurist | юрист |
| mechanic | mekhanik | механик |
| nurse | medsestra | медсестра |
| scientist | uchyony (m) | учёный |
| | uchyonaya (f) | учёная |
| student | student (m) | студент |
| | studentka (f) | студентка |
| teacher | uchitel'(m) | учитель |
| | uchitel'nitsa (f) | учительница |
| waiter | afitsyant (m) | официант |
| | afitsyantka (f) | официантка |
| writer | pisatel' (m) | писатель |
| | pisatel'nitsa (f) | писательница |

| What are you studying? | shto vy izuchaete? | Что вы изучаете? |
|---|---|---|
| I'm studying ... | ya izuchayu ... | Я изучаю ... |
| art | iskusstva | искусства |
| arts/humanities | gumanitarnye nauki | гуманитарные науки |
| business | biznes | бизнес |
| teaching | pedagogiku | педагогику |
| engineering | inzhenernye naukii | инженерные науки |
| languages | yazyki | языки |
| law | yurisprudentsiyu | юриспруденцию |
| medicine | meditsynu | медицину |
| Russian | ruskiy yazyk | русский язык |
| science | estestvennye nauki | естественные науки |

## RUDE GESTURES

Caution! The following gestures are all offensive:
- pointing at a person with your index finger (use an outstretched hand if you need to indicate something.)
- putting your thumb between your first and second fingers (called dulya, meaning 'get stuffed').
- putting a hand on your arm and raising your fist (the rudest of all).

## FEELINGS                          Чувства

Some Russians consider overt display of feelings as an indication of a poor upbringing. However, it depends on how well you know someone – Russian friendships are very open and intimate.

| I'm ... | ya ... | Я ... |
|---|---|---|
| afraid | bayus' | боюсь |
| angry | zlyus' | злюсь |
| boiling/hot | pagibayu at zhary | погибаю от жары |
| cold | zamyors (m) | замерз |
|  | zamyorzla (f) | замерзла |
| grateful | blagadaren (m) | благодарен |
|  | blagadarna (f) | благодарна |
| happy | shyasliv (m) | счастлив |
|  | shyasliva (f) | счастлива |
| hungry | goladen (m) | голоден |
|  | galadna (f) | голодна |
| in a hurry | speshu | спешу |
| keen to ... | khachu ... | хочу ... |
| sad | grushchyu | грущу |
| sleepy | sonny (m) | сонный |
|  | sonnaya (f) | сонная |
| sorry (condolence) | skarblyu | скорблю |
| sorry (regret) | sazhaleyu | сожалею |
| thirsty | khachu pit' | хочу пить |
| tired | ustal (m) | устал |
|  | ustala (f) | устала |
| well | chustvuyu sebya kharasho | чувствую себя хорошо |
| worried | bespakoyus' | беспокоюсь |
| What about you? | a vy? | А вы? |

## LANGUAGE DIFFICULTIES

## Языковой барьер

Do you speak English?
  vy gavarite
  pa-angliyski?

Вы говорите
по-английски?

Yes, I do.
  da

Да.

No, I don't.
  net

Нет.

Does anyone speak English?
  kto-nibud' gavarit
  pa-angliyski?

кто-нибудь говорит
по-английски?

I speak a little.
  ya nemnoga gavaryu

Я немного говорю.

Do you understand?
  vy panimaete?

Вы понимаете?

I (don't) understand.
  ya (ne) panimayu

Я (не) понимаю.

Could you speak more slowly?
  gavarite pa-medlenee,
  pazhalsta

Говорите по-медленнее,
пожалуйста.

Could you repeat that?
  paftarite,
  pazhalsta

Повторите,
пожалуйста.

Please write it down.
  zapishyte, pazhalsta

Запишите, пожалуйста.

How do you say (...)
in Russian?
  kak budet
  (...) pa-ruski

Как будет
(...) по-русски?

How do you pronounce this?
  kak eta praiznositsa?

Как это произносится?

What does (...) mean?
  shto abaznachaet
  slova (...) ?

Что обозначает
слово (...)?

## BAD RUSSIAN

Swearing in Russian is called mat' meaning
'mother' (see why below!). Just be careful ...

Get fucked!
(lit: fuck your mother)
   yob tvayu mat'!    Ёб твою мать!

Fuck off!
   atebis'!    Отъебись!

What the fuck for?
   na khuya?    На хуя?

Fuck all. (nothing)
   ni khuya    Ни хуя.

It's crap!
   khuynya!    Хуйня!

Dickhead!
   zalupa!    Залупа!

MEETING PEOPLE

## WRITING LETTERS

## Как написать письмо?

Once you get back home, you may want to drop a line to people you met. Here are a few lines to help you. See pg 77 for addresses.

| | |
|---|---|
| Dear ... | Дорогой (m) ...!<br>Дорогая (f) ...!<br>Дорогие (pl) ...! |
| I'm sorry it's taken me so long to write. | Извините за долгое молчание. |
| Thank you so much for your hospitality. | Огромное спасибо за Ваше гостеприимство. |
| I miss you. (sg/inf) | Мне тебя так не хватает! |
| I miss you. (pl) | Мне Вас так не хватает! |
| I had a fantastic time. | Я отлично провёл (m)/ провела (f) время. |
| My favourite place was ... | Больше всего мне понравилось ... |
| I hope to visit again. | Я надеюсь приехать еще раз. |
| Say 'hello' to ... (and ...) | Передавайте привет ... (и ...) |
| I'd love to see you again. | Мне бы очень хотелось увидеться снова. |
| Write soon! | Жду ответа!<br>(lit: I wait for reply) |
| All the best. | Всего хорошего. |
| With love. | С любовью. |

MEETING PEOPLE

# Средства передвижения

# GETTING AROUND

Despite Russia's size – when the sun's setting in Kaliningrad, it's rising in Vladivostok – the USSR has developed a comprehensive transport network of planes and trains. All cities have cheap and extensive public transport systems, including metros. The main problem you'll have with getting around is the weather.

## FINDING YOUR WAY

## Поиски нужного направления

| Where's the ...? | gde ...? | Где ...? |
|---|---|---|
| bus station | aftavagzal | автавакзал |
| train station | vagzal | вакзал |
| road to ... | daroga na ... | дорога на ... |

How do we get to ...?
kak dabrat'sa k ...?　　　Как добраться к ...?

Can we walk there?
tuda mozhna dabrat'sa　　Туда можно добраться
peshkom?　　　　　　　пешком?

Can you show me (on the map)?
pakazhyte mne　　　　　Покажите мне
pazhalsta (na karte)　　　пожалуйста (на карте).

How else can we get there?
kak eshcho tuda mozhna　Как ещё туда можно
dabrat'sa?　　　　　　　добраться?

| What ... is this? | shto eta za ...? | Что это за ...? |
|---|---|---|
| street | ulitsa | улица |
| city | gorat | город |
| village | derevnya | деревня |

GETTING AROUND

| What time does | f katoram chasu | В котором часу |
| the ... leave/arrive? | pribyvaet/ | прибывает/ |
| | atpravlyaetsa ... | отправляется ... |
| aeroplane | samalyot | самолёт |
| boat | karabl' | корабль |
| bus | aftobus | автобус |
| train (intercity) | poest | поезд |
| train (local/metro) | elektrichka | электричка |

## DIRECTIONS                Направления

While walking around town, you'll quickly realise that Russian drivers can be scary – a zebra crossing is apparently a signal for cars to speed up. By law, you have to cross a major road using an underground or above-ground pedestrian crossing, perekhot переход.

| Turn ... | pavernite ... | поверните ... |
| right | naprava | направо |
| left | naleva | налево |
| at the next corner | za ugal | за угол |
| at the traffic lights | na svetafore | на светофоре |

## Where? Где?

| straight ahead | pryama | прямо |
| behind | zzadi | сзади |
| in front of | fperedi | впереди |
| far | daleko | далеко |
| near | bliska | близко |
| opposite | naprotif | напротив |
| here | zdes' | здесь |
| there | tam | там |
| north | sever | север |
| south | yuk | юг |
| east | vastok | восток |
| west | zapat | запад |

# ADDRESSES                          Адреса

Russian addresses are written in reverse order to those in the west,
beginning with the country, then the city, the street, and finally
the name. It may be drawing a long bow, but some have surmised
this is to do with the individual being subsumed by the collectivist
Russian state.

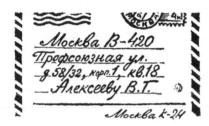

Москва В-420
Профсоюзная ул.
д.58/32, корп.1, кв.18
Алексееву В.Т.
Москва к-24

The first line states the city, in this case Moscow, moskva
Москва. This is followed by the postcode. The next line states
the street and ends with with ул, short for 'street'. Common
words for street names are:

| avenue | praspekt | проспект (пр.) |
| boulevard | bul'var | бульвар (бул.) |
| lane | pereulak | переулок (пер.) |
| square | ploshchyat' | площадь (пл.) |
| street | ulitsa | улица (ул.) |

The third line starts with д, short for дом, dom. This can mean
'house', but here it's used to mean a whole housing complex. The
next word корп., short for корпус, korpus, specifies one
building within the complex. Then кв. – квартира kvartira –
is the actual apartment. The final line is the person's name.

GETTING AROUND

## BUYING TICKETS

## Покупка билетов

Where can I buy a ticket?
gde mozhna kupit'
bilet na ...?

Где можно купить
билет на …?

We want to go to ...
my khatim paekhat' v ...

Мы хотим поехать в …

Do I need to book?
braniravat' nuzhna?

Бронировать нужно?

I need to book a seat to ...
mne nuzhna
zabraniravat'
mesta na ...

Мне нужно
забронировать
место на …

It's full.
fse mesta prodany

Все места проданы.

Can I get a stand-by ticket?
mozhna kupit'
stayachiy bilet?

Можно купить
стоячий билет?

| I'd like (a) ... | mne nada ... | Мне надо ... |
|---|---|---|
| one-way ticket | bilet v | билет в |
| | adin kanets | один конец |
| return ticket | bilet v | билет в |
| | oba kantsa | оба конца |
| two tickets | dva bileta | два билета |
| student's fare | bilet dlya | билет для |
| | studentaf | студентов |
| child's fare | detskiy bilet | детский билет |
| pensioner's fare | bilet dlya | билет для |
| | pensianeraf | пенсионеров |
| 1st class | f pervam klasse | в первом классе |
| 2nd class | va ftarom klasse | во втором классе |

# AIR   Путешествие самолётом

For all flights in Russia, foreigners must show their passport and
pay at a special rate. If you're with Intourist, you'll sit in a separate
lounge and may be seated before the locals.

Is there a flight to (Ryazan')?
  est' reys na (ryazan')?

Есть рейс на (Рязань)?

When's the next flight
to (Novgorod)?
  kagda sleduyushchiy reys
  na (novgarat)?

Когда следующий рейс
на (Новгород)?

How long does the flight take?
  kakava pradalzhytel'nast'
  palyota?

Какова
продолжительность
полёта?

What time do I have to check
in at the airport?
  f katoram chasu
  nachinaetsa registratsiya?

В котором часу
начинается
регистрация?

Where's the baggage claim?
  gde bagazhnae adelenie?

Где багажное
отделение?

GETTING AROUND

## At Customs  На таможне

All valuables and money must be declared when you enter Russia,
and you may be required to reconcile these with receipts when
you leave the country.

I have nothing to declare.
mne **ne**cheva dekla**ri**ravat'

Мне нечего
декларировать

I have something to declare.
mne **nuzh**na **shto**ta
zadekla**ri**ravat'

Мне нужно что-то
задекларировать

Do I have to declare this?
eta **nuzh**na
dekla**ri**ravat'?

Это нужно
декларировать?

This is all my luggage.
eta ves'moy ba**gazh**

Это весь мой багаж.

I didn't know I had to declare it.
ya ne znal (m)/**zna**la (f),
shto eta **na**da
dekla**ri**ravat'

Я не знал/знала,
что это надо
декларировать.

## BUS, TRAM, TROLLEY-BUS

To use a bus, tram or trolleybus, you'll need to buy a
strip of tickets which, once inside, you punch in a machine
on the wall. If it's crowded, you can ask someone to
punch it for you.

Please punch my ticket.
za**kam**pasti**ru**yte moy
bi**let**, **pazh**alsta

Закомпостируйте мой
билет, пожалуйста.

## BUS  Поездка на автобусе

Buses run the streets of most cities, but due to the permanent shortage of fuel, expect delays in schedules. Cities have a faster (but more expensive) alternative to standard buses called a 'fixed route taxi' marshrutnae taksi or marshrutka, which is actually a minibus and is usually red. Subways, or metro as they're called in Russia, are found in both St Petersburg and Moscow.

Where's the bus stop?
gde aftabusnaya astanofka? Где автобусная
остановка?

Which bus goes to ...?
kakoy aftobus idyot v ...? Какой автобус
идёт в ...?

Does this bus go to ...?
etat aftobus idyot v ...? Этот автобус
идёт в ...?

How often do buses come?
kak chyasta khodyat Как часто ходят
aftobusy? автобусы?

Where do I get the bus for ...?
gde astanavlivaetsa Где останавливается
aftobus na ...? автобус на ...?

| What time is the ... bus? | kagda budit ... aftobus ? | Когда будет ... автобус ? |
|---|---|---|
| next | sleduyushchiy | следующий |
| first | pervy | первый |
| last | pasledniy | последний |

Could you let me know
when we get to ...?
abyavite, pazhalsta, Объявите, пожалуйста,
kagda my padedem k ...? когда мы подъедем к...?

GETTING AROUND

## TRAIN                                           Поезд

Russian trains have four classes:

spal'ny vagon                              спальный вагон
   sleeping car – compartment shared by two or three people,
   with washing facilities
kupeyny vagon                              купейный вагон
   a simpler compartment for four
platskartny vagon                          плацкартный вагон
   the most basic sleeper with benches
obshchiy vagon                             общий вагон
   where you sit squeezed up on benches – usually for short
   distances (which for Russians can mean up to a day)

What station is this?
   kakaya eta astanofka?                   Какая это остановка?
What is the next station?
   kakaya sleduyushchaya                   Какая следующая
   astanofka?                              остановка?
Does this train stop at (...)?
   etat poest                              Этот поезд
   astanavlivaetsa v (...)?                останавливается в (...)?
The train is delayed/cancelled.
   poest apazdyvaet/atmenili               Поезд опаздывает/
                                           отменили.

How long will it be delayed?
   na skol'ka on apazdyvaet?               На сколько он
                                           опаздывает?

How long does the trip take?
   skol'ka vremeni uydyot                  Сколько времени уйдёт
   na etu paestku?                         на эту поездку?

| SIGNS |
| --- |

| ПЕРЕХОД НА ... | THIS WAY TO ... |
| ВЫХОД В ГОРОД | WAY OUT |

## TO ENTER THE METRO

To enter the metro, you need to buy a token, zheton, or a monthly ticket, called yediny bilet (which can be used on all forms of transport). Once through the turnstile, you can stay on the system for as long as you like.

A token, please.
adin zheton, pazhalsta       Один жетон,
                             пожалуйста.

monthly ticket
yediny bilet                 единый билет

Which line goes to (...)?
kakaya liniya idyot v (...)?  Как попасть в ...?

Is it a direct route?
eta pryamaya elektrichka?    Это прямая
                             электричка?

Is that seat taken?
eta mesta zanyata?           Это место занято?

I want to get off at ...
ya khachu vyti v ...         Я хочу выйти в ...

| | | |
|---|---|---|
| local/metro | elektrichka | электричка |
| intercity | poest | поезд |

GETTING AROUND

## TAXI                                    Такси

It's risky accepting a ride from drivers who approach you – find an official taxi with a checkerboard pattern down the side. Even then be prepared to be taken on roundabout routes and told that the meter 'isn't working'. Taxis parked outside hotels often charge US dollars. Don't expect the driver to do anything extra (like lift your luggage) without extra payment.

Is this taxi free?
svaboden?                              Свободен?
Please take me to ...
atvezite menya,                        Отвезите меня,
pazhalsta, v ...                       пожалуйста в ...
How much does it cost
to go to ...?
skol'ka stoit                          Сколько стоит
daekhat' do ...?                       доехать до ...?
How much is the fare?
skol'ka s menya?                       Сколько с меня?

### Instructions  Инструкции

Straight ahead!
pryama!                                Прямо!
The next street to the left/right.
na sleduyushchey                       На следующей улице
ulitse pavernite naleva/               поверните налево/
naprava!                               направо!
Please slow down.
ne tak bystra, pazhalsta!              Не так быстро,
                                       пожалуйста!
Please wait here.
padazhdite zdes', pazhalsta!           Подождите здесь,
                                       пожалуйста!
Stop here!
astanavites' zdes!                     Остановитесь здесь!
Stop at the corner.
astanavites' za uglom!                 Остановитесь за углом!

## THREE MEN OF ACTION

Stalin, Khruschev and Brezhnev were on a train. Suddenly it stopped in the middle of nowhere, and they were very annoyed. 'Shoot the driver!' ordered Stalin, but still the train didn't move. 'Rehabilitate the driver!' commanded Kruschev, but still nothing happened. Finally Brezhnev stood up and ordered: 'Pull down the blinds and pretend we're moving!'.

## BOAT                                    На корабле

A parakhot, пароход, is technically a steamboat (as opposed to a teplakhot, теплоход, which is powered by petrol), but is used generally to mean any ship. For river travel, Russia has a massive network of hydrofoils. A hydrofoil's called a ракета raketa, which literally means 'rocket'.

Where does the boat leave from?
    atkuda atkhodit karabl'?

Откуда отходит корабль?

What time does the boat arrive?
    f katoram chasu prikhodit karabl'?

В котором часу приходит корабль?

GETTING AROUND

## CAR    Путешествие на автомобиле

Hiring a car may be an option in Russia, although the choice is limited. You can get anywhere by car, as long as you can find fuel! Fill up the tank at every opportunity.

Petrol is measured in octane level aktanavae chislo, октановое число.

Where can I rent a car?
gde vzyat' mashynu
f prakat?

Где взять машину в прокат?

How much is it daily/weekly?
skol'ka stoit
adnadnevny/
nedel'ny prakat?

Сколько стоит однодневный/ недельный прокат?

Does that include insurance?
syuda fkhodit strakhofka?

Сюда входит страховка?

Can I park here?
zdes' mozhna pastavit'
mashynu?

Здесь можно поставить машину?

How long can we park here?
skol'ka zdes' mozhna
stayat'?

Сколько здесь можно стоять?

Does this road lead to ...?
eta daroga vedyot v ...?

Эта дорога ведёт в ...?

Where's the next petrol station?
gde blizhayshaya
zaprafka?

Где ближайшая заправка?

Please fill the tank.
zapolnite bak,
pazhalsta

Заполните бак, пожалуйста.

... litres.
... litraf

... литров

| Please check the ... | praver'te, pazhalsta ... | Проверьте, пожалуйста ... |
|---|---|---|
| oil | masla | масло |
| water | vodu | воду |
| tyre pressure | davlenie kalyos | давление колес |

**Useful Words** Полезные слова и выражения

| air | vozdukh | воздух |
| battery | batareya | батарея |
| brakes | tarmaza | тормоза |
| clutch | stseplenie | сцепление |

| driver's licence | vaditel'skiye prava | водительские права |
| engine | dvigatel' | двигатель |
| garage (for repairs) | aftamasterskaya | автомастерская |
| indicator | pavaroty | повороты |
| lights | fary | фары |
| main road | asnavnaya daroga | основная дорога |
| oil | masla | масло |
| puncture | prakol | прокол |
| radiator | radiatar | радиатор |
| roadmap | karta darok | карта дорог |
| seatbelt | remen' bezapasnasti | ремень безопасности |
| self-service | samaabsluzhyvanie | самообслуживание |
| speed limit | agranichenie skorasti | ограничение скорости |
| tyres | pakryshki | покрышки |
| windscreen | labavoe steklo | лобовое стекло |

GETTING AROUND

## Car Problems Поломка автомобиля

We need a mechanic.
nam nuzhen aftamekhanik    Нам нужен
автомеханик.

What make is it?
kakaya eto marka
mashiny?    Какая это марка
машины?

The car broke down at ...
mashyna slamalas' v ...    Машина сломалась в ...

The battery is flat.
batareya razryadilas'    Батарея разрядилась.

The radiator is leaking.
radiatar pratekaet    Радиатор протекает.

I have a flat tyre.
u menya lopnula pakryshka    У меня лопнула
покрышка.

The ... is overheating.
... peregrevaetsa    ... перегревается.

The ... isn't working.
... ne rabotaet    ... не работает.

I've lost my car keys.
ya pateryal (m)/pateryala (f)    Я потерял/потеряла
klyuchi at mayey    ключи от моей
mashyny    машины.

I've run out of petrol.
u menya konchilsa benzin    У меня кончился
бензин.

## MEETING PEOPLE

A good way to meet people on train trips is to
choose platskartny vagon, the most basic sleeper
carriage. Bring plenty of food on board to share
with your fellow passengers.

# BICYCLE                     На велосипеде

Russians don't ride bikes much, and you don't often see them
around big cities. Long-distance cycling in Russia has its positives
– great scenery, not many hills, not many cars, lots of cafes on
major roads. The drawbacks include bad roads, bad drivers and
bad gangs.

Is it within cycling distance?
 tuda mozhna daekhat'          Туда можно доехать
 na velasipede?                на велосипеде?
Where can I hire a bicycle?
 gde mozhna vzyat'             Где можно взять
 velasipet na prakat?          велосипед на прокат?
Where can I find second-hand
bikes for sale?
 gde pradayutsa                Где продаются
 paderzhannye                  подержанные
 velasipedy?                   велосипеды?
How much is it for 24 hours?
(standard period of hire)
 skol'ka stoit prakat          Сколько стоит прокат
 f sutki?                      в сутки?
I've got a flat tyre.
 u menya lopnula shyna         У меня лопнула шина.

GETTING AROUND

| | | |
|---|---|---|
| bike | velasipet | велосипед |
| brakes | tarmaza | тормоза |
| cycling | katat'sa na velasipede | кататься на велосипеде |
| handlebars | rul' | руль |
| helmet | shlem | шлем |
| inner tube | kamera | камера |
| lights | fary | фары |
| mountain bike | gorny velasipet | горный велосипед |
| padlock | navisnoy zamok | нависной замок |
| pump | nasos | насос |
| puncture | prakol | прокол |
| racing bike | spartivny velasipet | спортивный велосипед |
| saddle | sedlo | седло |
| tandem | tandem | тандем |
| wheel | kaleso | колесо |

# Жильё  ACCOMMODATION

## FINDING ACCOMMODATION

## В поисках жилья

| | | |
|---|---|---|
| I'm looking for a ... | ya ishchu ... | Я ищу ... |
| camping ground | kemping | кемпинг |
| hotel | gastinitsu | гостинницу |
| motel | matel' | мотель |
| room for rent | komnatu dlya syoma | комнату для съёма |
| youth hostel | apshchezhytie | общежитие |

| | | |
|---|---|---|
| Where can I find a ... hotel? | gde ... gastinitsa? | Где ... гостиница? |
| good | kharoshaya | хорошая |
| nearby | blizhayshaya | ближайшая |
| clean | chistaya | чистая |

| | | |
|---|---|---|
| Where's the ... hotel? | gde ... gastinitsa? | Где ... гостиница? |
| best | luchshaya | лучшая |
| cheapest | samaya deshovaya | самая дешёвая |

What's the address?
kakoy eyo adres?      Какой её адрес?
Could you write down the address please?
napishyte, pazhalsta, adres      Напишите, пожалуйста, адрес

---

### PLUG PROBLEMS

There's a truism that Russian hotels never have a plug in the washbasin. However, it's not due to any shortage – it's because Russians believe it's more hygienic to wash under running water.

ACCOMMODATION

## BOOKING AHEAD    Бронирование

Can I book a room?
mozhna zabraniravat' nomer?

Можно забронировать номер?

Do you have any rooms available?
u vas est' svabodnye nomera?

У вас есть свободные номера?

For (three) nights.
na (troe) sutak

на (трое) суток.

How much for ...? | skol'ka stoit prazhyvanie za ...? | Сколько стоит проживание за ...?
--- | --- | ---
one night | noch' | ночь
a week | nedelyu | неделю
two people | dvaikh | двоих

We'll be arriving at ...
my budem v ...

Мы будем в ...

My name is ...
maya familiya ...

Моя фамилия ...

ГОСТИНИЦА

---

### THE HOTEL RECEPTIONIST MAY SAY ...

u vas est' bron'?         Have you made a booking?
skol'ka chelavek?         How many people?
skol'ka sutak?            How many nights?
kagda vy syedite?         What day are you leaving?
patpishyte zdes'          Sign here.
paspart pazhalsta         Passport please.

## CHECKING IN                     Регистрация

| Do you have a/any ...? | u vas est' ...? | У вас есть ...? |
|---|---|---|
| rooms available | svabodnye nomera | свободные номера |
| room with two beds | dvumesnye nomera | двухместные номера |
| room with a double bed | nomera s dvuspal'ney kravat'yu | номера с двуспальней кроватью |
| single room | adnamesnaya nomer | одноместный номер |

I'd like to share a dorm.

ya by khatel (m)/khatela (f)
mesto v apshchezhytii

Я бы хотел/хотела
место в общежитии.

Sorry, we're full.

k sazhaleniyu,
svabodnykh mest net

К сожалению,
свободных мест нет.

| I want a room with a ... | ya by khatel (m)/ khatela (f) komnatu s ... | я бы хотел/ хотела комнату с ... |
|---|---|---|
| bathroom | vannoy | ванной |
| shower | dushem | душем |
| TV | televizaram | телевизором |
| window | aknom | окном |

ACCOMMODATION

ACCOMMODATION

Can I see it?
mozhna pasmatret'?
Можно посмотреть?

Are there any other rooms?
u vas est' drugie
nomera?
У вас есть другие
номера?

Where's the bathroom?
gde vannaya?
Где ванная?

Is there hot water all day?
garyachaya vada
byvaet tsely den'?
Горячая вода
бывает целый день?

Is there a discount for children/
students?
est' li skitka dlya
detey/studentaf?
Есть ли скидка для
детей/студентов?

It's fine. I'll take it.
kharasho, ya beru
Хорошо, я беру.

## REQUESTS & COMPLAINTS

Просьбы и пожелания

Do you have a safe where I can
leave my valuables?
u vas est' seyf, gde ya
magu khranit' svai
tsennasti?
У вас есть сейф, где я
могу хранить свои
ценности?

Where can I wash clothes?
gde mozhna
pastirat' adezhdu?
Где можно
постирать одежду?

Can we use the telephone?
mozhna pazvanit'?
Можно позвонить?

Can I have (another) ...
mozhna (yeshcho) ...
Можно (ещё) ...

My room is too dark.
v komnate slishkam
temno
В комнате слишком
темно.

| It's too … | v komnate ochen' … | В комнате очень … |
|---|---|---|
| cold/hot | kholadna/zharka | холодно/жарко |
| noisy | shumna | шумно |

I can't open/close the window.
ya ne magu atkryt'/   Я не могу открыть/
zakryt' akno   закрыть окно.

| This … isn't clean. | … gryaznaya | … грязная |
|---|---|---|
| sheet | prostyn' | простынь |
| pillow | padushka | подушка |
| pillow case | navalachka | наволочка |

Please change it/them.
smenite, pazhalsta   Смените,
пожалуйста.

## CHECKING OUT                  Отъезд

Can I pay by travellers cheque?
mozhna rasschitat'sa   Можно расплатиться
darozhnym chekam?   дорожным чеком?
Could I have the bill please?
mozhna paluchit'   Можно получить
shchyot?   счёт?
Could I have a receipt?
mozhna paluchit'   Можно получить
kvitantsiyu?   квитанцию?
There's a mistake in the bill.
menya apshchitali   Меня общитали.

**ACCOMMODATION**

ACCOMMODATION

## USEFUL WORDS

## Полезные слова и выражения

|  |  |  |
|---|---|---|
| air-conditioning | kanditsianer | кондиционер |
| bottle of water | butylka vady | бутылка воды |
| clean | chisty | чистый |
| face cloth | palatentsa dlya litsa | полотенце для лица |
| key | klyuch | ключ |
| lamp | nachnik | ночник |
| lock | zamok | замок |
| mosquito coil | sretstva at kamarof | средство от комаров |
| soap | myla | мыло |
| toilet | tualet | туалет |
| toilet paper | tualetnaya bumaga | туалетная бумага |
| towel | palatentse | полотенце |
| water (cold/hot) | vada (khalodnaya/ garyachaya) | вода (холодная/ горячая) |

## COMMUNAL LIVING

Most older apartments in Russian cities were communal. That is, a number of families shared a common bathroom, kitchen and telephone. Even when a family had their own flat, they may have had to share a telephone line with another apartment.

Recently, these communal flats have come to be viewed as prime real estate. It's just a matter of threatening or killing the inhabitants, fitting them out, and selling them to young entrepreneurs.

**LONGER STAY** Решили задержаться?

| Do you have a (room/flat) to rent ...? | u vas zdayotsya (komnata/ kvartira) ...? | У Вас сдаётся (комната/ квартира) ...? |
|---|---|---|
| for (two) people | na (dvukh) chelavek | на (двух) человек |
| for ... months | na ... mesyatsa | на ... месяца |
| near the (metro) | okala (metro) | около (метро) |
| in the city centre | f tsentre | в центре |

How much per (week/month)?
skol'ka v (nedelyu/mesyats)?
    Сколько в (неделю/месяц)?

car space
mesta dlya mashiny
    место для машины

contract
kantrakt
    контракт

deposit
zadatak
    задаток

security door
braniravannyye dveri
    бронированные двери

**PAPERWORK** Оформление документов

| family name | familiya | фамилия |
|---|---|---|
| given name | imya | имя |
| patronymic | otchestva | отчество |
| address | adres | адрес |
| date of birth | data razhdeniya | дата рождения |
| place of birth | mesta razhdeniya | место рождения |
| age | vozrast | возраст |
| sex | pol | пол |
| nationality | grazhdanstva | гражданство |
| profession | prafesiya | профессия |

ACCOMMODATION

**ACCOMMODATION**

| reason for travel | tsel' priyezda | цель приезда |
| religion | veraispavedanie | вероисповедание |
| marital status | semeynae palazhenie | семейное положение |
| single | ne zhenat (m) | не женат |
| | ne zamuzhem (f) | не замужем |
| married | zhenat (m) | женат |
| | zamuzhem (f) | замужем |
| divorced | razvedyon (m) | разведён |
| | razvedena (f) | разведена |
| widow/widower | vdava/vdavets | вдова/вдовец |
| identification | udastaverenie lichnasti | удостоверение личности |
| passport number | seriya i nomer pasparta | серия и номер паспорта |
| visa | viza | виза |
| baptismal certificate | svideytel'stva a khrishchenii | свидетельство о крещении |
| drivers licence | vaditel'skie prava | водительские права |
| customs | tamozhnya | таможня |
| immigration | pasportniy kantrol' | паспортный контроль |
| purpose of visit | tsel' priyezda | цель приезда |
| holiday | otpusk | отпуск |
| business | po biznesu | по бизнесу |
| visiting relatives | pasetit' radnykh | посетить родных |

## LOOKING FOR ...                 В поисках ...

| Where's a/the ... (around here)? | gdye (zdyes') ...? | Где (здесь) ...? |
|---|---|---|
| bank | bank | банк |
| consulate | konsul'stva | консульство |
| embassy | pasol'stva | посольство |
| post office | pochta | почта |
| telephone | telefonnaya | телефонная |
| booth | budka | будка |
| (public) | (abshchestvenny) | (общественный) |
| toilet | tualet | туалет |
| town square | tsentral'naya | центральная |
|  | ploshchad' | площадь |

## AT THE BANK                 В банке

An organised banking system only began to evolve in the 1990s. Regulation is still in its infancy, so there are good banks, as well as not so good banks.

Credit cards, and to a lesser extent EFTPOS, are common only in major cities – cash is the most popular way to pay. Although it's technically illegal to use foreign currency, some places demand US dollars.

| SIGNS | |
|---|---|
| БАНК | BANK |
| ОБМЕН ВАЛЮТЫ | CURRENCY EXCHANGE |
| ПОЧТА | POST OFFICE |
| ГЛАВПОЧТАМТ | CENTRAL POST OFFICE |
| ИНТЕРНЕТ-КАФЕ | INTERNET CAFÉ |

### PEOPLE ON THE STREET

| | | |
|---|---|---|
| crim | bandit | бандит |
| cop | musar | мусор |
| corpse | trup | труп |
| evangelist | evangilist | евангелист |
| hustler | kamivayazhor | коммивояжёр |
| petty crim | zhuchok | жучок |
| prostitute | prastitutka | проститутка |
| pimp | svodnik | сводник |

AROUND TOWN

You can change money legally – at a currency exchange, obmen valyuty, where you show your passport and fill out the official documentation – or illegally on the street. Be warned that the illegal option may often land you with counterfeit money, and without the receipt you'll need to declare on exiting the country.

Can I exchange money here?
zdes' mozhna
abmenyat' den'gi?

Здесь можно обменять
деньги?

Can I use my credit card?
mozhna vaspol'zavat'sa
kreditkoy?

Можно воспользоваться
кредиткой?

Please write it down.
zapishite, pazhalsta

Запишите, пожалуйста.

Can I have smaller notes?
mozhna paluchit' v
melkikh kupyurakh?

Можно получить в
мелких купюрах?

The automatic teller
swallowed my card.
avtamat proglatil
mayu kartachku

Автомат проглотил
мою карточку.

| I want to change (a) ... | ya khachu abmenyat' ... | Я хочу обменять ... |
|---|---|---|
| cash | nalichnye | наличные |
| money | den'gi | деньги |
| travellers cheque | darozhny chek | дорожный чек |

What's the exchange rate?
    kakoy kurs?    Какой курс?
What time does the bank open?
    kagda atkryvaetsa bank?    Когда открывается банк?

Where can I cash a travellers cheque?
    gdye mozhna obmenyat' darozhny chek na nalichnye den'gi?    Где можно обменять дорожный чек на наличные деньги?
Can I transfer money here from my bank?
    mozhna perevesti den'gi iz mayevo banka?    Можно перевести деньги из моего банка?
How long will it take to arrive?
    kak bystra den'gi pridut?    Как быстро деньги придут?

AROUND TOWN

---

## LISTEN UP

Russians can't be accused of wearing rose-coloured glasses. As you head around town, listen out for these words and phrases.

- tseny  prices
- defitsyt  shortages
- v narmal'nay strane
  how things work in a normal country (anywhere else)
- ran'she
  how things worked 'earlier' (in Soviet days)

### AT THE POST OFFICE      На почте

People have been complaining about the Russian postal system since the Central Post Office was established in 1714. Inbound mail is slow, unreliable, and handled by so many people that you'll be lucky to receive any parcel intact.

Outbound mail is faster. However, sending anything larger than a letter is time-consuming. You'll need to bring the items unwrapped and declare each one. Go to a central branch, as small branches don't send international parcels.

| I want to send a ... | ya khachu poslat' ... | Я хочу послать ... |
|---|---|---|
| letter | pis'mo | письмо |
| small parcel | banderol' | бандероль |
| large parcel | pasylku | посылку |
| telegram | telegrama | телеграмму |
| Please send it by ... | pashlyte, pazhalstav ... | Пошлите, пожалуйстав ... |
| air mail | avia | авиа |
| express mail | ekspres-pochtay | експресс-почтой |
| registered | zakaznoe pis'mo | заказное письмо |
| signed by receiver | s uvedomleniem | с уведомлением |
| regular post | abychnaya pochta | обычная почта |

**AROUND TOWN**

### THE CAPITALIST DREAM

The Russian post office is a monopoly that moguls in the west can only dream about. It is responsible for all communications (svyaz' связь), which include postal services, domestic and international calls, fax connections, and internet access. It owns all telecommunications infrastructure, distributes all government pensions and organises telegraphic transfers, as well as coordinating subscriptions to magazines. A finger in every pie.

What will it cost to send this to ...?

| skol'ka stoit peresylka ...? | Сколько стоит пересылка ...? |

I want to buy ... ya khachu kupit'... Я хочу купить ...

| greeting cards | pazdravitel'nye atkrytki | поздравительные открытки |
| postcards | atkrytki | открытки |
| stamps | marki | марки |
| envelope | kanvert | конверт |
| pen | ruchka | ручка |
| postcode | pachtovy indeks | почтовый индекс |
| mail box | pachtovy yashchik | почтовый ящик |

---

**DID YOU KNOW ...**

Kremlin kreml' кремль
The term 'Kremlin' actually refers to any walled fortress – there are other famous kremlins at Novgorod, Nizhniy Novgorod and Kazan.

St Basil's Cathedral
khram vasiliya blazhenava
Храм Василия Блаженного
The world-famous onion-domed cathedral on Red Square is called St Basil's Cathedral. Ivan the Terrible was so concerned the architects might build a more beautiful church for someone else that he had them blinded.

Red Square
krasnaya ploshchat'
Красная площадь
Red Square isn't red, and the name has nothing to do with the old Communist Regime – the word 'red' krasny formerly meant – 'beautiful' krasivy

**AROUND TOWN**

## TELECOMMUNICATIONS

## Телефонная связь

Computerisation developed slowly in Soviet times, due to isolation coupled with the Government's determination to develop a domestic 'cybernetics' industry. In one decade however, Russia has developed a world-class reputation in computer programming. The only thing lacking is capital.

Fax machines and internet access are available at the more prestigious hotels.

Can I use the telephone?
mozhna vaspol'zavat'sa telefonam?

Можно воспользоваться телефоном?

I want to call (England).
ya khachu pazvanit' v (angliyu)

Я хочу позвонить в (Англию).

I want to make an international call.
ya khachu pazvanit' za granitsu

Я хочу позвонить за границу.

The number is ...
nomer ...

Номер ...

How much does each minute cost?
skol'ka stoit minuta?

Сколько стоит минута?

| SIGNS | |
| --- | --- |
| ВХОД | ENTRANCE |
| ВЫХОД | EXIT |
| ГОРЯЧАЯ | HOT |
| ХОЛОДНАЯ | COLD |
| НЕ ВХОДИТЬ | NO ENTRY |
| НЕ КУРИТЬ | NO SMOKING |
| ОТКРЫТО | OPEN |
| ЗАКРЫТО | CLOSED |
| НЕ ... | ... PROHIBITED |
| ТУАЛЕТЫ | TOILETS |

AROUND TOWN

What's the code for (the US/Moscow)?
| | |
|---|---|
| kakoy kod (ameriki/maskvy)? | Какой код (Америки/Москвы)? |

It's engaged.
| | |
|---|---|
| zanyata | Занято. |

I've been cut off.
| | |
|---|---|
| menya prervali | Меня прервали. |

I need to get Internet access.
| | |
|---|---|
| mne nuzhna padklyuchit'sa k internetu | Мне нужно подключиться к интернету. |

I need to check my email.
| | |
|---|---|
| mne nuzhna praverit' mayu elektronuyu pochtu | Мне нужно проверить мою электронную почту. |

| | | |
|---|---|---|
| operator | aperatar | оператор |
| phone book | telefonnaya knishka | телефонная книжка |
| phone box | telefonnaya butka | телефонная будка |
| phonecard | telefonnaya kartachka | телефонная карточка |
| urgent | srochny | срочный |

## RUSSIAN ARCHITECTURE

| | | |
|---|---|---|
| altar | prestol | престол |
| arch(way) | arka | арка |
| bell | kolakal | колокол |
| cathedral | sabor | собор |
| church | tserkaf' | церковь |
| column | kalonna | колонна |
| cross | krest | крест |
| dome | kupal | купол |
| frescoe | freska | фреска |
| kremlin | kreml' | кремль |
| palace | dvarets | дворец |
| tower | bashnya | башня |

AROUND TOWN

**Making a Call** Как сделать звонок?

Hello. (answering a call)
 allo        Алло.
Hello, is ... there?
 pazavite, pazhalsta ...    Позовите, пожалуйста
Who's calling?
 izvinite, s kem ya gavariu?   Извините, с кем я говорю?
It's ...
 eta ...        Это ...
Yes, he/she is here.
 da, pazhalsta      Да, пожалуйста.

One moment, please.
 minutku        Минутку.
I'm sorry, he's/she's not here.
 izvinitye, evo/eyo netu    Извините, его/её нету.
What time will he/she be back?
 kagda on/ana vernyotsa?   Когда он/она
вернётся?
Please tell them ...
 peredayte,       Передайте,
 pazhalsta ...       пожалуйста...
I'll call back later.
 ia pereznanyu pozhe    Я перезвоню позже.

| **DID YOU KNOW ...** | In 1833, the first intercity postal system appeared in Russia. The first mail boxes appeared in 1848, and stamps in 1858. Little seems to have changed since. |
| --- | --- |

AROUND TOWN

## SIGHTSEEING

## Осмотр
## достопримечательностей

Where's the tourist office?
  gde turbyuro?

Где турбюро?

Do you have a local map?
  U vas est' karta gorada?

У вас есть карта
города?

I'd like to see ...
  ya khachu pasetit'...

Я хочу посетить ...

What time does it open?
  kagda atkryvaetsa?

Когда открывается?

What time does it close?
  kagda zakryvaetsa?

Когда закрывается?

What's that building?
  shto eta za zdanie?

Что это за здание?

What's this monument?
  shto eta za pamyatnik?

Что это за памятник?

Can we take photographs?
  mozhna sfatagrafiravat'?

Можно
сфотографировать?

I'll send you the photograph.
  ya vyshlyu vam fatagrafiyu

Я вышлю вам
фотографии.

Could you take a
photograph of me?
  sfatagrafiruyte menya,
  pazhalsta

Сфотографируйте меня,
пожалуйста.

**AROUND TOWN**

---

### WINTER ETIQUETTE

When you arrive at the theatre or a restaurant, make
sure you leave your coat, heavy boots and hat at the
garderop гардероб 'cloakroom', or people will see you
for the boorish foreigner that you are.

| | | |
|---|---|---|
| amusement park | park kul'tury | парк культуры |
| church | sabor | собор |
| cathedral | tserkaf' | церковь |
| cinema | kino | кино |
| concert | kantsert | концерт |
| crowded | lyudna | людно |
| exhibition | vystafka | выставка |
| kremlin | kreml' | кремль |
| mosque | mechet' | мечеть |
| museum | muzey | музей |
| palace | dvarets | дворец |
| park | park | парк |
| skating rink | katok | каток |
| statue | statuya | статуя |
| synagogue | sinagoga | синагога |
| town hall | meriya | мэрия |
| university | universitet | университет |
| war memorial | memarial | мемориал |

AROUND TOWN

## **DATING**                              На свидании
### **First Encounters** Будьте знакомы!

Can I have a light?
mozhna prikurit'?

Можно прикурить?

Let me give you a light?
razreshite vam pamoch'

Разрешите Вам помочь.
(lit: let me help)

Would you like a drink?
khatite vypit' samnoy?

Хотите выпить
со мной?

This place is great, isn't it?
zdes' klassna, pravda?

Здесь классно, правда?

This place is lousy, isn't it?
zdes' parshiva, pravda?

Здесь паршиво,
правда?

---

### **CLASSIC KNOCK BACKS**

| | |
|---|---|
| pravalivay! | Go away! |
| atyebis'! | Fuck off! |
| ya gey (m)/lezbianka (f) | I'm gay. |
| Ya ne gey (m)/lezbianka (f) | I'm not gay. |

What are they selling? (in a queue)
shto dayut?      Что дают?

You clearly appreciate (futurism/
constructivism/suprematism).
vam yavna nravitsya      Вам явно нравится
(futurizm/      (футуризм/
kanstruktivizm/      конструктивизм/
suprimatizm)      супрематизм).

Nice bum!
klassnaya popka!      Классная попка!

### LITTLE PIGEON.

Russians are affectionate, and have lots of terms to
show for it.

| | |
|---|---|
| galupchik (m)/galubushka (f) | Little pigeon. |
| lyubof' maya | My love. |
| solnyshka mayo | My sunshine. |
| slatkiy(m)/slatkaya (f) | Sweet. |
| zolotka | Golden one. |

## Getting Serious  Поговорим серьёзно

Can we meet again?
mozhna vstretit'sya
eshchyo ras?

Можно встретиться
ещё раз?

I like you a lot.
ty mne ochen'
nravishsya

Ты мне очень
нравишься.

I love you.
ya lyublyu tibya

Я люблю тебя.

I'm serious about you.
ya seryozen (m)/ seryozna (f)

Я серьёзен/серьёзна.

## INTIMATE RUSSIAN

I love you.
ya lyublyu tebya

Я люблю тебя.

You're beautiful.
ty krasivy (m)/
krasivaya (f)

Ты красивый/
красивая.

You're fantastic.
ty klassny (m)/
klassnaya (f)

Ты классный/
классная.

Kiss me.
patseluy menya

Поцелуй меня.

Hold me.
abnimi menya

Обними меня.

Use your tongue.
yazykom

Языком.

Use a condom.
aden' prezervativ

Одень презерватив.

Don't stop!
ni astanavlivaysa!

Не останавливайся!

Stop!
stoy!

Стой!

## DRESSING UP

Russians love dressing up, and it's quite a faux pas to head off to a party or concert without making the effort to wear either your best fur coat and jewellery (if you happen to be a woman) or a black shirt with beige shoes and matching brown tie (for men).

### Love Problems  Поговорим о любви

We need to talk.
   nam nuzhna pagavarit'        Нам нужно поговорить.

I'm sure we can sort this out.
   ya uveren (m)/uverena       Я уверен/уверена
   (f) my razberyomsa         мы  разберёмся.

I need time to think.
   mne nuzhna vrem          Мне нужно время
   ya padumat'             подумать.

I want to end our relationship.
   Ya khachu zakonchit'      Я хочу закончить
   nashu svyas'           нашу связь.

GOING OUT

# Увлечения INTERESTS

This chapter assumes you've got to know someone a little, and always uses the informal ty for 'you'. If it's your first conversation, or you're talking to someone older, it might be wise to use the formal vy (see pg 33).

## COMMON INTERESTS Хобби

What do you do in
your spare time?
  chem ty zanimaesh'sa f      Чем ты занимаешься в
  svabodnae vremya?           свободное время?
I like ...
  mne nravitsa ...            Мне нравится ...
I don't like ...
  mne ne nravitsa ...         Мне не нравится ...

| Do you like ...? | tebe nravitsa ...? | Тебе нравится ...? |
|---|---|---|
| art | iskustva | искусство |
| chess | igrat' f shakhmaty | играть в шахматы |
| cooking | gatovit' | готовить |
| dancing | tantsevat' | танцевать |
| dominoes | igrat' v damino | играть в домино |
| film | kino | кино |
| going out | byvat' v obshchestve | бывать в обществе |
| gymnastics | zanimat'sa gimnastikoy | заниматься гимнастикой |
| music | muzyka | музыка |
| playing cards | igrat' f karty | играть в карты |
| playing soccer | igrat' f fudbol | играть в футбол |
| playing sport | zanimat'sa sportam | заниматься спортом |
| reading books | chitat' knigi | читать книги |

INTERESTS

| shopping | khadit' pa magazinam | ходить по магазинам |
| skating | katat'sa na kan'kakh | кататься на коньках |
| skiing | katat'sa na lyzhakh | кататься на лыжах |
| swimming | plavat' | плавать |
| taking photos | fatagrafiravat' | фотографировать |
| the theatre | teatr | театр |
| travelling | puteshestvavat' | путешествовать |
| watching TV | smatret' televizar | смотреть телевизор |

## SPORT                                    Спорт

Do you like sport?
  tebe nravitsa sport?
Тебе нравится спорт?

I like playing sport.
  mne nravitsa zanimat'sa sportam
Мне нравится заниматься спортом.

I prefer to watch rather than play sport.
  ya predpachitayu smatret', a ne zanimat'sa sportam
Я предпочитаю смотреть, а не заниматься спортом.

| Do you play ...? | ty igraesh' v ...? | Ты играешь в ...? |
| Let's play ... | davay paigraem v ... | Давай |
| | | поиграем в ... |
| baseball | beysbol | бейсбол |
| basketball | basketbol | баскетбол |
| volleyball | valeybol | воллейбол |
| football (soccer) | fudbol | футбол |
| hockey | khakkey | хоккей |
| tennis | tennis | теннис |

INTERESTS

## SOCCER                                                    Футбол

Soccer, fudbol, is the national passion. Russian has patriotically
Russified most of the terminology that was originally borrowed
from English: halfback used to be khafbek хафбек but is now
paluzashchitnik полузащитник, literally 'half defence'.

| Who's playing? | kto igraet? | Кто играет? |
| Who's winning? | kto vidyot? | Кто ведёт? |
| What's the score? | kakoy shyot? | Какой счёт? |
| I support Spartak | ya baleyu za | Я болею за |
| | spartak | 'Спартак'. |
| Scum! | na myla! | на мыло! |
| | | (lit: 'Make |
| | | him into soap!) |
| first half | pervy taym | Первый тайм |
| second half | ftaroy taym | Второй тайм |
| goal | gol | гол |
| out | aut | аут |

---

### WALRUSING

During your stay in Russia, you might like to try zaplyv
morzhey, which roughly translates as 'walrusing'. It in-
volves swimming in holes in the ice during winter, excellent for the constitution.

INTERESTS

## ICE & SNOW     На льду и на снегу

| | | |
|---|---|---|
| skates | kan'ki | коньки |
| skis | lyzhy | лыжи |
| sled | sanki | санки |
| snowballs | sneshki | снежки |
| snowman | snezhnaya baba | снежная баба |
| shovel | lapata | лопата |
| galoshes | galoshy | галоши |
| felt boots | valenki | валенки |
| fur coat | shuba | шуба |
| (fur) hat | (mekhavaya) shapka | (меховая) шапка |
| scarf | sharf | шарф |
| gloves | perchatki | перчатки |

## CHESS     Шахматы

A serious game of chess should facilitate a serious friendship.

Shall we play chess?
    sygraem f shakhmaty?     Сыграем в шахматы?

| Check! | shakh! | шах! |
|---|---|---|
| Checkmate! | shakh i mat! | Шах и мат! |

| king | karol' | король |
|---|---|---|
| queen | ferz' | ферзь |
| rook | lad'ya | ладья |
| knight | kon' | конь |
| bishop | slon (lit: elephant) | слон |
| pawn | peshka | пешка |

**INTERESTS**

## MUSHROOMING В лес по грибы

Urban Russians make day trips to find mushrooms, griby, or berries, yagady, especially to preserve them for winter. Any self-respecting Russian knows many different types.

| basket | karzinka | корзинка |
|---|---|---|
| berries | yagady | ягоды |
| mushroom | grip (sg) | гриб |
| | griby (pl) | грибы |
| boletus | makhavik | моховик |
| edible boletus | baravik | боровик |
| picnic | piknik | пикник |

---

### RUSSIAN BATHS

For some clean healthy fun, head to the banya баня, 'communal bathhouse'. What makes a Russian banya different from a Turkish bath or a Finnish sauna is that Russians thrash themselves or their friends with a веник venik – a bunch of either oak or birch twigs – which detoxifies the body while releasing delightful forest aromas.

Bring a towel, shampoo, plastic shoes and tea (or beer). You need to buy your venik and then go to the parilka, steamroom. You should sit on a wooden bench and dip your venik into a bucket of hot water to soften it before the thrashing begins.

After five minutes or so, you can escape and immerse yourself in the cold pool. Then you can drink your tea and have a chat before starting all over again.

Russians wish each other good health, after the bathhouse, with the expression:

With light steam!
 s lyokhkim param! С лёгким паром!

INTERESTS

## CARDS                                        Карты

Maybe because of the climate, Russians love to play cards.

Do you play (poker)?
    ty igraesh' f (poker)?    Вы играете в (покер)?
I'll raise you.
    ya pavyshayu stafku    Я повышаю ставку.

| | | |
|---|---|---|
| bet | stafka | ставка |
| blackjack | achko | очко |
| cards | karty | карты |
| preference (Russian game like whist) | preferans | преферанс |
| clubs | trefy | трефы |
| diamonds | bubny | бубны |
| hearts | chervi | черви |
| spades | piki | пики |
| ace | tus | туз |
| two | dvoyka | двойка |
| three | troyka | тройка |
| four | chetvyorka | четвёрка |
| five | pyatyorka | пятёрка |
| six | shestyorka | шестёрка |
| seven | semyorka | семёрка |
| eight | vas'myorka | восьмёрка |
| nine | devyatka | девятка |
| ten | desyatka | десятка |
| jack | valet | валет |
| queen | dama | дама |
| king | karol' | король |
| joker | dzhoker | джокер |

# ART                                    Искусство

Many Russian art terms will be familiar to English speakers because they're from Latin, borrowed through other European languages.

| | | |
|---|---|---|
| architecture | arkhitektura | архитектура |
| icon painting | ikonapis' | иконопись |
| carving | reznaya rabota | резная работа |
| computer art | kamp'yutrernae iskustva | компьютерное искусство |
| decoration | addelka | отделка |
| design | dizayn | дизайн |
| painting | zhyvapis' | живопись |
| religious art | tserkovnae iskustva | церковное искусство |
| sculpture | skul'ptura | скульптура |

## Art Movements  Направления в искусстве

Early 20th century Russian art is considered to be some of the most brilliant ever, with artists including Kandinskiy Кандинский, Malevich Малевич and Shagal Шагал.

| | | |
|---|---|---|
| classicism | klasitsizm | классицизм |
| romanticism | ramantitsizm | романтизм |
| impressionism | imspresianizm | импрессионизм |
| expressionism | ekspresianizm | экспрессионизм |
| futurism | futurizm | футуризм |
| suprematism | suprematizm | супрематизм |
| constructivism | kanstruktivizm | конструктивизм |
| socialist realism | sotsialisticheskiy realizm | социалистический реализм |

## UNSTRESSED 'O'

Unless you want to affect a Volga accent, unstressed *o* should be pronounced a not o.

INTERESTS

## FAMILY                                        Семья

Often, three generations of Russians will live together under the same roof – 'the same roof' being a one or two bedroom flat.

Are you married?

| | |
|---|---|
| ty zamuzhem? (to a woman) | Ты замужем? |
| ty zhenat? (to a man) | Ты женат? |

I'm (not) married.

| | |
|---|---|
| ya (ne) zhenat (m)/ | Я (не) женат/ |
| zamuzhem (f) | замужем. |

## ASTROLOGY

Without doubt, the number one topic of conversation in Russia is the zodiac. Even business meetings can begin with a run down of everyone's sign and a summary of planetary positions (to help with strategic planning).

What's your sign?

| | |
|---|---|
| kakoy tvoy znak? | Какой твой знак? |

| My sign is ... | moy znak ... | Мой знак ... |
|---|---|---|
| Aries | oven | Овен |
| Taurus | tilets | Телец |
| Gemini | bliznetsy | Близнецы |
| Cancer | rak | Рак |
| Leo | lef | Лев |
| Virgo | deva | Дева |
| Libra | visy | Весы |
| Scorpio | skarpion | Скорпион |
| Sagitarius | strilets | Стрелец |
| Capricorn | kazirog | Козерог |
| Aquarius | vadaley | Водолей |
| Pisces | ryby | Рыбы |

I'm on the cusp.

| | |
|---|---|
| ya na styke znakaf | Я на стыке знаков. |

We're compatible!

| | |
|---|---|
| my idial'na padkhodim | мы идеально подходим |
| drug drugu! | друг другу! |

INTERESTS

Is your husband/wife here?
  tvoy mush/tvaya zhena zdes'?

Твой муж/твоя жена здесь?

Are you going out with anyone?
  ty fstrechaeshsa s kem-ta?

Ты встречаешься с кем-то?

I'm not going out with anyone.
  ya niskem ne fstrechayus'

Я ни с кем не встречаюсь.

How many children do you have?
  skol'ka u tebya detey?
  (to one person)
  skol'ka u vas detey?
  (to a couple)

Сколько у тебя детей?
Сколько у вас детей?

We don't have any children.
  u nas net detey

У нас нет детей.

How many siblings do you have?
  skol'ka u tebya brat'ef i sestyor?

Сколько у тебя братьев исестёр?

| I have (a) ... | u menya est' ... | У меня есть ... |
|---|---|---|
| brother | brat | брат |
| children | deti | дети |
| daughter | doch' | дочь |
| granddaughter | vnuchka | внучка |
| grandson | vnuk | внук |
| great-grandson | pravnuk | правнук |
| husband | mush | муж |
| sister | sestra | сестра |
| son | syn | сын |
| wife | zhena | жена |

## QUESTION FORMS

You can make any statement into a question simply by changing the intonation. Your voice should rise sharply and then fall near the end of the sentence. Don't try and change the word order.

INTERESTS

## RELATIVES       Родственники

| | | |
|---|---|---|
| mother | mat' | мать |
| father | atets | отец |
| aunt | tyotya | тётя |
| uncle | dyadya | дядя |
| grandfather | dedushka | дедушка |
| grandmother | babushka | бабушка |
| great-grandfather | pradedushka | прадедушка |
| great-grandmother | prababushka | прабабушка |
| nephew | plemyannik | племянник |
| niece | plemyannitsa | племянница |
| cousin (m) | dvayuradny brat | двоюродный брат |
| cousin (f) | dvayuradnaya | двоюродная |
| | sestra | сестра |

---

### SURNAMES & FAMILY HISTORY

Russia is the ultimate melting pot, and surnames may be the only clue to someone's background. Surnames ending in -ов/-ова, -of/-ova and -ин/-ина, -in/-ina are traditionally Russian:

| | | |
|---|---|---|
| Ivanov's son | Ivanof | Иванов |
| Ivanov's daughter | Ivanova | Иванова |

The ending -skiy, as in Razumofskiy, is often of Jewish or Polish origin. Names ending in -ко, -ko such as Шевченко Shefchenko, are usually Ukrainian.

In Caucasian languages, the ending of a name generally signifies someone's son or daughter, for example -швили -shvili as in Басилашвили Basilashvili (Georgian), and -ян -yan as in Хачатурян Khachaturyan (Armenian).

**In-Laws** Родня со стороны жены или мужа
English is impoverished when it comes to describing the in-laws.

brother-in-law (sister's husband)
   zyat'                          зять
brother-in-law (wife's brother)
   shurin                         шурин
brother-in-law (husband's brother)
   dever'                         деверь
sister-in-law (brother's wife)
   nevestka                      невестка
sister-in-law (husband's sister)
   zalofka                      золовка
sister-in-law (wife's sister)
   svayachenitsa           свояченица
father-in-law (husband's father)
   svyokar                     свёкор
father-in-law (wife's father)
   test'                          тесть
mother-in-law (husband's mother)
   svekrof'                     свекровь
mother-in-law (wife's mother)
   tyoshcha                    тёща

**INTERESTS**

## BAPTISMAL CERTIFICATES

Karl Marx famously labelled religion the 'opiate of the people', and one of the first decrees of the Bolshevik government was to separate Church and State. In the USSR, religion of any kind was persecuted, and many religious practices, such as baptism, were made illegal. Baptismal certificates still have no legal status, as opposed to official birth certificates and other civil documents.

INTERESTS

## PARTY ON

The Communist Party was central to Russian life for 70 years. To take part in any discussion about life ran'she раньше 'earlier', it's essential to know some key terms.

es-es-es-er CCCP
Union of Soviet Socialist Republics (USSR)

partiya партия
the (Communist) Party (not a get-together, which is called a вечеринка vecherinka). Only four per cent of the population were party members.

namenklatura номенклатура
the party elite, who had their own shops, apartment blocks, holiday houses, hairdressers, cars and so on. The word is still used for today's political elite, who enjoy similar privileges.

savet совет
'Soviet' (lit: council). In theory, a hierarchy of these councils represented the concerns of local villages, towns and regions. The highest body of public administration was the 'Supreme Soviet' verkhovny savet Верховный Совет, the national parliament.

partkom партком
Party Committee. Every workplace or college had its own partkom, which exercised ultimate control.

ka-ge-be КГБ
KGB, 'Committee for State Security', the secret police. This organisation had a network of millions of informants, and kept Soviet citizens in constant fear. The KGB general Oleg Kalugin once remarked that there was no sphere of life, from religion to sport, in which the KGB had no keen interest.

INTERESTS

## PARTY ON

The KGB was the offspring of ВЧК or Cheka, the 'All Russian Extraordinary Commission' (created after the Revolution), and НКВД or NKVD, the 'Peoples' Committee for Internal Affairs' (created under Stalin). KGB agents called themselves chekisty чекисты to signify that they were carrying on the great tradition of the Cheka.

paspart     паспорт
The internal passport Soviet citizens had to carry. Permission was once needed before travelling outside your locality. As farm workers weren't automatically issued with passports, they were tied to the farm.

prapiska     Прописка
'Permit for Residence'. This was a special stamp in your internal passport, which was required before you could live in a popular city. Bribery or fake marriage were the only ways to get one.

pyatiletka     пятилетка
The Five-Year Plan, the driving force of Soviet economic planning.

INTERESTS

## WEDDINGS                           Свадьбы

Most Russians still marry in a civil ceremony, and afterwards drive to famous local sights to be photographed (often a war memorial). After a toast, all the guests shout gor'ka! (lit: 'bitter', ironically wishing a sweet life together) and then start counting one, two, three ..., ras, dva, tri ..., for as long as the couple can kiss!

Congratulations!
  pazdravlyayu!                       Поздравляю!
To the bride and groom!
  za novobrachnykh!                   За новобрачных!
To a happy life together!
  zhelayu shaslivay
  semeynay zhyzni!                    Желаю счастливой
                                      семейной жизни!
What a beautiful ring!
  kakoe krasivae kal'tso!             Какое красивое
                                      кольцо!

Where are you going to live?
  gde vy budete zhyt'?                Где вы будете жить?

| engagement | pamolfka | помолвка |
|---|---|---|
| honeymoon | medovy mesyats | медовый месяц |
| wedding | svad'ba | свадьба |
| wedding cake | svadebny tort | свадебный торт |

# Покупки     **SHOPPING**

Be prepared for the 'three queue system' in many larger shops. When you choose an item, ask for a docket from the shop assistant by saying, vypishite, pazhalsta which literally means 'please write it out'.

Then take this docket to a cashier, kasa, where you pay and have your docket stamped. Finally, proceed to the counter with your docket and collect your purchase.

## LOOKING FOR ...      В поисках ...

| | | |
|---|---|---|
| Where can I buy ...? | gde mozhna kupit' ...? | Где можно купить ...? |
| Where is a ... around here? | gde zdes' ...? | Где здесь ...? |
| barber | mushskoy master | мужской мастер |
| bookshop | knizhny magazin | книжный магазин |
| camera shop | magazin fotatavarov | магазин фототоваров |
| chemist/pharmacy | apteka | аптека |
| department store | univermak | универмаг |
| supermarket | universam | универсам |
| laundry | prachechnaya | прачечная |
| market | rynak | рынок |
| souvenir shop | suvenirny magazin | сувенирный магазин |

### ATTENTION GRABBER

A polite way of attracting a shop assistant's attention is to say but'te dabry!, which is equivalent to 'Could you help me?'. You'll hear other expressions, however, especially devushka! Девушка!, (lit: Girl!), said to a female clerk of any age.

SHOPPING

## NAMES OF SHOPS

Bakery
bulachnaya БУЛОЧНАЯ

Books
knigi КНИГИ

Clothing
adezhda ОДЕЖДА

Department Store
univermak УНИВЕРМАГ

Dry Cleaning
khimchistka ХИМЧИСТКА

Electrical Goods
elektratavary ЭЛЕКТРОТОВАРЫ

Fashion
moda МОДА

Flowers
tsvety ЦВЕТЫ

Food Store
gastranom ГАСТРОНОМ

Hairdresser
parikhmakhershaya ПАРИКМАХЕРСКАЯ

Hardware
skabyanoy magazin СКОБЯНОЙ МАГАЗИН

Laundry
prachechnaya ПРАЧЕЧНАЯ

Liquor
likyora-vodachniye ЛИКЁРО-ВОДОЧНЫЕ
izdeliya ИЗДЕЛИЯ

Market
rynak РЫНОК

Pharmacy
apteka АПТЕКА

## NAMES OF SHOPS

**Photo supplies**
magazin          МАГАЗИН
fotatavarov      ФОТОТОВАРОВ

**Shoes**
obuf'            ОБУВЬ

**Souvenirs**
suveniry         СУВЕНИРЫ

**Supermarket**
universam        УНИВЕРСАМ

**Tobacconist**
tabachnye izdeliya   ТАБАЧНЫЕ ИЗДЕЛИЯ

**Toys**
igrushki         ИГРУШКИ

**SHOPPING**

## MAKING A PURCHASE          Покупки

I'd like to buy ...
    ya khatel (m)/
    khatela (f) by kupit' ...          Я хотел/хотела
                      бы купить ...

I'm just looking.
    ya prosta smatryu          Я просто смотрю.

How much is this?
    skol'ka eta stoit?          Сколько это стоит?

Can you write down the price?
    napishyte,          Напишите,
    pazhalsta, tsenu          пожалуйста, цену.

Do you have any others?
    u vas est' drugie?          У вас есть другие?

Can I look at it?
    pakazhyte,          Покажите,
    pazhalsta          пожалуйста.

I don't like it.
    mne eta ne nravitsa          Мне это не нравится.

Please write me out a docket.
(see pg 127)
    vypishite,          Выпишите,
    pazhalsta,          пожалуйста,
    kvitantsiyu          квитанцию.

Do you accept credit cards?
    vy prinimaete aplatu          Вы принимаете оплату
    kreditnay kartachkay?          кредитной карточкой?

Please wrap it.
    zavernite, pazhalsta          Заверните,
                      пожалуйста.

---

### THE SHOP ASSISTANT MAY SAY ...

| | |
|---|---|
| uplatite na kasse | Pay at the cashier. |
| u nas netu | We don't have any. |
| eta retka pastupaet | |
| k nam | It's in short supply. |

## BARGAINING

Поторгуемся?

I think it's too expensive.
   ya dumayu, eta
   ochen' doraga

Я думаю, это
очень дорого.

It's too much.
   eta ochen' mnoga

Это очень много.

Can you lower the price?
   vy mozhete snizit' tsenu?

Вы можете снизить
цену?

---

### THE LINE

There are two types of the Russian phenomenon ochered', which means 'line' or 'queue'.

One is the ochered' pa spisku, 'line on a list', which is the waiting period for something to be delivered. This could be a telephone connection, a flat, a car, furniture or anything else that's in short supply. You could be in one of these lines for – literally – years.

The most visible ochered' is a line of people waiting for goods. These are sometimes called a zhivaya ochered', or 'living line'. If you want to join the line, you must follow line etiquette. Go to the end of the line (which is sometimes hard to tell), and ask:

Who's the last in line?          Kto pasledniy?

Russian stores offer a variety of goods these days, but shopping still requires standing in long lines. Because goods are displayed behind a counter, you'll have to stay in a line to be served. Be ready to spend a fair time in the queue – salespeople could have more important things to do, like telephone their friends.

SHOPPING

## ESSENTIAL GROCERIES     Бакалея

Where can I find (a) ...?
gde pradayut ...?     Где лродают...?

| I'd like (a) ... | ya by khatel(m) | Я бы хотел |
| | khatela(f) kupit'... | хотела купить ... |
| batteries | batareyki | батарейки |
| bread | khlep | хлеб |
| butter | slivachnae masla | сливочное масло |
| cheese | syr | сыр |
| chocolate | shakalat | шоколад |
| eggs | yaytsa | яйца |
| flour | muku | муку |
| gas cylinder | gazavy balon | газовый баллон |
| ham | vetchinu | ветчину |
| honey | myot | мёд |
| margarine | margarin | маргарин |
| matches | spichki | спички |
| milk | malako | молоко |
| pepper | perets | перец |
| salt | sol' | соль |
| shampoo | shampun' | шампунь |
| soap | myla | мыло |
| sugar | sakhar | сахар |
| toilet paper | tualetnuyu bumagu | туалетную бумагу |
| toothpaste | zubnuyu pastu | зубную пасту |
| washing powder | stiral'ny parashok | стиральный порошёк |
| yogurt | yogurt | йогурт |

## WORKS OF ART

Works of art, such as books published before 1960, antiques or anything that looks old, need to be cleared by the local Customs Administration.

## SOUVENIRS        Сувениры

| abacus | shchyoty | счёты |
| amber | yantar' | янтарь |
| badge (pin) | znachok | значок |
| balalaika | balalayka | балалайка |
| chess set | shakhmaty | шахматы |
| fur hat | mekhavaya shapka | меховая шапка |
| handicrafts | zdeliya ruchnoy | изделия ручной |
|  | raboty | работы |
| icon | ikona | икона |
| jewellery | yuvelirnye | ювелирные |
|  | izdeliya | изделия |
| lace | kruzheva | кружева |
| peasant doll | matryoshka | матрёшка |
| poster | plakat | плакат |
| stamps | marki | марки |
| toy | igrushka | игрушка |
| vodka | votka | водка |

**SHOPPING**

---

### HOW MANY WOULD YOU LIKE?

If you want to buy a specific quantity of something, put one of the following words after the number.

| after 2, 3 and 4 | shtuki | штуки |
| after 5 and above | shtuk | штук |

Two, please.
dve shtuki, pazhalsta

Две штуки,
пожалуйста.

Eight, please.
vosem' shtuk,
pazhalsta

Восемь штук,
пожалуйста.

SHOPPING

## CLOTHING                    Одежда

These days, Russia has every boutique imaginable. However, these
are far removed from the shopping experience of normal Russians.
Affordable, fashionable clothes are still hard to get. Many Russians
know their family and friends' shoe sizes and measurements, just
in case they come across something good so they can buy up.

| | | |
|---|---|---|
| jacket | zhaket | жакет |
| jumper (sweater) | sviter | свитер |
| pants | bryuki | брюки |
| raincoat | plashch | плащ |
| shirt | rubashka | рубашка |
| shoes | tufli | туфли |
| socks | naski | носки |
| swimsuit | kupal'nik | купальник |
| T-shirt | fudbolka | футболка |
| underwear | bel'yo | бельё |

### THE SHOP ASSISTANT MAY NOT SAY ...

vam pamoch'?
    Can I help you?
vam zavernut'?
    Would you like me to wrap it for you?
spasiba za pakupki v ...
    Thank you for shopping at ...

## COLOURS

Цвета

| black | chyorny | чёрный |
|---|---|---|
| light blue | galuboy | голубой |
| dark blue | siniy | синий |
| brown | karishnevy | коричневый |
| green | zelyony | зелёный |
| grey | sery | серый |
| orange | aranzhevy | оранжевый |
| pink | rozavy | розовый |
| purple | purpurny | пурпурный |
| red | krasny | красный |
| white | bely | белый |
| yellow | zholty | жёлтый |
| dark ... | tyomna ... | темно- ... |
| light ... | svetla ... | светло- ... |

## TOILETRIES

Туалетные
принадлежности

| condoms | prezervativy | презервативы |
|---|---|---|
| deodorant | dezadarant | дезодорант |
| moisturising cream | uvlazhnyaushchiy krem | увлажняющий крем |
| razor blades | lezviya dlya brit'ya | лезвия для бритья |
| sanitary napkins | ginienicheskie salfetki | стерильные салфетки |
| shampoo | shampun' | шампунь |
| shaving cream | krem dlya brit'ya | крем для бритья |
| soap | myla | мыло |
| sunblock | sontsezashchitnyy krem | солнцезащитный крем |
| tampons | tampony | тампоны |
| toilet paper | tualetnaya bumaga | туалетная бумага |

SHOPPING

**SHOPPING**

## FOR THE BABY    Всё для младенца

| baby powder | detskaya prisypka | детская присыпка |
| bib | detskiy nagrudnik | детский нагрудник |
| disposable nappies | adnarazavye padguzniki | одноразовые подгузники |

| dummy/pacifier | soska | соска |
| feeding bottle | razhok | рожок |
| nappy | padguznik | подгузник |
| nappy rash cream | detskiy krem | детский крем |
| powdered milk | sukhoe malako | сухое молоко |
| tinned baby food | detskae pitanie v bankakh | детское питание в банках |

## RUSSIAN SIZES

Russian (and European) sizes are different from those in America and the UK. This is a rough guide.

| WOMEN'S SIZES | | | MEN'S SIZES | |
|---|---|---|---|---|
| Russia | UK | US | Russia | UK/US |
| 36 | 30 | 8 | 44 | 34 |
| 38 | 32 | 10 | 46 | 36 |
| 40 | 34 | 12 | 48 | 38 |
| 42 | 36 | 14 | 50 | 40 |
| 44 | 38 | 16 | 52 | 42 |
| 46 | 40 | 18 | 54 | 44 |

## STATIONERY & PUBLICATIONS

# Канцелярские товары

Is there a foreign-language bookshop here?

zdes' est' magazin inastranay knigi?

Здесь есть магазин иностранной книги?

Is there an English-language section?

u vas est' sektsiya angliyskay knigi?

У вас есть секция английской книги?

Is there a local entertainment guide?

u vas est' spisak mesnykh dastaprimechatel'nastey?

У вас есть список местных достопримечательностей?

SHOPPING

| Do you sell ...? | zdes' pradayutsa ...? | Здесь продаются ...? |
|---|---|---|
| magazines | zhurnaly | журналы |
| newspapers | gazety | газеты |
| postcards | atkrytki | открытки |
| dictionaries | slavari | словари |
| envelopes | kanverty | конверты |
| newspapers in English | gazety na angliyskam | газеты на английском |
| paper | bumaga | бумага |
| pen (ballpoint) | ruchka | ручка |
| stamps | marki | марки |
| ... maps | ... karty | ... карты |
| city | gorada | города |
| regional | oblasti | области |
| road | darok | дорог |

## MUSIC                     Музыка

I'm looking for a ... CD.
  ya ishchu disk ...        Я ищу диск ...
Do you have any ...?
  u vas est' ...?           У вас есть ...?
What's his/her best recording?
  kakoy samy luchshiy       Какой самый лучший
  evo/eyo disk?             его/её диск?

I heard a band/singer called ...
  ya slyshal (m)/           Я слышал/
  slyshala (f) grupu        слышала группу
  peftsa ...                певца ...
Can I listen to this CD here?
  zdes' mozhna              Здесь можно
  paslushat' disk?          послушать диск?
I need a blank tape.
  mne nuzhna                Мне нужна
  pustaya kaseta            пустая касета.

### NEW RUSSIANS

You can't help noticing the nouvelles riches of post-Soviet
Russia, the 'new Russians' novye ruskie новые русские,
for whom furs, gold, chauffeur-driven limos and even
bodyguards are de rigeur. The whole deregulation process
was so done in such a shabby manner that Russians rarely
trust anyone with money.

## PHOTOGRAPHY Фотография

In Russia you'll sometimes find GOST units rather than ASA or DIN. As a rule of thumb, they're slightly below ASA. GOST actually means 'State All-Union Standards'.

| GOST | ASA | DIN |
|------|-----|-----|
| 45   | 50  | 18  |
| 65   | 75  | 19  |
| 90   | 100 | 21  |
| 180  | 200 | 24  |
| 350  | 400 | 27  |

**SHOPPING**

How much is it to process this film?
skol'ka stoit
prayavit' etu plyonku?
Сколько стоит
проявить эту плёнку?

When will it be ready?
kagda ana budet gatova?
Когда она будет
готова?

I'd like a film for this camera.
mne nuzhna plyonka
dlya etava fotaparata
Мне нужна плёнка
для этого
фотоаппарата.

| battery | batereyka | батарейка |
|---------|-----------|-----------|
| B&W film | chyorna-belaya plyonka | чёрно-белая пленка |
| camera | fotaparat | фотоаппарат |
| colour film | tsvetnaya plyonka | цветная плёнка |
| film | plyonka | плёнка |
| flash/flash bulb | fspyshka | вспышка |
| lens | linza | линза |
| light meter | ekspanametr | экспанометр |
| slides | slaydy | слайды |
| videotape | videokaseta | видеокассета |

SHOPPING

## SMOKING     Табачные изделия

A packet of (Belamor) cigarettes,
please.
   pachku (belamora),
   pazhalsta

Пачку 'Беломора',
пожалуйста.

Are these cigarettes strong or mild?
   eti sigarety krepkie
   ili lyokhkie?

Эти сигареты крепкие
или лёгкие?

Do you have a light?
   mozhna prikurit'?

Можно прикурить?

Do you mind if I smoke?
   vy ne vazrazhaete,
   esli ya zakuryu?

Вы не возражаете,
если я закурю?

Please don't smoke.
   ne kurite, pazhalsta

Не курите, пожалуйста.

I'm trying to give up.
   ya pytayus' brosit' kurit'

Я пытаюсь бросить курить.

| | | |
|---|---|---|
| cigarettes | sigarety | сигареты |
| cigarette papers | papirosnaya bumaga | папиросная бумага |
| filtered | s fil'tram | с фильтром |
| lighter | zazhigalka | зажигалка |
| matches | spichki | спички |
| menthol | s mentolam | с ментолом |
| pipe | trupka | трубка |
| tobacco | tabak | табак |

## BEING HASSLED

I don't want one.
   ya ne khachu

Я не хочу.

I already have one.
   u menya uzhe est'

У меня уже есть.

Go away!    atstan'!

Отстань!

Police!    militsiya!

Милиция!

## SIGNS

| | |
|---|---|
| МАГАЗИН РАБОТАЕТ | OPENING HOURS |
| С ... ДО ... | FROM ... TO ... |
| ПЕРЕРЫВ НА ОБЕД | CLOSED FOR LUNCH |
| ВЫХОДНОЙ ДЕНЬ ПОНЕДЕЛЬНИК | CLOSED MONDAYS |
| ЗАКРЫТО НА РЕМОНТ | CLOSED FOR REPAIRS |

SHOPPING

SHOPPING

## RUSSIAN SALES

A dictionary will tell you that raspradazha распродажа means 'clearance sale'. However, in Russia, it usually means your workplace has obtained a shipment of something hard to get – such as imported shoes – and you can join a list to order a limited number of items to give to your family and friends.

## SIZES & COMPARISONS
## Размеры и сранения

| small | malen'kiy | маленький |
| big | bal'shoy | большой |
| heavy | tyazholy | тяжёлый |
| light | lyokhkiy | лёгкий |
| more | yeshchyo | ещё |
| little (amount) | nemnoga | немного |
| too much/many | slishkam mnoga | слишком много |
| many | mnoga | много |
| enough | dastatachna | достаточно |
| also | tozhe | тоже |
| a little bit | nemnoga | немного |

# Еда                                    **FOOD**

Russian food, at its best, is hearty and delicious. Soups such as borshch and Russian dumplings are well-known abroad. Central to every meal is bread – Russia has hundreds of varieties, and Russians will argue about their relative merits. Eggs and dairy products also feature heavily in Russian cuisine – who else would mix sour cream and mayonnaise?

Never pass up the opportunity to eat at a Russian home, for this is where you'll experience the heights of Russian cuisine. This is a truism amongst Russians themselves, and it represents the Russian tradition of sparing nothing in providing hospitality. It's reinforced by the fact that restaurant food in the Soviet Union was patchy at best, and even now restaurants differ widely in quality. Anyway, the purpose of eating out is less to taste exquisite food, than to enjoy a whole evening of socialising and entertainment, with multiple courses, drinking and dancing.

There are four main types of eateries in Russia.

restaran **ресторан**
    The most expensive (but not necessarily the best) place to eat is a restaurant. People usually go to restaurants in a group, and for special occasions. The atmosphere is boisterous, with live music and a dance floor.

kafe **кафе**
    Russian cafes aren't necessarily a place for drinking coffee, but often a cheaper restaurant serving light food

kanditerskaya **кондитерская**
    the place to go if you want coffee and cakes, the name literally means a 'pastry shop cafe'

stalovaya **столовая**
    canteens are no-fuss, self-service establishments which serve basic food

breakfast   zaftrak   завтрак

lunch   abed   обед
( the most substantial
meal of the day, usually
consisting of three courses)

dinner   uzhyn   ужин
(lighter than lunch,
but still substantial!)

> **PRIYATNAVA APETITA**
>
> It's polite to start a meal by saying priyatnava apetita! 'Bon appetit!'

## VEGETARIAN & SPECIAL MEALS
## Вегетарианские блюда

Vegetables are secondary in Russia, both through necessity (fresh vegetables are hard to get in winter) and preference. In fact, the concept of vegetarianism is totally alien to many people, so be prepared to stand your ground with waiters who insist that meat soup with some of the meat taken out is vegetarian. Also, Russians, being immensely hospitable, might not understand why you turn your nose up at the meal they've spent a week's salary on and two days preparing. A medical or religious excuse is probably the safest bet.

I'm a vegetarian.
   ya vegetarianets (m)   Я вегетарианец.
   ya vegetarianka (f)   Я вегетарианка.
I'm on a strict diet.
   ya na strogoy diete   Я на строгой диете.
I don't eat meat.
   ya ne em myasnova   Я не ем мясного.
I can't eat dairy products.
   ya ne em malochnava   Я не ем молочного.
Do you have any
vegetarian dishes?
   u vas est'   У вас есть
   vegetarianskie blyuda?   вегетарианские блюда?
Does this dish have meat?
   eto blyudo myasnoe?   Это блюдо мясное?

FOOD

Does it contain eggs?
  v etam blyude
  est' yaytsa?

В этом блюде
есть яйца?

I'm allergic to (nuts).
  u menya allergiya
  na (arekhi).

У меня аллергия
на (орехи).

Is there a kosher restaurant here?
  zdes' est' kasherny
  restaran?

Здесь есть кошерный
ресторан?

Is this kosher?
  eta kashernae?

Это кошерное?

## EATING OUT

Питание в
общественных местах

| Do you have | vas est' | У вас есть |
| a table ...? | stolik ...? | столик ...? |
| for two | na dvaikh | на двоих |
| for three | na traikh | на троих |

Can we see the menu?
  dayte, pazhalsta,
  menyu

Дайте, пожалуйста
меню.

Do I get it myself or do
they bring it to us?
  mne vzyat' samamu
  ili nam padadut?

Мне взять самому
или нам подадут?

**FOOD**

| Please bring (a/an/the) ... | prinesite, pazhalsta ... | Принесите, пожалуйста ... |
|---|---|---|
| ashtray | pepel'nitsu | пепельницу |
| bill | shyot | счёт |
| fork | vilku | вилку |
| knife | nosh | нож |
| plate | tarelku | тарелк |
| glass of water | stakan vody | стакан воды |
| with/ | so l'dom/ | со льдом/ |
| without ice | bez l'da | без льда |

Russian restaurant staff, no matter how surly, will expect a generous tip. Don't even think about asking if service is included, or you'll be landed with an additional charge.

## Useful Words   Полезные слова и выражения

| cup | chashka | чашка |
|---|---|---|
| fresh | svezhy | свежий |
| spicy | ostry | острый |
| stale | nesvezhy | несвежий |
| sweet | slatkiy | сладкий |
| toothpick | zubachistka | зубочистка |

FOOD

## TYPICAL DISHES   Национальные блюда

The following dishes are described in the order they appear in a traditional Russian meal. First of all are the cold hors d'oeuvres – in a restaurant these may be brought out without asking, so be prepared to send some back if you don't want to pay for them. This is followed by soup, called the 'first dish' pervye blyuda, then the main course, or ftarye blyuda 'second dish'. Finally comes dessert, dessert

**Hors d'Oeuvres** Холодные закуски

**икра (красная/чёрная)** ikra (krasnaya/chyornaya)
  caviar (red/black) – in Russia this means real sturgeon roe, and
  it's expensive

**баклажанная икра** baklazhannaya ikra
  (lit: eggplant caviar) this is an often spicy eggplant puree with
  other ingredients such as tomato, onion and garlic

**яйца** yaytsa
  stuffed and decorated hard-boiled eggs

**солёные огурцы** salyonye agurtsy
  cucumbers – usually pickled

**солёный арбуз** salyony arbus
  pickled watermelon

**селёдка** selyotka
  herrings – also pickled; occasionally in sour cream

**маринованные/** marinovanye/
**солёные грибы** salyonye griby
  marinated mushrooms

---

### RUSSIANS & THEIR WATERMELONS

Pickled watermelon is one of the most typical of
Russian recipes. Wash small-sized thin-skinned
watermelons and pierce them 10-15 times with a
wooden skewer. Place them into any wooden barrel
you have lying around and cover with pickling-juice
(one bucket of water and 700g of salt for every 10kg
of watermelons). Cover the barrel with a wooden lid
and put a weight on top to stop the watermelons
rising to the surface. Store in a cool place for a
month or two. Eat the pickled watermelons as a
zakuska, hors d'oeuvre, with vodka!

Watermelons sold in June and July can look
good, but it's because the growers inject them with
(sometimes deadly) nitrates, so wait until August!

---

FOOD

паштет    pashtet
  pâté or 'meat paste' – usually like liverwurst, not French pâté
салат    salat
  salad – usually safe for vegetarians. Tomatoes, onion and
  cucumber are the rule.
винегрет    vinegret
  boiled potato, carrot and beetroot, chopped and mixed with
  onion and pickles – sometimes called a 'winter salad', zimniy
  salat, because the ingredients are available in winter
блины со сметаной    bliny sa smetanay
  pancakes with sour cream, rolled up and baked
мясное ассорти    myasnoe asarti
  selection of cold meats
рыбное ассорти    rybnae asarti
  selection of cold fish delicacies

## Soups – 'First Dishes' Первые блюда
борщ    borshch
  beetroot soup. There are many varieties of borshch, including
  maskofskiy московский 'Moscow' and ukrainskiy
  украинский 'Ukrainian'. All, as a rule, include meat in meat
  stock. There's also zelyony borshch зелёный борщ
  'green borshch', which is made with sorrel. Russians usually
  add sour cream.
бульон    bul'on
  chicken broth, usually with noodles or meatballs (see soup
  extras below)
акрошка    akroshka
  cold soup with chopped pickles (and usually meat)
рассольник    rassol'nik
  for the offal lover – soup made with chopped pickles and kidney
уха    ukha
  simple broth made with fish and potatoes
щи    shchi
  soup made from fresh or pickled cabbage

солянка   salyanka
  hearty soup of vegetables with meat, myasnaya **мясная** or
  fish, rybnaya **рыбная**. The name roughly means 'salted',
  which is a fair description.
суп-лапша   sup-lapsha
  noodle soup, usually with chicken broth

| SOUP EXTRAS | | |
| --- | --- | --- |
| with noodles | vermishelevy | вермешелевый |
| with meat | myasnoy | с мясом |
| with fish | rybny | с рыбой |
| with meatballs | s frikadel'kami | с фрикадельками |

## Main Course – 'Second Dishes' Вторые блюда

говядина   gavyadina
  beef
бефстроганов   befstroganaf
  beef stroganov – braised beef with sour cream and mushrooms
биточки   bitochki
  meatballs, often served in tomato sauce
котлеты   katlety
  almost never 'cutlets', but rather meat rissoles
котлеты по-киевски   katlety pakiefski
  chicken Kiev – a chicken breast rolled and stuffed with butter,
  crumbed, and deep-fried
бифштекс   bifshteks
  steak
блинчики с мясом   blinchiki s myasam
  pancakes filled with meat
кебаб   kebap
  rissole with a Central Asian flavour
плов   plof
  another Central Asian specialty, related to Middle Eastern
  pilaf – rice with meat or vegetables, cooked in stock

FOOD

поджарка        padzharka
  roast meat, usually beef or pork
рагу        ragu
  stew of any description
сосиски        sasiski
  fried or boiled sausages. If boiled, they're usually served with
  pickled cabbage, along the lines of frankfurters and sauerkraut.
цыплёнок табака        tsyplyonak tabaka
  Caucasian dish of chicken flattened and grilled over charcoal
шашлык        shashlyk
  this can refer to any type of meat on a skewer, although
  traditionally lamb
шницель        shnitsel'
  Wiener schnitzel – veal coated in breadcrumbs and fried

## DESSERTS        Дессерт

Russians excel at baking – try cakes and pastries on any pretense.

оладьи        alad'i
  small fritters, often fried with fruit
мороженое        marozhenae
  ice-cream – Russia makes delicious icecream, and you can buy
  it almost anywhere at any time, for example, on a St Petersburg
  street in the middle of a snowstorm
пироженое        pirozhnae
  little pastries or biscuits
торт        tort
  large cake
компот        kampot
  fruit compote made from fresh or dried fruit

## SELF-CATERING    Самообслуживание

|  |  |  |
|---|---|---|
| bread (white/black) | khlep (bely/chyorny) | хлеб (белый/чёрный) |
| buckweat | grechka | гречка |
| butter | masla | масло |
| cheese | syr | сыр |
| chocolate | shakalat | шоколад |
| cereals | krupy | крупы |
| cottage cheese | tvarok | творог |
| cream | slifki | сливки |
| eggs | yaytsa | яйца |
| flour | muka | мука |
| ham | vetchina | ветчина |
| honey | myot | мёд |
| margarine | margarin | маргарин |
| milk | malako | молоко |
| oats | afsyanka | овсянка |
| pepper | perets | перец |
| rice | ris | рис |
| salt | sol' | соль |
| semolina | manka | манка |
| sour milk | prastakvasha | простокваша |
| sugar | sakhar | сахар |
| yogurt | yogurt | йогурт |
| sour cream | smetana | сметана |

FOOD

### COOKING METHODS

|  |  |  |
|---|---|---|
| baked | zapechyony | запечёный |
| boiled | varyony | варёный |
| fried | zharenay | жареный |
| grilled | v grile | в гриле |
| in sour cream | f smetane | в сметане |
| in tomato | f tamate | в томате |
| stuffed | farshirovanny | фаршированный |

## AT THE MARKET
## На рынке

While shops generally have fixed prices, you have to bargain at the market (see pg 131). Insist on samples, and watch out for tricks like overcharging, shortchanging, and disguising poor fruit and vegetables with a few nice pieces on top.

### Meat Мясо

| beef | gavyadina | говядина |
| liver | pechen' | печень |
| meat | myasa | мясо |
| mutton, lamb | baranina | баранина |
| pork | svinina | свинина |
| rabbit | krolik | кролик |
| tongue | yazyk | язык |
| veal | telyatina | телятина |

### Seafood Дары моря

| carp | karp | карп |
| fish | ryba | рыба |
| herring | sel't' | сельдь |
| perch | okun' | окунь |
| pike | shchuka | щука |
| salmon (or other red fish) | krasnaya ryba | красная рыба |
| sprats (tinned) | shproty | шпроты |

FOOD

## Vegetables & Fruit   Овощи и фрукты

| | | |
|---|---|---|
| beetroot | svyolka | свёкла |
| black radish | chyornaya red'ka | чёрная редька |
| cabbage | kapusta | капуста |
| carrots | markof' | морковь |
| cucumber | agurets | огурец |
| eggplant (aubergine) | baklazhan | баклажан |
| mushrooms | griby | грибы |
| onions | luk | лук |
| peas | garokh | горох |
| potatoes | kartoshka | картошка |
| radish | rediska | редиска |
| tomatoes | pamidory | помидоры |
| vegetables | ovashchi | овощи |

## Fruit   Фрукты

| | | |
|---|---|---|
| apples | yablaki | яблоки |
| berries | yagady | ягоды |
| blackberries | chernika | черника |
| blackcurrant | chyornaya smarodina | чёрная смородина |
| cherries | chireshnya | черешня |
| cranberries | brusnika | брусника |
| fruit | frukty | фрукты |
| lemon | limon | лемон |
| melon | arbus | арбуз |
| oranges | apel'siny | апельсины |
| redcurrant | krasnaya smarodina | красная смородина |
| wild strawberries | zemlyanika | земляника |

FOOD

## BLACK BREAD

Russia's most popular bread is black bread made from rye – dense, flavoursome and slightly sour. Don't be dismayed at the lack of hygenic handling at the bakery.

FOOD

## SPICES & CONDIMENTS

## Специи и приправы

| | | |
|---|---|---|
| bay leaf | lavrovy list | лавровый лист |
| chilli | gorkiy perets | горький перец |
| dill | ukrop | укроп |
| garlic | chesnok | чеснок |
| horseradish | khren | хрен |
| mustard | garchitsa | горчица |
| onions | luk | лук |
| parsley | petrushka | петрушка |
| pepper | perets | перец |
| salt | sol' | соль |
| sauce | sous | соус |

## USEFUL AMOUNTS

## Меры

| | | |
|---|---|---|
| How much/many? | skol'ka | Сколько? |
| Please give me ... | dayte pazhalsta ... | Дайте, пожалуйста ... |
| I need ... | mne nada ... | Мне надо ... |
| a little | nemnoga | немного |
| a few | neskal'ka | несколько |
| some | nemnoga | немного |
| a dozen | dyuzhina | дюжина |
| double | dvaynoye | двойное |
| | kalichestva | количество |
| enough | dastatachna | достаточно |

| | | |
|---|---|---|
| less | men'she | меньше |
| many; much; a lot | mnoga | много |
| more | bol'she | больше |
| too much | ochen' mnoga | очень много |
| a pair | para | пара |
| some | neskol'ka | несколько |
| a bottle of | butylka | бутылка |
| half a kilo of | pol-kilo | пол-кило |
| 100 grams | sto gram | 100 грамм |
| a jar | banka | банка |
| a kg | kilo | кило |
| a packet | paket | пакет |
| a slice of | lomtik | ломтик |
| a tin | banka | банка |

## RESTAURANT REVENGE

I didn't know you could make
borshch just from water.
    a ya i ne znal shta
    borshch **mozhet** byt'
    tol'ka na vade

А я и не знал,
что борщ может быть
только на воде.

I didn't realise you could make
meat rissoles from bread.
    ya ne znal shta
    myasnyye katlety
    byvayut khlebnymi

Я не знал,
что мясные катлеты
бывают хлебными.

I'm very sorry to hear all the
waiters died.
    vse afitsianty
    vymirli?

Все официанты
вымерли?

Can I have some pil'meney
with my sauce?
    mozhna li dabavit'
    chut'chut' pil'meney
    k sousu?

Можно ли добавить
чуть-чуть пельменей
к соусу?

**FOOD**

## DRINKS                    Всё о напитках

Russians toast before each round with the expression *za vashe zdarov'e!* 'To your health!', then while downing the vodka they say *pey dadna!* 'Drink to the bottom!'. After the second and subsequent toasts, it's a tradition to have a small bite of something, and Russian even has a special word, *zakusit'*, meaning 'eat something after drinking'!

In a restaurant or bar, if you're not after a bottle, *butylka*, you can order spirits by weight, for example 200 grams, *dvesti gram*. A handy phrase to know is:

Do you have any cold (wine/beer)?
    u vas est' khalodnae?        У вас есть холодное?

FOOD

### KVAS

Kvas khlebny (bread kvas) is an ancient, singularly Russian drink. Kvas is sweet and sour, made primarily from sugar and rye flour. It's the most popular drink in summer, believed to quench thirst, improve digestion and even benefit the human spirit. Napoleon himself said that the Russians defeated the French thanks to the fact they drank kvas.

It can be bought in bottles or from a huge tank on the street. The seller serves the kvas in a single glass, which they theoretically clean between customers.

## Alcoholic  Алкогольные напитки

| | | |
|---|---|---|
| beer | piva | пиво |
| champagne | shampanskae | шампанское |
| cocktail | kakteyl | коктейль |
| Cognac | kan'yak | коньяк |
| vodka | votka | водка |
| wine | vino | вино |
| red/white | krasnae/belae | красное/белое |
| sweet/dry | slatkae/sukhoe | сладкое/сухое |

## DRUNK RUSSIAN

Let's have a drink!
  davayte vyp'em!
To (eternal friendship)!
  za (vechnuyu druzhbu)!
I'm tipsy.
  ya vypifshiy (m)/
  vypifshaya (f)
I'm drunk.
  ya pyany (m)/pyanaya (f)

Давайте выпьем!

За (вечную дружбу)!

Я выпивший/
выпившая.

Я пьяный/пьяная.

Do you respect me?
(first sign of inebriation)
  ty menya uvazhaesh'?
I'm going to be sick.
  menya budet mutit'
I've got a hangover.
  ya apakhmelilsa (m)/
  apakhmelilas' (f)

Ты меня уважаешь?

Меня будет мутить.

Я опохмелился/
опохмелилась.

## Non-Alcoholic Безалкогольные напитки

| | | |
|---|---|---|
| fruit juice | sok | сок |
| lemonade/soft drink | limanat | лимонад |
| milk shake | malochny kakteyl | молочный коктейль |
| ryazhenka (fermented baked milk) | ryazhenka | ряженка |
| sour milk | prastakvasha | простокваша |
| ... water | ... vada | ... вода |
| mineral | mineral'naya | минеральная |
| boiled | kipyachyonaya | кипяченая |
| soda | gazirovannaya | газированная |
| coffee | kofe | кофе |
| Turkish coffee | kofe paturetski | кофе по-турецки |
| with/without milk | s malakom/ bez malaka | с молоком/ без молока |
| with/without sugar | s sakharam/ bes sakharu | с сахаром/ без сахару |
| (cup of) tea | (chashka) chayu | (чашка) чаю |
| herbal tea | chay is traf | чай из трав |

FOOD

# За городом **IN THE COUNTRY**

**CAMPING** Туризм

In Russia you can go to an official kemping 'camp site' which has basic facilities such as toilets, a shower, and perhaps a shop and a restaurant. These are mainly used by foreign tourists.

A more authentic Russian tradition is turizm, organised through a tourist club, turisticheskiy klup, which involves backpacking, setting up camp in the forest, and singing songs around the campfire with a guitar.

| | | |
|---|---|---|
| camping | turizm | туризм |
| campsite | kemping (with facilities) | кемпинг |
| | prival (in the wild) | привал |
| cooking pot | katelok | котелок |
| guitar | gitara | гитара |
| matches | spichki | спички |
| open fire | kastyor | костёр |
| rope | veryofka | верёвка |
| sleeping bag | spal'ny meshok | спальный мешок |
| tent | palatka | палатка |
| torch (flashlight) | fanarik | фонарик |
| | | |
| How much | skol'ka | Сколько |
| is it per ...? | stoit za ...? | стоит за |
|   person | adnavo chilaveka | одного человека |
|   tent | palatku | палатку |

Where can I hire a tent?
gde mozhna vzyat'
palatku f prakat?

Где можно взять
палатку в прокат?

Can we camp here? (in the wild)
zdes' mozhna zdelat' prival?

Здесь можно
сделать привал?

Are there shower facilities?
zdes' est' dush?

Здесь есть душ?

## HIKING　　Пешеходные маршруты

Where can I find out about
hiking trails?

gde mozhna paluchit'
infarmatsiyu a
turistskikh marshrutakh?

Где можно получить
информацию о
туристких маршрутах?

I'd like to talk to someone who
knows this area.

ya by khatel'(m)/
ya by khatela (f) pagavarit'
s kem-ta, kto znaet
etu mes'nast'

Я бы хотел/
хотела поговорить
с кем-то, кто знает
эту местность.

Is it dangerous to climb
this mountain?

vaskhazhdenie na
etu goru apasna?

Восхождение на
эту гору опасно?

Is there a hut up there?

tam naverkhu est'
staroshka?

Там наверху есть
сторожка?

Do we need a guide?

nam nuzhen pravadnik?

Нам нужен
проводник?

How long is the trail?

kakava pratyazhonnast'
marshruta?

Какова протяженность
маршрута?

Is the track well marked?

marshrut kharasho
pamechen?

Маршрут хорошо
помечен?

How high is the climb?

kak vysako my
padnimimsa?

Как высоко мы
поднимимся?

Which is the shortest route?
kakoy samy karotkiy put'?

Какой самый
короткий путь?

Which is the easiest route?
kaloy samy lyokhkiy put'?

Какой самый
лёгкий путь?

Is the path open?
trapa atkryta?

Тропа открыта?

When does it get dark?
kagda temneet?

Когда темнеет?

Is it very scenic?
eta krasivy marshrut?

Это красивый
маршрут?

Where can I hire mountain gear?
gde mozhna vzyat' f
prakat abmundiravanie
dlya vaskhazhdeniya v gory?

Где можно взять в
прокат обмундирование
для восхождения в горы?

Where can we buy supplies?
gde mozhna kupit' pradukty?

Где можно купить
продукты?

## DOWN ON THE COLLECTIVE FARM

In the USSR, there were two types of farms: the колхоз
kalkhos or 'collective farm', which farm workers
theoretically ran as a cooperative; and the совхоз
safkhos or 'state farm', which was run like a factory.

Although the distinction no longer exists, not much
on the surface has changed. Farms are still enormous,
but they're now owned or controlled by the new
moneyed class. Farm workers still feel disenfranchised,
putting much more effort into tending small private
plots, and 'borrowing' tools and fertilisers from their
employers when necessary.

IN THE COUNTRY

### On the Path  На маршруте

| | | |
|---|---|---|
| Where have you come from? | atkuda vy prishli? | Откуда вы пришли? |
| How long did it take you? | skol'ka vremeni eta u vas zanyalo? | Сколько времени это у вас заняло? |
| Are there any tourist attractions near here? | .pablizasti est' kakie-ta dastaprimechatel'nasti? | Поблизости есть какие-то достопримечательности? |
| Where's the nearest village? | gde blizhayshaya derevnya? | Где ближайшая деревня? |
| Does this path go to ...? | eta trapa vedyot k ...? | Эта тропа ведёт к ...? |
| I'm lost. | ya pateryalsa (m)/ pateryalas' (f) | Я потерялся/ потерялась. |
| Where can we spend the night? | gde mozhna perenachevat'? | Где можно переночевать? |
| Can I leave some things here for a while? | mozhna astavit' mai veshchi na vremya? | Можно оставить мои вещи на время? |

| | | |
|---|---|---|
| altitude | vysata | высота |
| backpack | ryugzak | рюкзак |
| binoculars | binokl' | бинокль |
| candles | svechi | свечи |
| to climb | vzbirat'sa | взбираться |
| compass | kompas | компас |
| downhill | sklon | склон |
| first-aid kit | aptechka | аптечка |
| gloves | perchatki | перчатки |

| | | |
|---|---|---|
| guide | pravadnik | проводник |
| hiking | turizm | туризм |
| hiking boots | turisticheskie batinki | туристические ботинки |
| hunting | akhota | охота |
| ledge | vystup | выступ |
| lookout | smatravaya plashchatka | смотровая площадка |
| map | karta | карта |
| mountain climbing | al'pinizm | альпинизм |
| pick | kirka | кирка |
| provisions | praviziya | провизия |
| rock climbing | skalalazanie | скалолазание |
| thick rope | tros | трос |
| thin rope | veryofka | верёвка |
| signpost | ukazatel'ny stolp | указательный столб |
| steep | krutoy | крутой |
| trek | perekhot | переход |
| uphill | v goru | в гору |
| to walk | khadit' | ходить |

## AT THE BEACH

На пляже

Swimming is forbidden at many Russian beaches because of pollution. Also, they're often pebbly. However, it doesn't matter because Russians like to stand at the beach to get an all-over tan.

**NO SWIMMING**

kupanie zapreshcheno!
Купание запрещено!

Can we swim here?
  zdes' mozhna plavat'?

Здесь можно плавать?

Is it safe to swim here?
  zdes' ne apasna plavat'?

Здесь не опасно плавать?

What time is high/low tide?
  f katoram chasu prilif/atlif?

В котором часу прилив/отлив?

Where can we change?
  gde mozhna pereadet'sa?

Где можно переодеться?

| | | |
|---|---|---|
| coast | berek | берег |
| fishing | pybnaya lovlya | рыбная ловля |
| reef | rif | риф |
| rock | skala | скала |
| sand | pesok | песок |
| sea | more | море |
| snorkelling | nyranie | ныряние |
| sunblock | zashchitny krem at sontsa | защитный крем от солнца |
| sunglasses | achki | очки (in context, people just say 'glasses') |
| surf | valnarez | волнорез |
| surfing | serfing | серфинг |

| surfboard | daska dlya serfinga | доска для серфинга |
| swimming | plavanie | плавание |
| towel | palatentse | полотенце |
| waterskiing | vodnye lyzhy | водные лыжи |
| waves | volny | волны |
| windsurfing | vintserfing | виндсерфинг |

## WEATHER        Погода

The climate in Russia is not as diverse as the country's huge size might suggest. Most places have a cold, continental climate (except for the southwest part of the country around the Black Sea and in the southeast near Vladivostok). In winter, the temperature in north-eastern Siberia can get down to -70°C. Moscow is more typical – it's warm and humid in summer (average 22°) and freezing in Winter (average –15°).

What's the weather like?
  kakaya pagoda?           Какая погода?

| Today it's ... | sevodnya ... | Сегодня ... |
| cloudy | oblachna | облачно |
| cold | kholadna | холодно |
| hot | zharka | жарко |
| warm | teplo | тепло |
| windy | vetrenna | ветренно |

It's raining heavily.
  idyou sil'ny dosht'      Идёт сильный дождь.
It's raining lightly.
  marasit               Моросит.

| storm | graza | гроза |
| sun | sontse | солнце |

**IN THE COUNTRY**

## TELL IT LIKE IT IS, VLAD

No Russian poet was as universally loved during his lifetime as the Pushkin of the Soviet Era, the poet, songwriter and performer, Vladimir Visotsky. He was uncompromising in his gritty descriptions of Soviet life, and many of his works were banned.

ПЕСНЯ О ДРУГЕ
   pesnya a druge          Song About a Friend

Если друг оказался вдруг
   esli druk akazalsa vdruk
   If a friend appears suddenly
И не друг, и не враг, а так ...
   i ne druk, i ne vrak, a tak
   Well a friend, not an enemy
Если сразу не разберёшь,
   esli srazu ne razberyosh
   If you can't figure out straight away
Плох он или хорош.
   plokh on ili kharosh
   If he's bad or good.
Парня в горы тяни – рискни,
   parnya v gary tyani-riskni
   Take this friend to the mountains, take this risk
Не бросай одного его, Пусть он в связке одной с тобой,
   ne brasay adnavo evo pust' on f svyaske adnoy s taboy
   Don't let go of him. Don't separate
Там поймёшь, кто такой.
   tam paymyosh', kto takoy
   Then you'll understand what he's like.
Если парень в горах не ах,
   esli paren' v garakh ne akh
   If this friend gasps
Если сразу раскис и вниз,
   esli srazu raskis i vnis
   If he suddenly becomes weak and drops
Шаг ступил на ледник и сник,
   shak stupil na lednik i snik
   He steps on the ice and slips

Оступился – и в крик.
astupilsa – i f krik
Stumbles – and shouts.

Значит, рядом с тобой чужой.
znachit, ryadam s taboy chuzhoy
It means there's a stranger next to you

Ты его не брани – гони,
ty evo ne brani, gani
Don't chastise him – just get rid of him

Вверх таких не берут и тут
verkh takikh ne berut i tut
You can't take a person like that up with you

О таких не поют.
a takikh ne payut
And we won't sing about them here.

Если он не скулил, не ныл,
esli on ne skupil, ne nyl
But even if he aches

Пусть он хмур был и зол, но шёл,
pust' on khmur byl i zol, no shol
Even if he's bad tempered and annoyed,
but still goes on

А когда ты упал со скал,
a kagda ty upal sa skal
When you fall from the cliff

Он стонал, но держал.
on stanal, no derzhal
He groans but still holds on.

Если шёл он с тобой, как в бой,
esli shol on s taboy tak v boy
If he goes with you as into battle

На вершине стоял хмельной,
na vershyne stayal khmel'noy
Stands drunk on the mountain top

Значит, как на тебя самого,
znzchit, kak na tebya samavo
It means you can depend on him

Положись на него.
palazhys na nevo
As you can on yourself

## GEOGRAPHICAL TERMS
## Немного географии

| | | |
|---|---|---|
| beach | plyash | пляж |
| bridge | most | мост |
| cave | peshchera | пещера |
| cliff | utyos | утёс |
| earthquake | zemletryasenie | землетрясение |
| farm | ferma (large) | ферма |
| | khazyaystva | хозяйство |
| | (belonging to a family) | |
| footpath | trapinka | тропинка |
| forest | les | лес |
| gap; narrow pass | gorny prakhot | горный проход |
| harbour | gavan' | гавань |
| hill | kholm | холм |
| hot spring | garyachiy | горячий |
| | istochnik | источник |
| island | ostraf | остров |
| lake | ozera | озеро |
| mountain | gara | гора |
| mountain path | gornaya trapa | горная тропа |
| pass | prakhot | проход |
| peak | vershyna | вершина |
| river | reka | река |
| sea | more | море |
| valley | dalina | долина |
| waterfall | vadapat | водопад |

## FAUNA
## Фауна

| | | |
|---|---|---|
| bear | medved' | медведь |
| beaver | babyor | бобёр |
| bird | ptitsa | птица |
| buffalo | buyval | буйвол |
| cat | koshka | кошка |
| | (general/female) | |
| | kot (male) | кот |

| chicken | tsyplyonak | цыплёнок |
| cockroach | tarakan | таракан |
| cow | karova | корова |
| crocodile | krakadil | крокодил |
| dog | sabaka | собака |
| dove/pigeon | golub' | голубь |
| European bison | zubr | зубр |
| fish | ryba | рыба |
| fly | mukha | муха |
| fox | lisa | лиса |
| goose | gus' | гусь |
| hare | zayats | заяц |
| horse | loshad' | лошадь |
| leech | piyafka | пиявка |
| lion | lef | лев |
| magpie | saroka | сорока |
| mink | norka | норка |
| monkey | abez'yana | обезьяна |
| mosquito | kamar | комар |
| nightingale | salavey | соловей |
| owl | sava | сова |
| pig | svin'ya | свинья |
| polar bear | bely medved' | белый медведь |
| polecat | kharyok | хорёк |
| rabbit | krolik | кролик |
| raven | varona | ворона |
| sable | sobal' | соболь |
| sheep | oftsy | овца |
| snake | zmeya | змея |
| sparrow | varabey | воробей |
| spider | pauk | паук |
| squirrel | belka | белка |
| stork | aist | аист |
| swallow | lastachka | ласточка |
| wolf | volk | волк |

## FLORA
## & AGRICULTURE

Флора

| agriculture | sel'skaye khazyaystva | сельское хозяйство |
|---|---|---|
| barley | yachmen' | ячмень |
| buckwheat | grichihka | гречиха |
| corn | kukuruza | кукуруза |
| crops | urazhay | урожай |
| flower | tsvitok | цветок |
| harvest (verb) | sabirat' urazhay | собирать урожай |
| leaf | list | лист |
| irrigation | arasheniye | орошение |
| rice | ris | рис |
| rye | rosh' | рожь |
| sugar beet | sakharnaya svekla | сахарная свекла |
| tobacco | tabak | табак |
| tree | deriva | дерево |
| wheat | pshinitsa | пшеница |

IN THE COUNTRY

# Всё о здоровье    **HEALTH**

Free healthcare was one of the USSR's greatest achievements.
Now, basic medicine is very scarce. Russians must supply their own
bandages and syringes, and it's often up to the family to look after
their sick.

## AT THE DOCTOR    У врача

| Where's a/the ...? | gde ...? | Где ...? |
|---|---|---|
| doctor | vrach | врач |
| hospital | bal'nitsa | больница |
| chemist | apteka | аптека |
| dentist | zubnoy vrach | зубной врач |

### Ailments  Недуги

I'm sick.
  ya baleyu    Я болею.
My friend is sick.
  moy druk (m)/
  maya padruga (f)baleyet    Мой друг/
  моя подруга болеет.
It hurts there.
  zdes' balit    Здесь болит.
I feel nauseous.
  menya tashnit    Меня тошнит.
I've been vomiting.
  menya rvyot    Меня рвёт.
I feel run down.
  mne ne mozhetsa    Мне не можется.
I can't sleep.
  mne ne spitsa    Мне не спится.
I'm shivery.
  menya marozit    Меня морозит.
I feel weak.
  u menya slabast'    У меня слабость.

HEALTH

## THE DOCTOR MAY SAY ...

| | |
|---|---|
| shto vas bespakoit?<br>What's the matter? | Что вас беспокоит? |
| balit?<br>Do you feel any pain? | Болит? |
| gde balit?<br>Where does it hurt? | Где болит? |
| zdes' balit?<br>Does it hurt here? | Здесь болит? |
| u vas est' mesyachnye?<br>Are you menstruating? | У вас есть месячные? |
| est' temperatura?<br>Do you have a<br>temperature? | Есть температура? |
| kak dolga u vas eta<br>sastayanie?<br>How long have you<br>been like this? | Как долго у вас<br>это состояние? |
| kagda poyavilis' boli?<br>When did the<br>problem start? | Когда появились боли? |
| u vas eta byla ran'she?<br>Have you had this<br>before? | У вас это было раньше? |
| vy prinimaete kakoe-ta<br>lekarstvo?<br>Are you on medication? | Вы принимаете<br>какое-то лекарство? |
| vy kurite?<br>Do you smoke? | Вы курите? |
| vy p'yote?<br>Do you drink? | Вы пьёте? |
| vy upatreblyaete<br>narkotiki?<br>Do you take drugs? | Вы употребляете<br>наркотики? |

**HEALTH**

---

### THE DOCTOR MAY SAY ...

| | |
|---|---|
| u vas est' allergiya na ...? <br> Do you have an allergy to ...? | У Вас есть аллергия на...? |
| vy beremenny? <br> Are you pregnant? | Вы беременны? |
| prinimayte ... <br> Take ... | Принимайте ... |
| adnu/dve tabletki <br> one/two tablets | одну/две таблетки |
| do/posle yedy <br> before/after meals | до/после еды |
| dva/tri raza v den' <br> two/three times a day | два/три раза в день |

---

| I have (a/an) ... | u menya ... | У меня ... |
|---|---|---|
| allergy | alergiya | аллергия |
| anaemia | malakrovie | малокровие |
| burn | azhok | ожог |
| cancer | rak | рак |
| cold | prastuda | простуда |
| constipation | zapor | запор |
| cough | kashel' | кашель |
| diarrhoea | panos | понос |
| fever | temperatura | температура |
| gastroenteritis | atravlenie | отравление |
| headache | galavnaya bol' | головная боль |
| heart condition | balezn' serdtsa | болезнь сердца |
| indigestion | rastroystvo zhelutka | расстройство желудка |
| infection | infektsia | инфекция |
| lice | fshy | вши |
| migraine | migrein | мигрень |
| pain | bol' | боль |

HEALTH

| sore throat | balit gorla | болит горло |
| sprain | rastiazhenie svyazak | растяжение связок |
| stomachache | balit zheludak | болит желудок |
| thrush | malochnitsa | молочница |
| toothache | zubnaya bol' | зубная боль |
| travel sickness | marskaya balezn' | морская болезнь |
| venereal disease | enericheskaya balezn' | венерическая болезнь |
| worms | glisty | глисты |

БОЛЬНИЦА

## Useful Phrases  Полезные выражения

I feel better/worse.
  ya chustvuyu sebya
  luche/khuzhe.

Я чувствую себя лучше/хуже.

This is my usual medicine.
  ya abychna prinimayu
  eta lekarstva

Я обычно принимаю это лекарство.

I've been vaccinated.
  ya privit (m)/privita (f)

Я привит/привита.

I don't want a blood transfusion.
  ya ne khachu, shtoby
  mne perelivali krof'

Я не хочу, чтобы мне переливали кровь.

Can I have a receipt for my insurance?
  dayte kvitantsiyu dlya
  mayey strakhofki?

Дайте квитанцию для моей страховки?

**HEALTH**

## WOMEN'S HEALTH — Женские заболевания

Could I see a female doctor?
mozhna zapisat'sa na
priyom k
zhenshchine-vrachu?

Можно записаться на
приём к
женщине-врачу?

I'm pregnant.
ya beremenna

Я беременна.

I think I'm pregnant.
ya dumayu, shto ya
beremenna

Я думаю, что я
беременна.

I'm on the Pill.
ya prinimayu
prativazachatachnye
tabletki

Я принимаю
противозачаточные
таблетки.

I haven't had my period for ...
weeks.
u menya ... nedel'
zadershka

У меня ... недель
задержка.

| | | |
|---|---|---|
| abortion | abort | аборт |
| cystitis | tsistit | цистит |
| diaphragm | diafragma | диафрагма |
| IUD | spiral' | спираль |
| mamogram | mammagramma | маммограмма |
| menstruation | menstruatsiya | менструация |
| miscarriage | vykidysh | выкидыш |
| pap smear | mazok | мазок |
| period pain | balezennye | болезненные |
| | mesyachnye | месячные |
| the Pill | prativazachatachnye | противозачаточные |
| | tabletki | таблетки |
| premenstrual | predmenstrual'ny | предменструальный |
| tension | sindrom | синдром |
| thrush | malochnitsa | молочница |
| ultrasound | ul'trazvuk | ультразвук |

HEALTH

## SPECIAL HEALTH NEEDS

### Особые состояния пациента

| I have ... | u menya ... | У меня ... |
|---|---|---|
| diabetes | diabet | диабет |
| | sakharnaya (medical term) | сахарная |
| | balezn' (common term) | болезнь |
| asthma | astma | астма |
| anaemia | anemiya (medical term) | анемия |
| | malakrovie (common term) | малокровие |

| I'm allergic to ... | u menya allergiya na ... | У меня аллергия на ... |
|---|---|---|
| antibiotics | antibiotiki | антибиотики |
| aspirin | aspirin | аспирин |
| bees | pchelinyy ukus | пчелиный укус |
| codeine | kadein | кодеин |
| dairy products | malochnye pradukty | молочные продукты |
| penicillin | penitsilin | пеницилин |
| pollen | pyl'tsu | пыльцу |

I have a skin allergy.
   u menya kozhnaya allergiya

У меня кожная аллергия.

I've had my vaccinations.
   mne delali privivki

Мне делали прививки.

I have my own syringe.
   u menya svoy shprits

У меня свой шприц.

I'm on medication for ...
   ya prinimayu lekarstva ot ...

Я принимаю лекарство от ...

I need a new pair of glasses.
   mne nuzhny achki

мне нужны очки

| | | |
|---|---|---|
| addiction | privykanie | привыкание |
| bite | prikus | прикус |
| blood test | analis krovi | анализ крови |
| contraceptive | prativazachatachnae | противозачаточное |
| | sretstva | средство |
| injection | inyektsiya | инъекция |
| | (medical term) | |
| | ukol | укол |
| | (common term) | |
| injury | travma | травма |
| vitamins | vitaminy | витамины |
| wound | rana | рана |

HEALTH

## SICK TALK

What's the matter?
  shto s vami?                     Что с Вами?
I hope it's nothing serious.
  nadeyus', nichevo               Надеюсь, ничего
  seryoznava!                     серьёзного!
Get well soon!
  vyzdaravlivayte!                Выздоравливайте!
Bless you! (after sneezing)
  but'te zdarovy!                 Будьте здоровы!

HEALTH

## ALTERNATIVE TREATMENTS
## Альтернативная медицина

| acupuncture | akupunktura (medical term) | аккупунктура |
| | igloukalyvanie (common term) | иглоукалывание |
| aromatherapy | apomaterapiya | ароматерапия |
| faith healer | narodny tselitel | народный целитель |
| herbalist | travnik | травник |
| homeopathy | gomeopatiya | гомеопатия |
| massage | masash | массаж |
| meditation | meditatsiya | медитация |
| naturopath | naturapat | натуропат |
| reflexology | refleksalogiya | рефлексология |
| yoga | yoga | йога |

## PARTS OF THE BODY
## Наши органы

| ankle | galenastopny sustaf | голеностопный сустав |
| appendix | appenditsit | аппендицит |
| arm | ruka | рука |
| back | spina | спина |
| bladder | machevoy puzyr' | мочевой пузырь |
| blood | krof' | кровь |
| bone | kost' | кость |
| chest | grudnaya kletka | грудная клетка |
| ears | ushy | уши |
| eye | glas | глаз |
| finger | palets | палец |
| foot | stapa | стопа |
| hand | kist' | кисть |
| head | galava | голова |
| heart | sertse | сердце |
| kidney | pochka | почка |
| knee | kalena | колено |
| legs | nogi | ноги |

| liver | pechen' | печень |
| lungs | lokhkie | лёгкие |
| mouth | rot | рот |
| muscle | myshtsa | мышца |
| ribs | ryobra | рёбра |
| shoulder | plecho | плечо |
| skin | kozha | кожа |
| stomach | zheludak | желудок |
| teeth | zuby | зубы |
| throat | gorla | горло |
| vein | vena | вена |

HEALTH

## AT THE DENTIST
I have a toothache.
   u menya balit zup
I have a hole.
   u menya dyra v zube
I've lost a filling.
   u menya vypala plomba
I've broken my tooth.
   u menya slamalsa zup
My gums hurt.
   u menya balyat dyosny
I don't want it pulled out.
   ya ne khachu udalyat' zup
Please give me an anaesthetic.
   abezbol'te, pazhalsta

Ouch!
   oy!

## У зубного врача

У меня болит зуб.

У меня дыра в зубе.

У меня выпала пломба.

У меня сломался зуб.

У меня болят дёсны.

Я не хочу удалять зуб.

Обезбольте,
пожалуйста.

Ой!

HEALTH

## AT THE CHEMIST                        В аптеке

I need something for ...
  mne nuzhna shto-ta ot ...         Мне нужно что-то от ...
Do I need a prescription for this?
  dlia etava nuzhen retsept?        Для этого нужен
                                    рецепт?

How many times a day
(do I take it)?
  skol'ka ras v den'                Сколько раз в день
  (prinimat'eta lekarstva)?         (принимать это
                                    лекарство)?

| | | |
|---|---|---|
| antibiotics | antibiotiki | антибиотики |
| antiseptic | antiseptik | антисептик |
| aspirin | aspirin | аспирин |
| bandage | bint | бинт |
| Band-Aids | plastyr' | пластырь |
| condoms | prezervativy | презервативы |
| cotton wool | vata | вата |
| cough medicine | sretstva at kashlya | средство от кашля |
| gauze | marlya | марля |
| laxatives | slabitel'nye | слабительные |
| painkillers | boleutalyayushchie | болеутоляющие |
| rubbing alcohol | meditsinski spirt | медицинский спирт |
| sleeping pills | snatvornae | снотворное |

# Особые
# Нужды     SPECIFIC NEEDS

In Russia, where even medical necessities such as aspirin are in short supply, there are few facilities for disabled people. Locals must depend on foreign donors or the charity of businesspeople. Most people, however, will do anything they can to assist you.

## DISABLED TRAVELLERS
### Туристы инвалиды

I'm disabled.
  ya invalit

Я инвалид.

I need assistance.
  mne nuzhna pomashch'

Мне нужна помощь.

What services do you have for disabled people?
  kakie vidy usluk vy akazyvaete invalidam

Какие виды услуг вы оказываете инвалидам?

Is there wheelchair access?
  u vas est' prispasablenie dlya invalidnay kalyaski?

У вас есть приспособление для инвалидной коляски?

I'm deaf. Speak more loudly, please.
  ya glukhoy (m)/ glukhaya (f) gavarite gromche, pazhalsta

Я глухой/глухая. Говорите громче, пожалуйста.

---

## JUST SAY DA

Just say да da? 'yes?' at the end of a sentence to make a question: вы турист, да? vy turist, da? 'You're a tourist, aren't you?', 'So are you a tourist?'.

SPECIFIC NEEDS

I can lipread.
ya panimayu rech' pa
dvizheniyu gup

Я понимаю речь по
движению губ.

I have a hearing aid.
u menya slukhavoy
apparat

У меня слуховой
аппарат.

Does anyone here know
sign language?
zdes' kto-to znaet yazyk
glukhanemykh?

Здесь кто-то знает
язык глухонемых?

Are guide dogs permitted inside?
mozhna vayti s sabakay
pavadyryom?

Можно войти с
собакой-поводырём?

| braille books | knigi s shriftom Braylya | книги с шрифтом Брайля |
| disabled person | invalit | инвалид |
| guide dog | sabaka-pavadyr' | собака-поводырь |
| wheelchair | kresla dlya invalidaf | кресло для инвалидов |

## GAY TRAVELLERS
### Туристы гомосексуалисты

Since 1997, homosexuality has no longer been a crime in Russia but gay people should be wary of widespread ignorance and, at worst, open and violent hostility. Services such as publications and phone services are in their infancy. There's a thriving gay culture of course, but it's completely underground.

Where are the gay hangouts?
gde tusuyutsa gei?

Где тусуются геи?

Is there a gay street/district?
est' li ulitsa/mesta,
gde tusuyutsa gei?

Есть ли улица/место,
где тусуются геи?

Are we likely to be harassed?
na nas mogut napast'
zdes'?

На нас могут напасть
здесь?

**SPECIFIC NEEDS**

## THE BLUE LINE

Russian, like English, has a range of words meaning 'gay'. Inside the gay community, gey is the norm. The word for 'blue', galaboy, used to be common (the Blue Line on the St Petersburg metro became something of a hangout) but it's now out of fashion. The word gomik (from gomoseksualist, 'homosexual') is abusive.

Is there a gay bookshop
around here?
pablizasti est' knizhny
magazin dlya geyev?

Поблизости есть
книжный магазин для
геев?

Is there a local gay guide?
u vas est' mesny
putevaditel' dlya geyev?

У вас есть местный
путеводитель для геев?

SPECIFIC NEEDS

Where can I buy some gay/
lesbian magazines?
   gde mozhna kupit'
   zhurnaly dlya
   geyev/lesbianak?

Где можно
купить журналы для
геев/лесбианок?

Is there a gay telephone hotline?
   est' li telefonnaya sluzhba
   dlya geyev?

Есть ли телефонная
служба для геев?

## TRAVELLING WITH THE FAMILY

## Путешествуя с семьёй

Be prepared for Russian babushkas to pinch your children on the
cheek and scold you for not dressing them warmly enough.

Are there facilities for babies?
   est' li mesta,
   aborudavannye dlya
   uhoda za mladentsami?

Есть ли места,
оборудованные для
ухода за младенцами?

Do you have a child minding
service?
   u vas est' sluzhba pa
   prismotru za det'mi?

У вас есть служба по
присмотру за детьми?

Where can I find a
(English-speaking) babysitter?
   gde mozhna nayti nyanyu
   (gavaryashchuyu
   pa-angliyski)?

Где можно найти
няню, (говорящую
по-английски)?

Can you put an (extra) bed/
cot in the room?
   mozhna pastavit'
   dapalnitel'nuyu
   kravat'/koyku v nomer?

Можно поставить
дополнительную
кровать/койку в
номер?

I need a car with a child seat.
   mne nuzhna mashyna s
   kreslam dlya perevozki
   detey

Мне нужна машина с
креслом для перевозки
детей.

Is it suitable for children?
    eta rasshitanna na detey?

Это рассчитано на
детей?

Are there any activities for
children?
    est' li razlicheniya dlya
    detey?

Есть ли развлечения
для детей?

Is there a family discount?
    est' li simeynaya skitka?

Есть ли семейная
скидка?

Are children allowed in?
    detyam fkhot razreshchyon?

Детям вход разрешён?

Do you have a children's menu?
    u vas est' detskaye menyu?

У вас есть детское
меню?

**SPECIFIC NEEDS**

## LOOKING
## FOR A JOB

## В поисках
## работы

Despite economic instability, it is possible to find work in Russia,
but don't expect top conditions. Most expats arrange work through
a foreign company with a branch in Moscow or St Petersburg.

Where can I find local job
advertisements?
    gde reklamiruyetsa rabota?

Где рекламируется
работа?

Do I need a work permit?
    nuzhna imet' razreshenie
    na rabotu?

Нужно иметь
разрешение на работу?

I've come about the position
advertised.
    ya prishöl (m)/prishla (f)
    pa abyavleniyu na rabotu

Я пришёл/пришла
по объявлению.

I'm ringing about the position
advertised.
    ya zvanyu pa povadu
    abyavleniya a rabote

Я звоню по поводу
объявления о работе.

SPECIFIC NEEDS

I've had experience.
u menya est' rabochiy stash

У меня есть рабочий стаж.

What is the wage?
kakaya budet zarplata?

Какая будет зарплата?

Do I have to pay tax?
s menya budut snimat'
padakhodny nalok?

С меня будут снимать подоходный налог?

| I can start ... | ya magu vyti ... | Я могу выйти ... |
|---|---|---|
| today | sevodnya | сегодня |
| tomorrow | zaftra | завтра |
| next week | na sleduyushchey nedele | на следующей неделе |

## Useful Words   Полезные слова

| apprenticeship | uchenichestva | ученичество |
|---|---|---|
| casual | vremeny | временный |
| employee | sluzhashchiy | служащий |
| employer | pabotadatel' | работодатель |
| full-time | na polnuyu stafku | на полную ставку |
| job | rabota | работа |
| occupation/trade | prafesiya | профессия |
| part-time | na polstafki | на пол-ставки |
| resume/cv | rezyume/ aftabiagrafiya | резюме/ автобиография |
| traineeship | praktika | практика |
| work experience | praizvotstvennaya praktika | производственная практика |

## UNSCRUPULOUS MEANS

In shady circles, you may hear the word barysh барыш, which means a profit made from possibly unscrupulous means.

## ON BUSINESS

По бизнесу

| We're attending a ... | my na ... | мы на ... |
|---|---|---|
| conference | kanferentsii | конференции |
| meeting | sabranii | собрании |
| trade fair | targovay | торговой |
| | yamarke | ярмарке |

I'm doing a course.
ya uchyus'
Я учусь.

I have an appointment with ...
u menya vstrecha s ...
У меня встреча с ...

Here's my business card.
vot maya vizitnaya
kartachka
Вот моя визитная
карточка.

I need an interpreter.
mne nuzhen perevotchik
Мне нужен переводчик.

I need to use a computer.
mne nuzhen kamp'yuter
Мне нужен компьтер.

I need to send a fax/email.
mne nuzhna atpravit'
faks/imeyl
Мне нужно отправить
факс/имейл.

**SPECIFIC NEEDS**

## Useful Words Полезные слова

| cellular | radio | радио |
|---|---|---|
| mobile | mabil'ny | мобильный |
| phone | telefon | телефон |
| client | klient | клиент |
| colleague | kalega | коллега |
| distributor | distribyutar | дистрибьютер |
| email | imeyl | имейл |
| exhibition | vystafka | выставка |
| manager | menedzer | менеджер |
| occupation | prafesiya | профессия |
| profit | dakhot | доход |
| proposal | predlazhenie | предложение |

**SPECIFIC NEEDS**

## ON TOUR

We're part of a group.
my f sastave turgrupy

We're on tour.
my puteshestvuem

I'm with the ...   ya s ...
| band | grupay |
| crew | ekipazham |
| group | turgrupay |
| team | kamanday |

Please speak with our manager.
abratites' k rukavaditelyu
nashey grupy, pazhalsta

We've lost our equipment.
my paterali nashi
instrumenty

We're playing on (Saturday).
my igraem f (subotu)

| We sent | my paslali |
| equipment | nashi |
| on this ... | instrumenty ... |
| bus | aftobusam |
| flight | etim reysam |
| train | poezdam |

## На гастролях

Мы в составе
тургруппы.

Мы путешествуем.

Я с ...
группой
экипажем
тургруппой
командой

Обратитесь к
руководителю нашей
группы, пожалуйста.

Мы потеряли наши
инструменты.

Мы играем в (субботу).

Мы послали
наши
инструменты ...
автобусом
этим рейсом
поездом

---

### ME TARZAN

Russian doesn't use 'to be' byt быть in the
present tense, so 'I'm Sonya' is just 'I Sonya'
ya Sonya Я Соня.

## Film & TV Crews Киносъёмка

We're on location.
   my na nature           Мы на натуре.
We're filming!
   my snimaem!           Мы снимаем!
Can we film here?
   zdes' mozhna snimat'?    Здесь можно снимать?

We're making a ... my delaem ...    Мы делаем ...

| | | |
|---|---|---|
| documentary | dakumental'ny fil'm | документальный фильм |
| film | khudozhestvenny fil'm | художественный фильм |
| TV series | televizionny serial | телевизионный сериал |

SPECIFIC NEEDS

### THEY MAY SAY ...

| | |
|---|---|
| yablaku negde upast' | It's packed (lit: nowhere for an apple to fall) |
| khot' sharom pakati | It's completely empty. (lit: you could roll a ball through it) |
| sem' pyatnits na nedele | They can never make up their mind. (lit: seven Fridays in their week) |
| tyoplae mestechka | A cushy position. (lit: a warm little place) |
| at nevo tolku kak at kazla malaka | Like getting blood from a stone. (lit: you can get as much benefit from him as you can get milk from a he-goat) |

SPECIFIC NEEDS

## PILGRIMAGE & RELIGION

### Всё о религии

The Russian Orthodox Church is the largest Christian demomination in Russia. Since the breakup of the atheist USSR, the Church's popularity has been growing, and it's even quite fashionable for young people to wear paraphernalia like crosses.

Orthodox Churches are beautifully decorated. Services include ancient and mystical rituals, with candles, incense and haunting, unaccompanied singing. The Russian Church is often seen to be nationalistic and resistant to outside influences.

What religion are you?
kakovo vy veraispavedaniya? Какого вы
вероисповедания?

| I'm ... | ya ispaveduyu ... | Я исповедую ... |
|---|---|---|
| Buddhist | budizm | буддизм |
| Christian | khristianstva | христианство |
| Hare Krishna | krishnaizm | кришнаизм |
| Hindu | induizm | индуизм |
| Jewish | yudaizm | иудаизм |
| Muslim | islam | ислам |

I'm not religious.
ya neveruyushchiy (m) Я неверующий
ya neveruyushchaya (f) я неверующая.
I'm not practising.
ya ne sablyudayu traditsii Я не соблюдаю
традиции.

I think I believe in God.
ya dumayu, shto Я думаю, что я верю в
ya veryu v boga Бога.
I believe in destiny/fate.
ya veryu f sud'bu Я верю в судьбу.
I'm interested in astrology/
philosophy.
ya uvlikayus' Я увлекаюсь
astralogiey/ астрологией/
filasofiey философией.

I'm an atheist.
ya ateist (m)/ateistka (f)      Я атеист/атеистка.

I'm agnostic.
ya agnostik      Я агностик.

Can I attend this service?
mozhna paprisutstvavat'
na sluzhbe?      Можно
поприсутствовать на
службе?

Can I pray here?
zdes' mozhna pamalit'sa?      Здесь можно
помолиться?

Where can I pray/worship?
gde mozhna pamalit'sa?      Где можно
помолиться?

Where can I make confession
(in English)?
gde mozhna ispavedavat'sa
(pa-angliyski)?      Где можно
исповедоваться
(по-английски)?

Can I receive communion here?
mozhna zdes'
prichyastit'sya?      Можно здесь
причаститься?

**SPECIFIC NEEDS**

| baptism/christening | khreshchenie | крещение |
|---|---|---|
| church | tserkaf' | церковь |
| communion | prichyastie | причастие |
| confession | ispaved' | исповедь |
| funeral | pokharany | похороны |
| god | bok | Бог |
| monk | manakh | монах |
| prayer | malitva | молитва |
| priest | sveshchenik | священник |
| religious procession | religioznaya pratsesiya | религиозная процессия |
| sabbath | shabat | шабат |
| saint | svyatoy | святой |
| shrine | mesta paklanenie | место поклонения |
| temple | khram | храм |

SPECIFIC NEEDS

## TRACING ROOTS & HISTORY

## В поисках своих корней

(I think) my ancestors lived in this area.

    (ya dumayu, shto) mai pretki zhyli zdes'

(Я думаю, что) мои предки жили здесь.

I'm looking for my relatives.

    ya ishchyu svaikh rotsvennikaf

Я ищу своих родствеников.

I have/had a relative who lives around here.

    u menya est'/byl rotsvennik, katory zhyvyot gde-ta zdes'

У меня есть/был родственник, который живёт где-то здесь.

Is there anyone here by the name of ...?

    zdes' est' kto-ta pa familii ...?

Здесь есть кто-то по фамилии ...?

I'd like to go to the cemetary.

    ya by khatel(m)/ khatela (f) skhadit' na kladbishche

Я бы хотел/хотела сходить на кладбище.

My (father) fought/died here in the war.

    moy (atets) vaeval/pagip zdes' vavremya vayny

Мой (отец) воевал/ погиб здесь во время войны.

My (grandmother) nursed in the war.

    maya (babushka) byla medsestroy vavremya vayny

Моя (бабушка) была медсестрой во время войны.

# TIME, DATES & FESTIVALS
# Время и даты. Праздники

## TELLING THE TIME  Всё о времени

The simplest way to tell the time, as in English, is to say the hour and then the minutes. There's no need to say 'It is ...' in a Russian sentence.

What time is it?
  katory chas?  Который час?

It's eight fifty-five.
  vosem' pit'desyat' pyat'  Восемь пятьдесят
                  пять. (lit: eight fifty-five)

The form of 'o'clock' changes depending on the number before it.

o'clock  chas  час
It's one o'clock.  chas  час

Numbers two to four take chasa часа.

It's two o'clock.  dva chasa  два часа.
It's three o'clock.  tri chasa  три часа.
It's four o'clock.  chetire chasa  четыре часа.

Numbers five and up take chasov часов.

It's five o'clock.  pyat' chasov  пять часов.
It's seven o'clock.  sem' chasov  семь часов.
It's nine o'clock.  devyat' chasov  девять часов.
(It's) twelve o'clock.  dvenadtsat'  двенадцать
              chasov  часов.

'Half past' in Russian literally means 'half of' the *next* hour.

Half past one.  palftarova  пол-второго.
                          (lit: half-of-the second)
Half past three.  palchetvortava  пол-четвёртого.
                          (lit: half-of-the fourth)

**DAYS**     Название дней недели

Unlike English, Russian doesn't use capital letters for months or for days of the week.

| Monday | panedel'nik | понедельник |
| Tuesday | ftornik | вторник |
| Wednesday | sreda | среда |
| Thursday | chetverk | четверг |
| Friday | pyat'nitsa | пятница |
| Saturday | subota | суббота |
| Sunday | vaskresen'e | воскресенье |

**MONTHS**     Название месяцев

| January | yanvar' | январь |
| February | fevral' | февраль |
| March | mart | март |
| April | april' | апрель |
| May | may | май |
| June | iyun' | июнь |
| July | iyul' | июль |
| August | avgust | август |
| September | sentabr' | сентябрь |
| October | aktabr' | октябрь |
| November | nayabr' | ноябрь |
| December | dekabr' | декабрь |

**SEASONS**     Времена года

| summer | | |
| leta | лето | |
| autumn | | |
| osen' | осень | |
| winter | | |
| zima | зима | |
| spring | | |
| vesna | весна | |

**WORD STRESS**

Like English, Russian strongly stresses one syllable in a word. The stressed syllable is shown in bold.

TIME, DATES & FESTIVALS

# DATES

Даты

What's the date today?
    kakoe sevodnya chislo?    Какое сегодня число?

As with clock times, you don't translate 'It is ...'. The ending -ae -oe on the number is equivalent to English '-th'.

It's 18 October.
    vasemnadtsatae aktyabrya    Восемнадцатое
                                октября.

## PRESENT
В настоящем

| now | seychas | сейчас |
|---|---|---|
| today | sevodnya | сегодня |
| this morning | sevodnya utram | сегодня утром |
| tonight | sevodnya vecheram | сегодня вечером |
| this week | na etay nedele | на этой неделе |
| this year | v etam gadu | в этом году |

## PAST
В прошлом

| day before yesterday | pazafchera | позавчера |
|---|---|---|
| yesterday | fchera | вчера |
| yesterday morning | fchera utram | вчера утром |
| last night | fchera vecheram | вчера вечером |
| last week | na proshlay nedele | на прошлой неделе |
| last year | f proshlam gadu | в прошлом году |

## FUTURE
В будущем

| tomorrow | zaftra | завтра |
|---|---|---|
| day after tomorrow | paslezaftra | послезавтра |
| next week | na sleduyushchey nedele | на следующей неделе |
| tomorrow morning | zaftra utram | завтра утром |
| tomorrow afternoon | zaftra dnom | завтра днём |
| tomorrow evening | zaftra vecheram | завтра вечером |
| next year | v sleduyushchem gadu | в следующем году |

TIME, DATES &
FESTIVALS

## DURING THE DAY                                                    Днём

| day | den' | день |
|---|---|---|
| early | rana | рано |
| dawn | rassvet | рассвет |
| sunrise | vaskhod sontsa | восход солнца |
| morning | utra | утро |
| noon | polden' | полдень |
| afternoon | posle abeda | после обеда |
| sunset | zakhod sontsa | заход солнца |
| night | noch' | ночь |
| midnight | polnach' | полночь |

## NATIONAL                            Национальные
## HOLIDAYS                            праздники

### New Year   Новый год

1 January is Russia's most important secular holiday, and a highlight
of the social calendar. Friends and family gather for a sumptuous
feast on New Year's Eve, and just before midnight turn on Radio
Moscow to listen for the Kremlin bells signalling 12 o'clock.
Everyone toasts with champagne, wishing each other a happy New
Year, s novym godam! с новым годом!

Grandfather Frost, ded maros Дед Мороз, a familiar-look-
ing figure with a red coat and white beard, brings presents to all
good children.

### Russian Orthodox Christmas   Рождество

7-8 January. This celebration has the most significance in rural
areas, where many rituals reflect older pagan beliefs. On Christmas
Eve, children go from house to house singing a mixture of songs,
some in praise of Christ, and others to celebrate a good harvest.
On Christmas day, a pig may be slaughtered to ensure successful crops.

### Day of Defence of the Motherland; 'Army Day'

День защиты Отечества. День Российской Армии.
23 February is of great significance to Russian men, since most
have served in the army. In fact, it's a de facto 'men's day', when
women buy flowers for the men in their lives.

## Women's Day Восьмое марта

Also called 'Mothers' Day', this celebration held on 8 March calls for men to give flowers to women, and boys to give a present to their female teachers. The men in a household may cook dinner to make up for the other 364 days.

The celebration has little of the political significance it has in the West, and is losing the function it had in the USSR, when the newspapers ran stories of motherhood heroines.

## Russian Orthodox Easter Пасха

March/April. Unlike in Western countries, Easter is of far greater significance than Christmas. It signals the end of Lent, and Orthodox families gather for lavish celebrations.

Russian Easter starts on the Saturday evening. The faithful bring paskha пасха (a special cream cheese cake) and kulich кулич (a sweet bread) to the church to be blessed. Just before midnight the priest opens the doors and announces khristos vaskrese! Христос воскресе! 'Christ is risen!' to which the congregation respond vaistinu vaskrese! Воистину воскресе! 'He is truly risen!'. The priest then leads a procession around the church three times, in a symbolic search for Christ's body – which they never find.

TIME, DATES & FESTIVALS

### ANTI-SEMITISM & THE HOLOCAUST

On the eve of the Nazi invasion, June 22, 1941, there were about five million Jews in the former USSR. It's thought that the total number of Jews killed was around three million. However, the word Holocaust never appeared in the Soviet media. Only in recent years have words like 'catastrophe' katastrofa and 'annihilation' unichtozhenie been used.

### Victory Day   День победы

Held on 9 May, this day commemorates victory over the Nazis in WWII, remembered by Russians as the Great Patriotic War. Over 20 million people in the former USSR were killed – not a single family escaped the tragedy. It is a day for military parades and gatherings of veterans to remember their fallen comrades. You may be cynical about the authorities' motives in reminding people of this day, but you will deeply offend people if you say so.

### 7 November   Седьмое ноября

This was formerly the anniversary of the Great October Socialist Revolution – October because the Western calendar was only introduced later – when Lenin and the Bolsheviks seized power from the provisional government.

This is still a holiday, but doesn't have a new name yet! It's a focal point for supporters of the former regime, who are nostalgic for the days when workers were actually paid, and grandmother didn't need to pay protection money to the mafia.

TIME, DATES &
FESTIVALS

# NUMBERS & AMOUNTS

## NUMBERS                                     Цифры

Numbers are written the same as English numerals.

### Cardinal Numbers Количественные
                     числительные

| | |
|---|---|
| 1 | adin (m); adna (f); adno (n); often ras when counting |
| 2 | dva (m/n); dve (f) |
| 3 | tri |
| 4 | chetiri |
| 5 | pyat' |
| 6 | shest' |
| 7 | sem' |
| 8 | vosem' |
| 9 | deviat' |
| 10 | desiat |
| 11 | adinnadtsat' |
| 12 | dvenadtsat' |
| 13 | trinadtsat' |
| 14 | chetirnadtsat' |
| 15 | piatnadtsat' |
| 16 | shestnadsat' |
| 17 | semnadsat' |
| 18 | vasemnadtsat' |
| 19 | devyatnadtsat' |
| 20 | dvadtsat' |
| 21 | dvadtsat' adin (m); adna (f); adno (n) |
| 22 | dvadtsat' dva (m/n); dve (f) |
| 23 | dvadtsat' tri |
| 30 | tridtsat' |
| 40 | sorak |
| 50 | pyat'desyat |

| | |
|---|---|
| 60 | shest'dye**syat** |
| 70 | **sem**'desyat' |
| 80 | **vo**sem'desyat |
| 90 | devya**no**sta |
| 100 | sto |
| 1000 | **ty**syacha |
| one million | million |

## Ordinal Numbers  Порядковые числительные

| | (m) | (f) | (n) |
|---|---|---|---|
| 1st | **per**vy | **per**vaya | **per**voye |
| 2nd | fta**roy** | fta**ra**ya | fta**ro**ye |
| 3rd | **tre**tiy | tre**tya**ya | **tre**tyeye |

## DECIMALS  Десятичные дроби

Decimals in standard Russian are complicated! Although it's not actually correct, a foreigner can read out numbers one by one and still be understood.

A comma is like an English decimal point. The number 2,5 means 'two and a half'.

| | | |
|---|---|---|
| point | **za**pyataya | запятая |
| | | (lit: comma) |

## FRACTIONS  Дроби

| | | |
|---|---|---|
| 1/4 | chet**vert**' | четверть |
| 1/3 | tret' | треть |
| 1/2 | pala**vi**na | половина |
| 2/3 | dve **tre**ti | две трети |
| 3/4 | tri chet**ver**ti | три четверти |

# Чрезвычайные ситуации
# EMERGENCIES

## GENERAL

Выражения в чрезвычайных
ситуациях

| | | |
|---|---|---|
| Stop it! | pekratite! | Прекратите! |
| Go away! | idite atsyuda! | Идите отсюда! |
| Thief! | vor! | Вор! |
| Fire! | pazhar! | Пожар! |
| Watch out! | astaozhna! | Осторожно! |

It's an emergency.
eta srochna

Это срочно.

Could you help us please?
pamagite, pazhalsta

Помогите,
пожалуйста.

Could I please use the telephone?
mozhna vaspol'zavat'sa
telefonam?

Можно
воспользоваться
телефоном?

I'm lost.
ya pateryalsa (m)/
pateryalas' (f)

Я потерялся/
потерялась.

Where are the toilets?
gdye zdes' tualyet?

Где здесь туалет?

## NO CONTINUOUS FORMS

Russian doesn't have continuous forms – so 'I work'
and 'I'm working' are the same in Russian – ya
rabotayu я работаю.

**EMERGENCIES**

## POLICE                                    Милиция

Call the police!
  vyzavite militsiyu!            Вызовите милицию!
Where's the police station?
  gde militseyskiy uchastak?     Где милицейский
                                 участок?

We want to report an offence.
  my khatim zayavit'            Мы хотим заявить
  v militsiyu                    в милицию.
I've been raped/assaulted.
  menya iznasilavali/           Меня изнасиловали/
  pabili                         побили.
I've been robbed.
  menya agrabili                Меня ограбили.

| My ... was/were stolen. | u menya ukrali ... | У меня украли ... |
|---|---|---|
| backpack | ryukzak | рюкзак |
| bags | bagazh | багаж |
| handbag | sumku | сумки |
| money | den'gi | деньги |
| paper | dakumenty | документы |
| travellers cheques | darozhnye cheki | дорожные чеки |
| passport | paspart | паспорт |
| wallet | bumazhnik | бумажник |

### ANY COMMENTS?

You can comment on any situation by using the ending
o/a -o/-a (unstressed) on an adjective:

| kharasho! | Хорошо! | Good! OK! |
| interesna! | Интересно! | Interesting! |
| skushna! | Скучно! | Boring! |

EMERGENCIES

My possessions are insured.

mai veshchi zastrakhovany — Мои вещи застрахованы.

What am I accused of?

f chyom menya abvinyayut? — В чём меня обвиняют?

You'll be charged with ...

vas asudyat za … — Вас осудят за …

| She/He will be charged with ... | yeyo/evo asudyat za … | Её/его осудят за … |
|---|---|---|
| anti-government activity | anti-pravitel'stvenye deystivya | анти-правительственные действия |
| assault | nasilie | насилие |
| disturbing the peace | narushenie pakoya | нарушение покоя |
| possession (of illegal substances) | khranenie zapreshchyoykh predmetaf | хранение запрещенных предметов |
| illegal entry | nelegal'ny vest | нелегальный въезд |
| murder | ubiystva | убийство |
| having no visa | bezvizavy vest | безвизовый въезд |
| overstaying his/her visa | prasrochenaya visa | просроченная виза |
| rape | isnasilavanie | иснасилование |
| robbery/theft | agrablenie | ограбление |
| shoplifting | varafstvo v magazine | воровство в магазине |
| traffic violation | narushenie pravil darozhnava dvizheniya | нарушение правил дорожного движения |
| working without a permit | rabota bes razresheniy | работа без разрешений |

I'm sorry; I apologise.
  izvinitye, pazhalsta

Извините,
пожалуйста.

I didn't realise I was
doing anything wrong.
  ya ne znal (m)/znala (f)
  shto ya delayu shto-ta
  nepravil'na

Я не знал/знала
что я делаю что-то
не правильно.

I didn't do it.
  ya etava ne delal (m)/
  delala (f)

Я этого не делал/
делала.

We're innocent.
  my ne vinavaty

Мы не виноваты.

We are foreigners.
  my inastrantsy

Мы иностранцы.

I want to contact my
embassy/consulate.
  ya khachu abratit'sa f
  svayo pasol'stva
  konsul'stva

Я хочу обратиться в
своё посольство/
консульство.

Can I call someone?
  mozhna pazvanit'?

Можно позвонить?

I need a lawyer who
speaks English.
  mne nuzhen advakat,
  gavaryashchi na
  angliskam yazyke

Мне нужен адвокат,
говорящий на
английском языке.

Is there a fine we can pay
to clear this?
  mozhna zaplatit' shtraf za
  etat prastupak?

Можно заплатить
штраф за этот
проступок?

Can we pay an on-the-spot fine?
  mozhna zaplatit' shtraf
  na meste?

Можно заплатить
штраф на месте?

EMERGENCIES

I understand.
  ya panimayu              Я понимаю.
I don't understand.
  ya ne panimayu           Я не понимаю.
I know my rights.
  ya znayu svai prava      Я знаю свои права.

| | | |
|---|---|---|
| arrested | arestovan (m) | арестован |
| | arestovana (f) | арестована |
| cell | tyuremnaya | тюремная |
| | kamera | камера |
| embassy | pasol'stva | посольство |
| consulate | konsul'stva | консульство |
| fine (payment) | shtraf | штраф |
| guilty | vinoven (m) | виновен |
| | vinovna (f) | виновна |
| lawyer | advakat | адвокат |
| not guilty | ne vinoven (m) | не виновен |
| | ne vinovna (f) | не виновна |
| police officer | militsianer | милиционер |
| police station | adelenie militsii | отделение |
| | | милиции |
| prison | tyur'ma | тюрьма |
| trial | sud | суд |

## ABC TOURS

For the benefit of rich businesswomen, there are numerous agencies hiring out men as escorts. Officially this is a non-sexual service. A male escort is classified as 'A', 'B' or 'C'. Category A (the most expensive) meets three criteria: pleasant appearance, a car, and knowledge of a foreign language. Category B means the absence of one of these three criteria; and category C means the absence of two.

**EMERGENCIES**

## HEALTH                           Здоровье

Call a doctor!
vyzavite vracha!                    Вызовите врача!

Call an ambulance!
vyzavite skoruyu                    Вызовите скорую
pomashch!                           помощь!

I'm ill.
ya bolen (m)/bal'na (f)             Я болен/больна.

My friend is ill.
moy priyatel' zabalyel (m)/         Мой приятель заболел/
maya priyatel'                      моя приятельница
nitsa zabalyela (f)                 заболела.

I have medical insurance.
u menya est' meditsynskaya          У меня есть
strakhofka                          медицинская страховка.

## SOME RULES OF THUMB!

You will be understood if you pick words straight out of this dictionary. However, these rules of thumb will help you get your message across even more effectively. See the grammar chapter (pg 23) for more details.

To make a noun plural, add the suffix -y, ы to a consonant, or replace a final -a, a with -y, ы.

Adjectives are in the masculine form (usually -y, ый). If you're describing a woman, or a noun ending in -a, a, change this ending to -aya, ая.

Verbs are usually given in two forms. To describe an ongoing action, use the first form (imperfective). To describe a finished action, use the second form (perfective).

# A

| | | |
|---|---|---|
| abacus | shyoty | счёты |
| able (to be);can | moch'/smoch' | мочь/смочь |

Can I (enter)?
mozhna (vayti)?
**Можно (войти)?**

Can you (help me)?
vy mozhete (pamoch' mne)
**Вы можете (помочь мне)?**

| | | |
|---|---|---|
| aboard | na bartu | на борту |
| abortion | abort | аборт |
| above | nat | над |
| abroad | za granitsey | за границей |
| to accept | prinimat'/prinyat' | принимать/принять |
| accident | neshasny sluchay | несчастный случай |
| accommodation | pameshchenie | помещение |
| across | cherez | через |
| adaptor | adapter | адаптер |
| addiction | pagubnaya | пагубная |
| (to drugs) | privychka | привычка |
| address | adres | адрес |
| administration | administratsiya | администрация |
| admission (by ticket) | fkhot (pa biletam) | вход (по билетам) |
| to admit | fpuskat'/fpustit' | впускать/впустить |
| adult | vzrosly/vzroslaya | взрослый/взрослая |
| advantage | preimushchestva | преимущество |
| advice | savet | совет |
| aeroplane | samalyot | самолёт |
| to be afraid of | bayat'sa | бояться |
| after | posle | после |

**A**

|  |  |  |
|---|---|---|
| (in the) afternoon | dnyom | днём |
| again | apyat' | опять |
| against | protif | против |
| age | vozrast | возраст |
| aggressive | agresivny | агрессивный |
| (a while) ago | nedavna | недавно |
| (half an hour) ago | (palchasa) tamu nazat | (пол-часа) тому назад |
| to agree | saglashat'sa/ saglasit'sa | соглашаться/ согласиться |

I don't agree.
ya ne saglasen (m)/saglasna (f)
Я не согласен/согласна

Agreed!
dagavarilis'!
Договорились!

| agriculture | sel'skae khazyaystva | сельское хозяйство |
|---|---|---|
| ahead | fperyot | вперёд |
| AIDS | spit | СПИД |
| air | vozdukh | воздух |
| air-conditioner | kanditsianer | кондиционер |
| air mail | aviapochta | авиапочта |
| airport | aeraport | аэропорт |
| airport tax | nalok na vzlyot | налог на вылет |
| alarm clock | budil'nik | будильник |
| alcoholism | alkagalizm | алкоголизм |
| all | fse | все |
| allergy | alergiya | аллергия |
| to allow | pazvalyat'/pazvolit' | позволять/позволить |

It's allowed.
razresheno
Разрешено.

It's not allowed.
zapreshcheno
Запрещено.

| almost | pachti | почти |
|---|---|---|
| alone | adin (m)/adna (f) | один/одна |
| already | uzhe | уже |
| also | tozhe | тоже |
| altitude | vysata | высота |
| always | fsegda | всегда |
| amateur | lyubitel'skiy | любительский |
| ambassador | pasol | посол |
| among | mezhdu | между |
| anarchist | anarkhist (m)/anarkhistka (f) | анархист/анархистка |
| ancient | drevniy | древний |

**D I C T I O N A R Y**

| and | i | и |
| --- | --- | --- |
| angry | serdity | сердитый |
| animals | zhyvotnye | животные |
| annual | ezhegodny | ежегодный |
| answer | atvet | ответ |
| ant | muravey | муравей |
| antinuclear | prativayaderny | противоядерный |
| antiques | antikvaryat | антиквариат |
| appointment (business) | fstrecha | встреча |
| appointment (doctor) | vizit | визит |
| archaeological | arkhealagicheskiy | археологический |
| architecture | arkhitektura | архитектура |
| to argue | sporit' | спорить |
| arm | ruka | рука |
| armaments | vaaruzhenie | вооружение |
| army | armiya | армия |
| to arrive | priezhat'/priekhat' | приезжать/приехать |
| arrivals | pribytie | прибытие |
| art | iskustva | искусство |
| art gallery | kartinnaya galereya | галлерея |
| artist | khudozhnik (m)/khudozhnitsa (f) | художник/художница |
| ashtray | pepel'nitsa | пепельница |
| to ask (for something) | prasit'/paprasit' | просить/попросить |
| to ask (a question) | sprashivat'/sprasit' | спрашивать/спросить |
| aspirin | aspirin | аспирин |
| asthmatic | asmatik | астматик |
| atheist | ateist | атеист |
| atmosphere | atmasfera | атмосфера |
| aunt | tyotya | тётя |
| automatic teller (ATM) | bankafskiy aftamat | банковский автомат |
| autumn | osen' | осень |
| avenue | praspekt | проспект |
| awful/horrible/terrible | uzhasny | ужасный |

## B

| baby | rebyonak | ребёнок |
| --- | --- | --- |
| babysitter | nyanya | няня |
| back (body) | spina | спина |
| back (behind) | zzadi | сзади |
| backpack | ryugzak | рюкзак |
| bad | plakhoy | плохой |
| bag | meshok | мешок |
| baggage | bagash | багаж |
| baggage claim | stoyka vydachi | стойка выдачи |
|  | bagazha | багажа |

| bakery | bulachnaya | булочная |
| balcony | balkon | балкон |
| ball (sport) | myach | мяч |
| the Baltics | pribaltika | Прибалтика |
| band (music) | grupa | группа |
| bandage | bint | бинт |
| bank | bank | банк |
| baptism | kreshchenie | крещение |
| bar | bar | бар |
| basket | karzina | корзина |
| bath | vanna | ванна |
| bathhouse | banya | баня |
| bathing suit (f) | kupal'nik | купальник |
| bathing suit (m) | plafki | плавки |
| bathroom | vannaya | ванная |
| battery | batereya | батарея |
| to be | byt' | быть |
| beautiful | krasivy | красивый |
| because | patamu shto | потому, что |
| bed | pastel' | постель |
| bedbug | klop | клоп |
| bedroom | spal'nya | спальня |
| before | do | до |
| beggar | nishchiy (m)/nishchaya (f) | нищий/нищая |
| to begin | nachinat'/nachat' | начинать/начать |
| behind | za | за |
| bell (church) | kolakal | колокол |
| below | pod | под |
| berries | yagady | ягоды |
| beside | ryadam s | рядом с |
| best | samy luchshiy | самый лучший |
| a bet | pari | пари |
| better | luchshe | лучше |
| between | mezhdu | между |
| Bible | bibliya | Библия |
| bicycle | velasipet | велосипед |
| big | bal'shoy | большой |
| bill (account) | shyot | счёт |
| biodegradable | z bia-dabafkami | с био-добавками |
| bird | ptitsa | птица |
| birth certificate | svidetel'stva a razhdenii | свидетельство о рождении |
| birthday | den' razhdeniya | день рождения |
| bite (dog, insect) | ukus | укус |
| black | chyorny | чёрный |
| black market | chyorny rynak | чёрный рынок |

| blanket (thin) | plet | плед |
| blanket (thick) | zimnee adeyala | зимнее одеяло |
| to bleed | istekat' krov'yu | истекать кровью |
| to bless | blagaslavyat'/blagaslavit' | благословлять |

**Bless you!** (when sneezing)
bud'te zdarovy!
**Будьте здоровы!**

| blind | slepoy | слепой |
| blood | krof' | кровь |
| blood group | grupa krovi | группа крови |
| blood pressure | kravyanoe davlenie | кровяное давление |
| to board (ship, etc) | sadit'sa/sest' | садиться/сесть |
| boarding pass | pasadachny talon | посадочный талон |
| boat | lotka | лодка |
| body | tela | тело |

**Bon appétit!**
priyatnava apetita!
**Приятного аппетита!**

**Bon voyage!**
shyaslivava puti!
**Счастливого пути!**

| book | kniga | книга |
| to book | zakazyvat'/zakazat' | заказывать/заказать |
| bookshop | knizhny magazin | книжный магазин |
| boots | sapagi | сапоги |
| border | granitsa | граница |
| boring | skuchny | скучный |
| to borrow | brat'/vzyat' na vremya | брать/взять на время |
| both | oba (m)/obe (f) | оба/обе |
| bottle | butylka | бутылка |
| bottle opener (beer) | atkryvalka | открывалка |
| bottle opener (wine) | shtopar | штопор |
| (at the) bottom | na dne | на дне |
| box | karopka | коробка |
| boy | mal'chik | мальчик |
| boyfriend | paren' | парень |
| branch (bank etc) | filial | филиал |
| bread | khlep | хлеб |
| to break | lamat'/slamat' | ломать/сломать |
| breakfast | zaftrak | завтрак |
| to breathe | dyshat' | дышать |
| a bribe | vzyatka | взятка |
| to bribe | davat'/dat' vzyatku | давать/дать взятку |
| bridge | most | мост |

| | | |
|---|---|---|
| brilliant | blestyashchiy | блестящий |
| to bring | prinasit'/prinesti | приносить/принести |
| broken (doesn't work) | slomanny | сломанный |
| bucket | vedro | ведро |
| Buddhist | budist (m)/ | буддист/ |
| | budistka (f) | буддистка |
| bug | zhuk | жук |
| to build | stroit'/pastroit' | строить |
| building | zdanie | здание |
| bureaucracy | byurakratiya | бюрократия |
| bus | aftobus | автобус |
| bus station | aftavagzal | автовокзал |
| bus stop | astanofka | остановка |
| business | biznes | бизнес |
| business person | biznesmen (m) | бизнесмен |
| | zhenshchina-biznesmen (f) | женщина-бизнесмен |
| busker | ulichny muzykant | уличный музыкант |
| busy | zanyat (m)/zanyata (f) | занят/занята |
| but | no | но |
| butterfly | babachka | бабочка |
| buttons | pugavitsy | пуговицы |
| to buy | pakupat'/kupit' | покупать/купить |

I'd like to buy ...
ya by khatel (m)/khatela (f) kupit' ...
я бы хотел/хотела купить ...

Where can I buy (a ticket)?
gde mozhna kupit' (bilet)?
Где можно купить (билет)?

## C

| | | |
|---|---|---|
| calendar | kalendar' | календарь |
| camera | fotoaparat | фотоаппарат |
| camera shop | fotomagazin | фотомагазин |
| to camp | raspalagat'sa/ | располагаться/ |
| | raspalazhyt'sa | расположиться |

Can we camp here?
zdes' mozhna raspalazhyt'sa?
Здесь можно расположиться?

| | | |
|---|---|---|
| can (to be able) | moch'/smoch' | мочь/смочь |

We can do it.
my mozhem zdelat' eta
Мы можем сделать это.

I can't do it.
ya ne magu zdelat' eta
**Я не могу сделать это.**

| | | |
|---|---|---|
| can (aluminium) | banka | банка |
| can opener | atkryvashka | открывашка |
| to cancel | atmenyat'/atmenit' | отменять/отменить |
| candle | svecha | свеча |
| car | mashyna | машина |
| carpark | aftastayanka | автостоянка |
| car registration | registratsiya mashyny | регистрация машины |
| to care (about) | zabotit'sa (o) | заботиться (о) |
| to care (for) | ukhazhyvat' (za) | ухаживать (за) |
| cards | karty | карты |

Careful!
astarozhna!
**Осторожно!**

| | | |
|---|---|---|
| caring | zabotlivy | заботливый |
| to carry | nesti/pdnesti | нести/понести |
| carton | kartonka | картонка |
| cartoon | mul'tfil'm | мультфильм |
| cashier | kasir | кассир |
| cassette | kaseta | кассета |
| cat | koshka | кошка |
| cathedral | sabor | собор |
| Catholic | katolik (m)/katalichka (f) | католик/католичка |
| cave | peshchera | пещера |
| to celebrate | praznavat' | праздновать |
| centimetre | santimetr | сантиметр |
| ceramics | keramika | керамика |
| chair | stul | стул |
| champagne | shampanskae | шампанское |
| championships | chempianat | чемпионат |
| chance | shans | шанс |
| to change | menyat'/abmenyat' | менять/обменять |
| change (coins) | melach' | мелочь |
| charming | acharavatel'ny | очаровательный |
| to chat up | ubaltyvat'/ubaltat' | убалтывать/уболтать |
| cheap | deshovy | дешёвый |
| cheap hotel | deshovaya gastinitsa | дешёвая гостинница |
| a cheat | mashenik | мошенник |

Cheat!
abman
**Обман!**

| | | |
|---|---|---|
| to check | praveryat'/praverit' | проверять/проверить |
| checkpoint | kantrol'ny punkt | контрольный пункт |

| cheese (hard) | syr | сыр |
| chemist | apteka | аптека |
| chess | shakhmaty | шахматы |
| chest | grudnaya kletka | грудная клетка |
| chewing gum | zhevatel'naya rezinka | жевательная резинка |
| chicken | kuritsa | курица |
| child | pebyonak | ребёнок |
| children | deti | дети |
| chocolate | shakalat | шоколад |
| to choose | vybirat'/vybrat' | выбирать/выбрать |
| Christian | khristianin (m)/khristianka (f) | христианин/христианка |
| Christmas | razhdestvo | Рождество |
| Christmas Eve | sachel'nik | Сочельник |
| church | tserkaf' | церковь |
| cigarette papers | papirosnaya bumaga | папиросня бумага |
| cigarette (Russian style) | papirosa | папироса |
| cigarette (Western style) | sigareta | сигарета |
| cinema | kino | кино |
| circus | tsyrk | цирк |
| city | gorat | город |
| city centre | tsentr gorada | центр города |
| class | klas | класс |
| class system | klasavaya sistema | классовая система |
| clean | chisty | чистый |
| clean hotel | chistaya gastinitsa | чистая гостинница |
| client | klient | клиент |
| cliff | utyos | утёс |
| to climb | padnimat'sa/padnyat'sa | подниматься/подняться |
| cloakroom | garderop | гардероб |
| clock | chasy | часы |
| to close | zakryvat'/zakryt' | закрывать/закрыть |
| closed | zakryta | закрыто |
| clothing | adezhda | одежда |
| cloud | oblaka | облако |
| clown | kloun | клоун |
| coast | berek | берег |
| coat | pal'to | пальто |
| cocaine | kakain | кокаин |
| coin | maneta | монета |
| a cold | prastuda | простуда |
| cold (adj) | khalodny | холодный |

It's cold.
kholadna
**Холодно.**

| cold water | khalodnaya vada | холодная вода |

| colleague | kalega | коллега |
|---|---|---|
| college | tekhnikum | техникум |
| colour | tsvet | цвет |
| comb | raschyoska | расчёска |
| to come | prikhadit'/priyti | приходить/прийти |
| comedy | kamediya | комедия |
| comfortable | uyutny | уютный |
| comics | komiksy | комиксы |
| companion (travelling) | paputchik (m)/paputchitsa (f) | попутчик/попутчица |
| company | kampaniya | компания |
| compass | kompas | компас |
| a concert | kantsert | концерт |
| confession (religious) | ispaved' | исповедь |
| to confirm (a booking) | pattverzhdat'/pattverdit' | подтверждать/подтвердить |

Congratulations!
Pazdravlyayu!
**Поздравляю!**

| connections (contacts) | svyazi | связи |
|---|---|---|
| conservative | kanservativny | консервативный |
| constipation | zapor | запор |
| constitution | kanstitutsiya | конституция |
| consulate | konsul'stva | консульство |
| contact lenses | kantaktnye linzy | контактные линзы |
| contraceptives | prativazachatachnye sretstva | противозачаточные средства |
| contract | kantrakt | контракт |
| to cook | gatovit'/prigatovit' | готовить/приготовить |
| cool (person) (col) | krutoy | крутой |

Cool! (col)
klassna!
**Классно!**

| cooperative (business) | kaaperatif | кооператив |
|---|---|---|
| corner | ugal | угол |
| corrupt | korumpiravany | коррумпированный |
| to cost | stoit' | стоить |

How much does it cost to go to ...?
skol'ka stoit paestka v ...?
**Сколько стоит поездка в ...?**

It costs a lot.
eta doraga
**Это дорого.**

| cotton | khlopak | хлопок |
|---|---|---|

| country (nation) | strana | страна |
| a cough | kashel' | кашель |
| to count | shchitat'/pashchitat' | считать/посчитать |
| coupon | talon | талон |
| court (legal) | sut | суд |
| court (tennis) | kort | корт |
| cow | karova | корова |
| crafts | remyosla | ремёсла |
| crafty | khitry | хитрый |
| crazy | sumashetshiy | сумасшедший |
| credit card | kreditnaya kartachka | кредитная карточка |
| creep (slang) | merskiy tip | мерзкий тип |
| cricket | kriket | крикет |
| cross (religious) | krest | крест |
| cross (angry) | serdity | сердитый |
| cross-country trail | daroshka | дорожка |
| a cuddle | abyatie | объятие |
| cup | chashka | чашка |
| cupboard | bufet | буфет |
| curator | khranitel' | хранитель |
| current affairs | politicheskie sabytiya i novasti | политические события и новости |
| customs | tamozhnya | таможня |
| to cut | rezat'/narezat' | резать/нарезать |
| to cycle | ezdit' na velasipede | ездить на велосипеде |

| dad | papa | папа |
| daily | ezhednevny | ежедневный |
| dairy products | malochnye pradukty | молочные продукты |
| to dance | tantsevat' | танцевать |
| dancing | tantsy | танцы |
| dangerous | apasny | опасный |
| dark | tyomny | тёмный |
| date (time) | chislo | число |
| to date (someone) | fstrechat'sa s | встречаться с |
| date of birth | data razhdeniya | дата рождения |
| daughter | doch' | дочь |
| dawn | rasvet | рассвет |
| day | den' | день |
| day after tomorrow | poslezaftra | послезавтра |
| day before yesterday | pazafchera | позавчера |

In (six) days.
cheres (shest') dney
через (шесть) дней.

| dead | myortvy | мёртвый |

| deaf | glukhoy | глухой |
| to decide | reshat'/reshyt' | решать/решить |
| deck (of cards) | kaloda | колода |
| deck (of ship) | paluba | палуба |
| deep | glubokiy | глубокий |
| deer | alen' | олень |
| deforestation | vyrupka lesa | вырубка леса |
| degree (academic) | stepen' | степень |
| degree (measurement) | gradus | градус |
| delay | zadershka | задержка |
| delicatessen | kulinariya | кулинария |
| delirious | bisvyazny | бессвязный |
| democracy | demakratiya | демократия |
| demonstration | demanstratsiya | демонстрация |
| dentist | zubnoy vrach | зубной врач |
| to deny | atritsat' | отрицать |
| to depart | uezhat'/uekhat' | уезжать/уехать |
| department store | univermak | универмаг |
| departure | atest | отъезд |
| descendant | patomak | потомок |
| desert | pustynya | пустыня |
| design | dizayn | дизайн |
| destination | mesta naznacheniya | место назначения |
| to destroy | razrushat'/razrushit' | разрушать/разрушить |
| diabetic | diabetik | диабетик |
| dial tone | gudok | гудок |
| diarrhoea | panos | понос |
| diary | dnevnik | дневник |
| dice | igral'nye kosti | игральные кости |
| dictionary | slavar' | словарь |
| to die | umeret' | умереть |
| different | drugoy | другой |
| difficult | trudny | трудный |
| dining car | vagon-restaran | вагон-ресторан |
| dinner (evening meal) | uzhyn | ужин |
| direct | pryamoy | прямой |
| director | direktar | директор |
| dirty | gryazny | грязный |
| disabled | invalit | инвалид |
| disadvantage | nevygada | невыгода |
| discount | skitka | скидка |
| to discover | atkryvat'/atkryt' | открывать/открыть |
| discrimination | diskriminatsiya | дискриминация |
| disease | balezn' | болезнь |
| diving | padvodnae plavanie | подводное плавание |

I feel dizzy.
u menya kruzhytsa galava
**У меня кружится голова.**

| | | |
|---|---|---|
| to do | delat'/zdelat' | делать/сделать |

What are you doing?
shto vy delaete?
**Что вы делаете?**

| | | |
|---|---|---|
| doctor | vrach | врач |
| dog | sabaka | собака |
| dole | pasobie pa bezrabotitse | пособие по безработице |
| dolls | kukly | куклы |
| door | dver' | дверь |
| dope (drugs) | narkotiki | наркотики |
| double | dvaynoy | двойной |
| double bed | dvuspal'naya kravat' | двуспальняя кровать |
| double room | komnata na dvaikh | комната на двоих |
| dozen | dyuzhyna | дюжина |
| drama | drama | драма |
| dramatic (exciting) | dramaticheskiy | драматический |
| to dream | videt' son | видеть сон |
| dress | plat'e | платье |
| a drink | napitak | напиток |
| to drink | pit'/vypit' | пить/выпить |
| to drive | byt' za rulyom | быть за рулём |
| driver's licence | vaditel'skie prava | водительские права |
| drug (illegal) | narkotik | наркотик |
| drug addiction | pristrastie k narkotikam | пристрастие к наркотикам |
| drug dealer | narkodiler | нарко-диллер |
| drums | barabany | барабаны |
| drunk (sloshed) | p'yany | пьяный |
| to dry (clothes) | sushyt'/vysushyt' | сушить/высушить |

## E

| | | |
|---|---|---|
| each | kazhdy | каждый |
| ear | ukha | ухо |
| early | ranniy | ранний |

It's early.
rana
**рано.**

| | | |
|---|---|---|
| to earn | zarabatyvat'/ zarabotat' | зарабатывать/ заработать |
| earrings | ser'yoshki | серёжки |

| ears | ushy | уши |
| Earth | zemlya | земля |
| earth (soil) | pochva | почва |
| earthquake | zemletryasenie | землетрясение |
| east | vastok | восток |
| easy | lyokhkiy | лёгкий |
| to eat | est'/sest' | есть/съесть |
| economy | ekanomiya | экономия |
| editor | redaktar | редактор |
| education | abrazavanie | образование |
| elections | vybary | выборы |
| electricity | elektrichestva | электричество |
| embarrassed | smushchony | смущённый |
| embassy | pasol'stva | посольство |
| emergency | avariya | авария |
| employee | sluzhashchiy (m)/ | служащий/ |
| | sluzhashchaya (f) | служащая |
| employer | rabotadatel' | работодатель |
| empty | pustoy | пустой |
| end | kanets | конец |
| endangered species | zhyvotnye, | животные, |
| | zanesyonnye f krasnuyu | занесённые в красную |
| | knigu | книгу |
| engagement | pamolfka | помолвка |
| engine | mator | мотор |
| engineer | inzhiner | инженер |
| English | angliyskiy | английский |
| to enjoy (oneself) | naslazhdat'sa/ | наслаждаться/ |
| | nasladit'sa | насладиться |
| enough | dastatachna | достаточно |

Enough!
davol'na!
Довольно!

| to enter | fkhadit'/vayti | входить/войти |
| entertaining | zabavny | забавный |
| envelope | kanvert | конверт |
| environment | akruzhayushchaya sreda | окружающая среда |
| epileptic | epileptik | эпилептик |
| equal opportunity | ravnye vazmozhnasti | равные возможности |
| equality | ravnapravie | равноправие |
| equipment | abarudavanie | оборудование |
| European | evrapeyskiy | европейский |
| euthanasia | eftanaziya | эвтаназия |
| evening | vecher | вечер |
| every day | kazhdy den' | каждый день |

**F**

For example ...
naprimer ...
Например ...

| excellent | atlichny | отличный |
| exchange bureau | abmen valyuty | Обмен Валюты |
| to exchange | menyat'/abmenyat' | менять/обменять |
| exchange rate | abmenny kurs | обменный курс |
| excluded | isklyuchaya | исключая |

Excuse me.
izvinite, pazhalsta
Извините, пожалуйста.

| exhibition | vystafka | выставка |
| exit | vykhat | выход |
| expensive | daragoy | дорогой |
| exploitation | ekspluatatsiya | эксплуатация |
| express | ekspres | экспресс |
| eye | glas | глаз |

# F

| face | litso | лицо |
| factory | fabrika | фабрика |
| factory worker | rabochiy (m)/rabochaya (f) | рабочий/рабочая |
| fall (autumn) | osen' | осень |
| family | sem'ya | семья |
| famous | znamenity | знаменитый |
| fan (machine) | ventilyator | вентилятор |
| fans (of a team) | balel'shchiki | болельщики |
| far | dalyokiy | далёкий |
| farm | ferma | ферма |
| farmer | fermer | фермер |
| fast (quick) | bystry | быстрый |
| to fast | pastit'sa | поститься |
| fat | tolsty | толстый |
| father | atets | отец |
| fault (someone's) | vina | вина |
| faulty | ashybachny | ошибочный |
| fear | strakh | страх |
| feast | pir | пир |
| to feel | chustvavat' | чувствовать |
| feelings | chustva | чувства |
| fence | zabor | забор |
| festival | festival' | фестиваль |
| fever/temperature | likharatka | лихорадка |
| few | mala | мало |
| fiancée/fiancé | nevesta/zhenikh | невеста/жених |

D I C T I O N A R Y

| fiction | khudozhistvenaya litiratura | художественная литература |
|---|---|---|
| field | pole | поле |
| fight | draka | драка |
| to fight | drat'sa/padrat'sa | драться/подраться |
| to fill | napalnyat'/napolnit' | наполнять/ наполнить |
| film (for camera) | plyonka | плёнка |
| films (movies) | kino | кино |
| filtered (cigarettes) | sigarety s fil'tram | сигареты с фильтром |
| to find | nakhadit'/nayti | находить/найти |
| a fine | shtraf | штраф |
| finger | palets | палец |
| fire (for heat) | agon' | огонь |
| fire (emergency) | pazhar | пожар |
| firewood | drava | дрова |
| first | pervy | первый |
| first-aid kit | sanitarnaya sumka | санитарная сумка |
| fish | ryba | рыба |
| flag | flak | флаг |
| flat (land, etc) | ploskiy | плоский |
| flea | blakha | блоха |
| flashlight | fanarik | фонарик |
| flight | palyot | полёт |
| floor | pol | пол |
| floor (storey) | etash | этаж |
| flour | muka | мука |
| flower | tsvetok | цветок |
| fly | mukha | муха |

It's foggy.
tumana
**Туманно.**

| folk art | narodnae iskustva | народное искусство |
|---|---|---|
| to follow | sledavat'/ pasledavat' | следовать/ последовать |
| food | eda | еда |
| foot | naga | нога |
| football (soccer) | fudbol | футбол |
| footpath | tratuar | тротуар |
| foreign | inastranny | иностранный |
| forest | les | лес |
| forever | nafsegda | навсегда |
| to forget | zabyvat'/zabyt' | забывать/забыть |

I forget.
ya zabyl (m)/zabyla (f)
**Я забыл/забыла.**

Forget about it!; Don't worry!
Nichevo strashnava!
**Ничего страшного!**

| | | |
|---|---|---|
| to forgive | prashchat'/prastit' | прощать/простить |
| fortnight | dve nedeli | две недели |
| fortune teller | gadalka | гадалка |
| foyer | faye | фойе |
| free (not bound) | svabodny | свободный |
| free (gratis) | besplatny | бесплатный |
| Friday | pyatnitsa | пятница |
| friend | druk (m)/padruga (f) | друг/подруга |
| frozen foods | svezhimarozhini pradukty | свежемороженые продукты |
| fruit picking | zbor fruktaf | сбор фруктов |
| full | polny | полный |

It's fun.
vesela
**Весело.**

| | | |
|---|---|---|
| for fun | zabavy radi | забавы ради |
| to have fun | veselit'sa | веселиться |
| funeral | pokharany | похороны |
| fur | mekh | мех |
| fur hat | shapka | шапка |
| future | budushcheye | будущее |

# G

| | | |
|---|---|---|
| game (games) | igra | игра |
| game (sport) | sport | спорт |
| a game show | pakazatel'naya igra | показательная игра |
| garbage | musar | мусор |
| gardening | sadavotstva | садоводство |
| garden | sad | парк |
| gas cartridge | gazavy balon | газовый баллон |
| gate | varota | ворота |
| gay | gey | гей |
| general | opshiy | общий |

Get lost!
ischezni!
**Исчезни!**

| | | |
|---|---|---|
| gift | padarak | подарок |
| gig | rok-kantsert | рок-концерт |
| girl (pre-teen) | devochka | девочка |
| girl (teenage) | devushka | девушка |

| girlfriend | padruga | подруга |
| to give | davat'/dat' | давать/дать |

Could you give me ...?
dayte, pazhalsta ...
Дайте, пожалуйста ...

| glass | stakan | стакан |
| glasnost | glasnast' | гласность |
| to go | itti/payti | идти/пойти |

Let's go.
pashli!
Пошли!

Go straight ahead. (on foot)
idite pryama!
Идите прямо!

Go straight ahead. (taxi)
et'te pryama!
Едьте прямо!

| to go out with | khadit' s | ходить с |
| goal (sport) | gol | гол |
| goalkeeper | vratar' | вратарь |
| goat | kazyol | козел |
| God | bok | Бог |
| gold | zolata | из золота |

Good afternoon.
dobry den'
Добрый день.

Good evening.
dobry vecher
Добрый вечер.

Good health!; Cheers!
vashe zdarov'e!
Ваше здоровье!

| good hotel | kharoshaya gastinitsa | хорошая гостинница |

Good luck!
Shyasliva!
Счастливо!

Good morning.
dobrae utra
Доброе утро.

Goodbye.
da svidaniya
До свидания.

| | | |
|---|---|---|
| government | pravitel'stva | правительство |
| grandchild | vnuk (m)/vnuchka (f) | внук/внучка |
| grandfather | dedushka | дедушка |
| grandmother | babushka | бабушка |
| grapes | vinagrat | виноград |
| grass | trava | трава |
| grave | magila | могила |
| great | velikiy | великий |

Great!
Atlichna!
Отлично!

| | | |
|---|---|---|
| green | zelyony | зелёный |
| grey | sery | серый |
| to guess | dagadyvat'sya/ dagadat'sya | догадаться/ догадываться |
| guide(person) | git | гид |
| guidebook | putevaditel' | путеводитель |
| guidedog | sabaka-pavadyr' | собака-поводырь |
| guitar | gitara | гитара |
| gym | spartzal | спортзал |
| gymnastics | gimnastika | гимнастика |

# H

| | | |
|---|---|---|
| hair | volasy | волосы |
| hairbrush | shchyotka dlya valos | щётка для волос |
| half | palavina | половина |
| half a litre | pol-litra | пол-литра |
| to hallucinate | galyutsiniravat' | галлюцинировать |
| ham | vetchina | ветчина |
| hammer | molat | молот |
| hand | ruka | рука |
| handbag | sumachka | сумочка |
| handmade | ruchnoy raboty | ручной работы |
| handsome | krasivy | красивый |
| happy | shyaslivy | счастливый |

Happy birthday!
z dnyom razhdeniya!
С днём рождения!

| | | |
|---|---|---|
| harbour | gavan' | гавань |
| hard (difficult) | trudny | трудный |
| hard to get | defitsytny | дефицитный |
| harrassment | ushchimleniye praf | ущемление прав |
| harvest | urazhay | урожай |
| hash | gashysh | гашиш |

| to have | u ... est' | у ... есть |
| | | |

Do you have ...?
u vas est' ...?
**У Вас есть ...?**

I have ...
u menya est' ...
**У меня есть ...**

| hayfever | sennaya likharatka | сенная лихорадка |
| he | on | он |
| head | galava | голова |
| headache | galavnaya bol' | головная боль |
| health | zdarov'e | здоровье |
| to hear | slyshat'/uslyshat' | слышать |
| hearing aid | slukhavoy aparat | слуховой аппарат |
| heart | serttse | сердце |
| heat | zhara | жара |
| heating | ataplenie | отопление |
| heavy | tyazholy | тяжёлый |

Hello.
zdrastvuyte!
**Здравствуйте!**

Hello! (answering telephone)
allo!
**Алло!**

Help!
pamagite!
**Помогите!**

| to help | pamagat'/pamoch' | помогать/помочь |
| herbs | travy | травы |
| herbalist | spetsialist pa travam | специалист по травам |
| here | zdes' | здесь |
| heroin | gerain | героин |
| high | vysokiy | высокий |
| high school | srednyaya shkola | средняя школа |
| to hike | khadit' pishkom | ходить пешком |
| hiking | pakhot | поход |
| hill | kholm | холм |
| Hindu | indus (m)/induska (f) | индус/индуска |
| to hire | brat'/vzyat' naprakat | брать/взять напрокат |
| to hitchhike | puteshestvovat' aftastopam | путешествовать автостопом |
| HIV positive | vich infetsiravany | ВИЧ инфецированный |
| holiday | praznik | праздник |
| holidays | otpusk | отпуск |

| | | |
|---|---|---|
| Holy Week | svyataya nedelya | Святая Неделя |
| homeless | bezdomny | бездомный |
| homeopathy | gomeopatiya | гомеопатия |
| homosexual | gomoseksualist | гомосексуалист |
| honey | myot | мёд |
| honeymoon | medovy mesyats | медовый месяц |
| hooligan | khuligan | хулиган |
| horrible/awful/terrible | uzhasny | ужасный |
| horse | loshad' | лошадь |
| horse riding | verkhavaya ezda | верховая езда |
| hospital | bal'nitsa | больница |
| hot (weather) | zharkiy | жаркий |

It's hot.
zharka
жарко.

I'm hot.
mne zharka
Мне жарко.

| | | |
|---|---|---|
| hot water | garyachaya vada | горячая вода |
| house | dom | дом |
| housework | rabota pa domu | работа по дому |
| how | kak | как |

How do I get to ...?
kak dabrat'sa da ...?
Как добраться до ...?

How do you say ...?
kak skazat' ...?
Как сказать ...?

| | | |
|---|---|---|
| to hug | abnimat'/abnyat' | обнимать/обнять |
| human rights | prava chelaveka | права человека |
| a hundred | sto | сто |
| hungry | goladen (m)/galadna (f) | голоден/голодна |
| husband | mush | муж |
| hyperinflation | giperinflyatsiya | гиперинфляция |

## I

| | | |
|---|---|---|
| I | ya | я |
| ice | lyot | лёд |
| ice axe | ledarup | ледоруб |
| icecream | marozhenae | мороженое |
| ice hockey | khakey nal'du | хоккей на льду |
| ice skating | katanie na kan'kakh | катание на коньках |
| icon | ikona | икона |

| | | |
|---|---|---|
| identification | ustanavleniye lichnosti | установление личности |
| idiot | durak | дурак |
| if | esli | если |
| ill | bolen (m)/bal'na (f) | болен/больна |
| immigration | imigratsiya | иммиграция |
| important | vazhny | важный |

It's (not) important.
(ne) vazhna.
(Не) Важно.

| | | |
|---|---|---|
| to be in a hurry | speshyt' | спешить |
| in front of | naprotif | напротив |
| incense | ladan | ладан |
| included | fklyucheno | включено |
| incomprehensible | nepanyatny | непонятный |
| indicator | ukazatel' | указатель |
| indigestion | rastroystva pishchevaveniya | растройство пищеварения |
| industry | pramishlenast' | промышленность |
| inequality | neravenstva | неравенство |
| inflation | inflyatsiya | инфляция |
| informant | asvedamitel' (m)/ asvedamitel'nitsa (f) | осведомитель/ осведомительница |
| to inject | delat'/zdelat' ukol | делать/сделать укол |
| injection | inektsiya | инъекция |
| injury | travma | травма |
| inside | vnutri | внутри |
| instructor | instruktar | инструктор |
| insurance | strakhavanie | страхование |
| intense | napryazhony | напряжённый |
| interesting | interesny | интересный |
| intermission | pereryf | перерыв |
| international | mezhdunarodny | международный |
| interview | interv'yu | интервью |
| island | ostraf | остров |
| itch | zut | зуд |
| itinerary | marshrut | маршрут |

## J

| | | |
|---|---|---|
| jail | t'yurma | тюрьма |
| jar | banka | банка |
| jealous | revnivy | ревнивый |
| jeans | dzhynsy | джинсы |
| jeep | dzhyp | джип |
| jewellery | yuvelirnye izdeliya | ювелирные изделия |

| | | |
|---|---|---|
| Jewish | evreyskiy | еврейский |
| job | rabota | работа |
| job advertisement | ab'yavlenie a rabote | объявление о работе |
| jockey | zhakey | жокей |
| joke | shutka | шутка |
| to joke | shutit'/pashutit' | шутить/пошутить |
| journalist | zhurnalist (m)/ | журналист/ |
| | zhurnalistka (f) | журналистка |
| journey | puteshestvie | путешествие |
| judge | sud'ya | судья |
| juice | sok | сок |
| to jump | prygat'/prygnut' | прыгать/прыгнуть |
| jumper (sweater) | dzhemper | джемпер |
| justice | spravedlivast' | справедливость |

## K

| | | |
|---|---|---|
| key | klyuch | ключ |
| keyboard | klaviatura | клавиатура |
| KGB | ka-ge-be | КГБ |
| kick | udaryat/udarit' | ударятв/ударитв |
| | nagoy | ногой |
| kick off | nachala | начало |
| to kill | ubivat'/ubit' | убивать/убить |
| kind | dobry | добрый |
| kindergarten | detskiy sat | детский сад |
| king | karol' | король |
| kiss | patseluy | поцелуй |
| to kiss | tselavat'/pafselavat' | целовать/поцеловать |
| kitchen | kukhnya | кухня |
| kitten | katyonak | котенок |
| knee | kalena | колено |
| knife | nosh | нож |
| to know | znat' | знать |

I don't know.
ya ne znayu
Я не знаю.

| | | |
|---|---|---|
| Koran | karan | Коран |
| Kremlin | kreml' | Кремль |

## L

| | | |
|---|---|---|
| labour camp | trudavoy lager' | трудовой лагерь |
| lace | kruzheva | кружева |
| lake | ozera | озеро |

| | | |
|---|---|---|
| land | zemlya | земля |
| language | yazyk | язык |
| large | bal'shoy | большой |
| last | pasledniy | последний |
| last month | f proshlam mesyatse | в прошлом месяце |
| last night | fchera vecheram | вчера вечером |
| last week | na proshlay nedele | на прошлой неделе |
| last year | f proshlam gadu | в прошлом году |
| late | pozniy | поздний |
| laugh | smekh | смех |
| launderette | prachechnaya | прачечная |
| law | zakon | закон |
| lawyer | advakat | адвокат |
| laxatives | slabitel'nae | слабительное |
| lazy | lenivy | ленивый |
| leader | rukavaditel' | руководитель |
| to learn | uchit'/vyuchit' | учить/выучить |
| leather | kozha | кожа |
| leathergoods | izdeliya iz kozhi | изделия из кожи |
| ledge | vystup | выступ |
| left (not right) | leva | лево |
| left luggage | kamera khraneniya | камера хранения |
| left-wing | levy | левый |
| leg | naga | нога |
| legalisation | legalizatsiya | легализация |
| lens | linza | линза |
| Lent | velikiy post | Великий Пост |
| lesbian | lezbianka | лесбианка |
| less | men'she | меньше |
| letter | pis'mo | письмо |
| liar | lgun (m)/lgun'ya (f) | лгун/лгунья |
| library | bibliateka | библиотека |
| lice | fshy | вши |
| license | litsenziya | лицензия |
| to lie (down) | lezhat' | лежать |
| life | zhyzn' | жизнь |
| lift (elevator) | lift | лифт |
| a light | lampa | лампа |
| light (adj) | svetly | светлый |
| light (sun/lamp) | svet | свет |
| light bulb | lampachka | лампочка |
| lighter | zazhygalka | зажигалка |
| to like | lyubit' | любить |
| line | liniya | линия |
| lips | guby | губы |
| lipstick | gubnaya pamada | губная помада |

| to listen | slushat' | слушать |
| little (small) | malen'kiy | маленький |
| a little (amount) | nemnoga | немного |
| to live (somewhere) | zhyt' | жить |

Long live ...!
da zdrastvuyet ...!
Да здравствует ...!

| local | mesny | местный |
| local/city bus | reysavy aftobus | рейсовый автобус |
| location | mestanakhazhenie | местонахождение |
| lock | zamok | замок |
| to lock | zapirat'/zaperet' | запирать/запереть |
| long | dlinny | длинный |
| long distance | dal'ny | дальний |
| to look | smatret'/pasmatret' | смотреть/посмотреть |
| to look after | prismatrivat'/ | присматривать/ |
| | prismatret' | присмотреть |
| to look for | iskat' | искать |
| loose change | melach' | мелочь |
| to lose | teryat'/pateryat' | терять/потерять |
| loser | neudachnik | неудачник |
| loss | paterya | потеря |
| a lot | mnoga | много |
| loud | gromkiy | громкий |
| to love | lyubit' | любить |
| lover | lyubovnik (m)/lyubovnitsa (f) | любовник/любовница |
| low | niskiy | низкий |
| loyal | verny, predany | верный |
| luck | shchast'e, vizenie | счастье |
| lucky | shaslivy | счастливый |
| luggage | bagash | багаж |
| luggage lockers | kamera-aftamat | камера-автомат |
| lump | shyshka | шишка |
| lunch | abet | обед |
| lunchtime | abediny piriryf | обеденный перерыв |
| luxury | roskash' | роскошь |

# M

| machine | mashyna | машина |
| mad | sumashedshiy | сумасшедший |
| made (of) | zdelany iz | сделанный из |
| magazine | zhurnal | журнал |
| magician | fokusnik | фокусник |
| mail | pochta | почта |
| mailbox | pachtovy yashchik | почтовый ящик |

| main road | glavnaya daroga | главная дорога |
| main square | tsentral'naya ploshchat' | центральная площадь |
| majority | bal'shinstvo | большинство |
| to make | delat'/sdelat' | делать/сделать |
| make-up | kasmetika | косметика |
| man | mushchina | мужчина |
| manual worker | rabochiy (m)/rabochaya (f) | рабочий/рабочая |
| many | mnoga | много |

Many happy returns!
dolgikh let zhyzni!
**Долгих лет жизни!**

| map | karta | карта |

Can you show me on the map?
pakazhyte, pazhalsta, na karte
**Покажите, пожалуйста, на карте.**

| market | rynak | рынок |
| marriage | brak | брак |
| to marry | | |
| (take a wife) | zhenit'sa | жениться |
| (take a husband) | vykhadit'/ | выходить/ |
| | vyti zamush | выйти замуж |
| marvellous | izumitel'niy | изумительный |
| mass (Orthodox) | abednya | обедня |
| massage | massash | массаж |
| mat (door) | palavik | половик |
| match (sport) | mach | матч |
| matches | spichki | спички |

It doesn't matter. (no problem)
nichevo
**Ничего.**

It doesn't matter. (any one is OK)
fsyo ravno.
**Всё равно.**

What's the matter?
f chyom dela?
**В чём дело?**

| mattress | matrats | матрац |
| maybe | mozhet byt' | может быть |
| May Day | pervae maya | Первое Мая |
| mayor | mer | мэр |
| meat dumplings | pil'meney | пельмени |
| mechanic | mekhanik | механик |
| medal | medal' | медаль |
| medicine | lekarstva | лекарство |

| meditation | meditatsiya | медитация |
|---|---|---|
| to meet | fstrechat'/fstrechit' | встречать/встретить |
| menstruation | menstruatsiya | менструация |
| menu | menyu | меню |
| message | zapiska | записка |
| metal | metal | метал |
| midnight | polnach' | полночь |
| migraine | migren' | мигрень |
| military | vaenny | военный |
| military service | vaennaya sluzhba | военная служба |
| milk | malako | молоко |
| mind | um | ум |
| mineral water | mineral'naya vada | минеральная вода |
| mink | norka | норка |
| minute | minuta | минута |

Just a minute.
minutku
**Минутку.**

In (five) minutes.
cheres (pyat') minut
**Через (пять) минут.**

| mirror | zerkala | зеркало |
|---|---|---|
| miscarriage | vykidysh | выкидыш |
| to miss (feel absence) | taskavat' pa | тосковать по |
| mistake | ashipka | ошибка |
| to mix | smeshyvat'/smeshat' | смешивать/смешать |
| mobile phone | sotaviy telefon | сотовый телефон |
| modem | modem | модем |
| monastery | manastyr' | монастырь |
| money | den'gi | деньги |
| month | mesyats | месяц |
| this month | v etam mesyatse | в этом месяце |
| monument | pamyatnik | памятник |
| moon | luna | луна |
| more | bol'she | больше |
| morning (6 am – 1pm) | utra | утро |
| mosque | mechet' | мечеть |
| mother | mat' | мать |
| motorboat | matornaya lotka | моторная лодка |
| motorcycle | matatsykl | мотоцикл |
| motorway | shase | шоссе |
| mountain | gara | гора |
| mountain bike | gorniy velasipet | горный велосипед |
| mountain range | gornaya gryada | горная гряда |
| mountaineering | al'pinizm | альпинизм |
| mouse | mysh' | мышь |

| | | |
|---|---|---|
| mouse (computer) | myshka | мышка |
| mouth | rot | рот |
| movie | fil'm | фильм |
| mud | slyakat' | слякоть |
| Mum | mama | Мама |
| muscle | muskul | мускул |
| museum | muzey | музей |
| music | muzyka | музыка |
| musician | muzykant | музыкант |
| Muslim | musul'manin (m)/ | мусульманин/ |
| | musul'manka (f) | мусульманка |
| mute | nemoy | немой |
| mystic | mistik | мистик |
| mystical | misticheskiy | мистический |

## N

| | | |
|---|---|---|
| name (person) | imya | имя |
| name (thing) | nazvanie | название |
| name day | imeniny | именины |
| nappy | padguznik | подгузник |
| national park | zapavednik | заповедник |
| nationality | natsianal'nast' | национальность |
| nature | priroda | природа |
| naturopath | naturapat | натуропат |
| nausea | tashnata | тошнота |
| near | bliska ot | близко от |
| nearby hotel | blizhayshaya | ближайшая |
| | gastinitsa | гостинница |
| necessary | nuzhny | нужный |
| necklace | azherel'e | ожерелье |
| to need | nuzhdat'sa v | нуждаться в |
| needle (sewing) | igla | игла |
| needle (syringe) | shprits | шприц |
| never | nikagda | никогда |
| new | novy | новый |
| news | novasti | новости |
| newsagency | gazetny kiosk | газетный киоск |
| newspaper | gazeta | газета |
| New Year | novy got | Новый год |
| New Year's Eve | navagodnyaya noch' | Новогодняя ночь |
| next | sleduyushchiy | следующий |
| next month | f sleduyushchem mesyatse | в следующем месяце |
| next to | ryadam s | рядом с |
| next week | na sleduyushchey nedele | на следующей неделе |
| next year | f budushchem gadu | в будущем году |

| nice | mily | милый |
| nickname | prozvishche | прозвище |
| night | noch' | ночь |
| nightmare | kashmar | кошмар |
| no | net | нет |
| noise | shum | шум |
| noisy | shumny | шумный |
| noon | polden' | полдень |
| north | sever | север |
| nose | nos | нос |
| notebook | blaknot | блокнот |
| nothing | nichevo | ничего |

Not yet.
net eshchyo
Нет еще.

| novel (book) | raman | роман |
| now | seychas | сейчас |
| nuclear energy | yadernaya energiya | ядерная энергия |
| nun | manakhinya | монахиня |
| nurse | medsestra | медсестра |

# O

| ocean | akean | океан |
| offence | prastupak | проступок |
| office | kantora | контора |
| office worker | sluzhayshchiy | служащий |
| offside | ofsayt | офсайт |
| often | chasta | часто |
| oil (cooking) | masla | масло |
| OK | kharasho | хорошо |
| old | stary | старый |
| old city | stary gorat | старый город |
| Olympic Games | alimpiyskie igry | олимпийский игры |
| on | na | на |
| on time | vovremya | вовремя |
| once | adin ras | один раз |
| open | atkryty | открытый |
| to open | atkryvat'/atkryt' | открывать/открыть |
| opening | atkrytie | открытие |
| opera house | operny teatr | оперный театр |
| operation | aperatsiya | операция |
| opinion | mnenie | мнение |
| opposite | protif | против |
| or | ili | или |
| oral | usny | устный |

| | | |
|---|---|---|
| orange (colour) | aranzhevy | оранжевый |
| orchestra | arkestr | оркестр |
| order | paryadak | порядок |
| to order | zakazyvat'/ zakazat' | заказывать/ заказать |
| ordinary | abyknaveny | обыкновенный |
| orgasm | argazm | оргазм |
| original | ariginal'ny | оригинальный |
| Orthodox Church | pravaslavnaya tserkaf' | православная церковь |
| other | drugoy | другой |
| outside | snaruzhy | снаружи |
| over | nat | над |
| overcoat | pal'to | пальто |
| overdose | peredazirovka | передозировка |
| owner | vladelets | владелец |
| oxygen | kislarot | кислород |
| ozone layer | azonavy sloy | озоновый слой |

## P

| | | |
|---|---|---|
| package | pasylka | посылка |
| packet (cigarettes) | pachka | пачка |
| padlock | navisnoy zamok | нависной замок |
| page | stranitsa | страница |
| a pain | bol' | боль |
| painful | balit | болит |
| painkillers | boleutalyaushchie | болеутоляющие |
| to paint | krasit'/pakrasit' | красить/покрасить |
| painter | khudozhnik | художник |
| painting (the art) | zhyvapis' | живопись |
| paintings | kartiny | картины |
| pair (a couple) | para | пара |
| palace | dvarets | дворец |
| pan | skavarada | сковорода |
| pap smear | mazok | мазок |
| paper | bumaga | бумага |
| paraplegic | paralizovany | парализованный |
| parcel | pasylka | посылка |
| parents | raditeli | родители |
| a park | park | парк |
| to park | stavit'/pastavit' mashynu | ставить/поставить машину |
| parliament (Russian) | duma | Дума |
| part | chast' | часть |
| party (fiesta!) | vecherinka | вечеринка |

|  |  |  |
|---|---|---|
| party (politics) | partiya | партия |
| passenger | pasazhyr | пассажир |
| passport | paspart | паспорт |
| past | proshlae | прошлое |
| path | trapinka | тропинка |
| patient (adj) | terpelivy | терпеливый |
| to pay | platit'/zaplatit' | платить/заплатить |
| payment | aplata | оплата |
| peace | mir | мир |
| peak | pik | пик |
| peasant | krest'yanin (m)/ krest'yanka (f) | крестьянин/ крестьянка |
| pedestrian | pishikhot | пешеход |
| pen (ballpoint) | ruchka | ручка |
| pencil | karandash | карандаш |
| penis | penis | пенис |
| people | lyudi | люди |
| pepper | perets | перец |
| performance | spektakl' | спектакль |
| performance art | stsenicheskoye iskustva | сценическое искусство |
| permafrost | vechnaya merzlata | вечная мерзлота |
| permanent | pastayany | постоянный |
| permit (piece of paper) | razreshenie | разрешение |
| person | chelavek | человек |
| personality | lichnast' | личность |
| to perspire | patet'/fspatet' | потеть/вспотеть |
| petition | petitsiya | петиция |
| petrol | benzin | бензин |
| pharmacy | apteka | аптека |
| phone book | telifonaya kniga | телефонная книга |
| phone box | telifonaya butka | телефонная будка |
| phonecard | telifonaya kartachka | телефонная карточка |
| photo | snimak | снимок |

Can I take a photo?
mozhna vas sfatagrafiravat'?
**Можно вас сфотографировать?**

|  |  |  |
|---|---|---|
| photographer | fatograf | фотограф |
| photography | fatagrafiya | фотография |
| pickaxe | kirka | кирка |
| to pick up | padnimat'/padnyat' | поднимать/поднять |
| pie | pirok | пирог |
| pig | svin'ya | свинья |
| pill | tabletka | таблетка |
| pillow | padushka | подушка |
| pillowcase | navalachka | наволочка |
| pipe | truba | труба |

P

| place | mesta | место |
|---|---|---|
| place of birth | mesta razhdeniya | место рождения |
| plain | prastoy | простой |
| plane | samalyot | самолёт |
| planet | planeta | планета |
| plant | rastenie | растение |
| plastic | plastmassa | пластмасса |
| plate | taryelka | тарелка |
| play (theatre) | p'esa | пьеса |
| to play | igrat' | играть |
| player (sports) | spartsmen (m)/ | спортсмен/ |
| | spartsmenka (f) | спортсменка |
| playing cards | karty | карты |
| to play cards | igrat' f karty | играть в карты |
| plug (bath) | propka | пробка |
| plug (electricity) | vilka | вилка |
| pocket | karman | карман |
| poetry | paeziya | поэзия |
| to point | ukazyvat'/ukazat' | указывать/указать |
| police | militsiya | милиция |
| politics | palitika | политика |
| politicians | palitiki | политики |
| pollution | zagryazneniye | загрязнение |
| | akruzhayushchey sredy | окружающей среды |
| pool (swimming) | basseyn | бассейн |
| pool (game) | pul'ka | пулька |
| poor | bedny | бедный |
| popular | papulyarny | популярный |
| port | port | порт |
| portrait sketcher | partretny eskiz | портретный эскиз |
| possible | vazmozhny | возможный |

It's (not) possible.

eta (ne) vazmozhna

Это (не) возможно.

| postcard | atkrytka | открытка |
|---|---|---|
| post code | pachtovy indeks | почтовый индекс |
| poster | plakat | плакат |
| post office | pochta | почта |
| power | vlast' | власть |
| prayer | malitva | молитва |
| to prefer | predpachitat'/ | предпочитать/ |
| | predpachest' | предпочесть |
| pregnant | beremennaya | беременная |
| to prepare | prigatavlivat'/ | приготавливать/ |
| | prigatovit' | приготовить |
| present (gift) | padarak | подарок |

| presenter (TV, etc) | vedushchiy | ведущий |
| pretty | kharoshenkiy | хорошенький |
| price | tsena | цена |
| pride | gordast' | гордость |
| priest | svyashchenik | священник |
| prison | tyur'ma | тюрьма |
| private | chasny | частный |
| privatisation | privatizasiya | приватизация |
| to produce | praizvadit' | производить |
| producer (film) | pradyuser | продюссер |
| profession | prafessiya | профессия |
| profit | pribyl' | прибыль |
| program | pragrama | программа |
| promise | abeshchanie | обещание |
| proposal | predlazhenie | предложение |
| to protect | zashchishchat'/zashchitit' | защищать/защитить |
| protected forest | zapavednik | заповедник |
| protection racket | reket | рэкет |
| protest | pratest | протест |
| to protest | pratestavat' | протестовать |
| public toilet | apshchestveny tualet | общественный туалет |
| to pull | tyanut'/patyanut' | тянуть/потянуть |
| pump | nasos | насос |
| puncture | prakol | прокол |
| to punish | nakazyvat'/ nakazat' | наказывать/ наказать |
| puppy | shchenok | щенок |
| pure | chisty | чистый |
| purple | purpurny | пурпурный |
| to push | talkat'/talknut' | толкать/толкнуть |

| qualifications | kvalifikatsii | квалификации |
| quality | kachestva | качество |
| quarantine | karantin | карантин |
| quarrel | sora | ссора |
| quarter | chetvert' | четверть |
| queen | karaleva | королева |
| question | vapros | вопрос |
| to question | daprashyvat'/ daprasit' | допрашивать/ допроситв |
| question (topic) | vapros | вопрос |
| queue | ochered' | очередь |

| quick | bystry | быстрый |
| quiet | tikhiy | тихий |
| to quit | brasat'/brosit' | бросать/бросить |

## R

| rabbit | krolik | кролик |
| race (ancestry) | rasa | раса |
| race (sport) | bek | бег |
| racing bike | gonachny velasipet | гоночный велосипед |
| racism | rasizm | расизм |
| racquet | raketa | ракета |
| radiator | radiatar | радиатор |
| railroad | zheleznaya daroga | железная дорога |
| railway station | vagzal | вокзал |
| rain | dosht' | дождь |

It's raining.
idyot dosht'
Идёт дождь.

| rally | manifestatsiya | манифестация |
| rape | iznasilavanie | изнасилование |
| rare | retkiy | редкий |
| a rash | syp' | сыпь |
| rat | krysa | крыса |
| rate of pay | stafka zarabatnay platy | ставка заработной платы |
| raw | syroy | сырой |
| razor | britva | бритва |
| razor blades | lezviya | лезвия |
| to read | chitat'/prachitat' | читать/прочитать |
| ready | gatof (m)/gatova (f) | готов/готова |
| reason | prichina | причина |
| receipt | kvitantsiya | квитанция |
| to receive | paluchat'/paluchit' | получать/получить |
| recent | nedavniy | недавний |
| recently | nedavna | недавно |
| to recognise | uznavat'/uznat' | узнавать/узнать |
| to recommend | rekamendavat' | рекомендовать |
| recording | zapis' | запись |
| recycling | utilizatsiya | утилизация |
| red | krasny | красный |
| red tape | byurakratizm | бюрократизм |
| referee | referi | рефери |
| reference | rekamendatsiya | рекомендация |
| reflection (mirror) | atrazhenie | отражение |
| reflection (thinking) | razmyshlenie | размышление |

| refrigerator | khaladil'nik | холодильник |
| refugee | bezhenets (m)/bezhenka (f) | беженец/беженка |
| refund | vazvrashchenie denek | возвращение денег |
| to refuse | atkazyvat'/atkazat' | отказывать/ отказать |
| regional | regional'ny | региональный |
| to regret | sazhalet' | сожалеть |
| relationship | svyaz' | связь |
| to relax | raslablyatsa/ raslabitsa' | расслабляться/ расслабиться |
| religion | religiya | религия |
| religious | religiozny | религиозный |
| to remember | pomnit'/fspomnit' | помнить/ вспоминить |
| remote | dal'niy | дальний |
| rent | arendnaya plata | арендная плата |
| to rent | arendavat' | арендовать |
| to repeat | paftaryat'/paftarit' | повторять/ повторить |
| republic | respublika | республика |
| to reserve | zakazyvat'/ zakazat' | заказывать/ заказать |
| resignation | atstafka | отставка |
| respect | uvazhenie | уважение |
| rest (relaxation) | odykh | отдых |
| rest (what's left) | astatak | остаток |
| to rest | adykhat'/adakhnut' | отдыхать/ отдохнуть |
| resumé | rezyume | резюме |
| retired | na pensii | на пенсии |
| to return | vazvrashchat'sa/ vernut'sa | возвращаться/ вернуться |
| return (ticket) | abratny (bilet) | обратный (билет) |
| review | retsenziya | рецензия |
| revolution | revalyutsiya | революция |
| rhythm | ritm | ритм |
| rich (wealthy) | bagaty | богатый |
| rich (food) | zhyrny | жирный |
| right (not left) | naprava | направо |
| right (correct) | pravil'ny | правильный |

You're right.
vy pravy.
Вы правы.

| civil rights | grazhdanskiye prava | гражданские права |
| right-wing | pravy | правый |
| ring (on finger) | kal'tso | кольцо |

| to ring | zvanit'/pazvanit' | звонить/позвонить |
|---|---|---|

I'll give you a ring.
ya vam pazvanyu
Я вам позвоню.

| rip-off | grabyosh | грабёж |
|---|---|---|
| risk | risk | риск |
| river | reka | река |
| road (main) | daroga | дорога |
| road map | karta darog | карта дорог |
| to rob | krast'/abakrast' | красть/обокрасть |
| rock | skala | скала |
| rock climbing | skalalazanie | скалолазание |
| rock group | rok grupa | рок-группа |
| romance | ramans | романс |
| room | komnata | комната |
| room (hotel) | nomer | номер |
| rope/string | veryofka | верёвка |
| round | krugly | круглый |
| rubbish | musar | мусор |
| rug | kavyor | ковёр |
| ruins | razvaliny | развалины |
| rules | pravila | правила |
| to run | bezhat'/pabezhat' | бежать/побежать |

## S

| sad | grusny | грустный |
|---|---|---|
| safe (adj) | bezapasny | безопасный |
| a safe | seyf | сейф |
| safe sex | bezapasny seks | безопасный секс |
| saint | svyatoy | святой |
| Saint's Day | imeniny | именины |
| salary | zarplata | зарплата |
| (on) sale | f pradazhe | в продаже |
| salt | sol' | соль |
| same | tot zhe (m)/ta zhe (f) | тот же/та же |
| sand | pisok | песок |
| sanitary napkins | ginienicheskie salfetki | гигенические салфетки |
| Saturday | subota | суббота |
| sauna | sauna | сауна |
| to save | spasat'/spasti | спасать/спасти |
| to say | gavarit'/skazat' | говорить/сказать |
| scarf | sharf | шарф |
| school | shkola | школа |
| science | nauka | наука |

| scientist | uchyony (m)/uchyonaya (f) | учёный/учёная |
| scissors | nozhnitsy | ножницы |
| to score (sport) | zabivat'/zabit' gol | забивать/забить гол |
| scoreboard | tablo | табло |
| screen | ekran | экран |
| sculpture | skul'ptura | скульптура |
| sea | more | море |
| sea/travel sickness | marskaya balezn' | морская болезнь |
| seaside | berek morya | берег моря |
| seat | mesta | место |
| seatbelt | rimen' | ремень |
| second (time) | sekunda | секунда |
| second | ftaroy | второй |
| secretary | sikritarsha | секретарша |
| to see | videt'/uvidet' | видеть/увидеть |

We'll see!
pasmotrim!
**Посмотрим!**

I see. (understand)
panyatna
**Понятно.**

See you later.
Paka
**Пока.**

See you tomorrow.
da zaftra
**До завтра.**

| (to be) self-employed | rabotat' na sebya | работать на себя |
| selfish | egoistichny | эгоистичный |
| self-service | samaapsluzhyvanie | самообслуживание |
| to sell | pradavat'/pradat' | продавать/продать |
| to send | pasylat'/paslat' | посылать/послать |
| sensible | razumny | разумный |
| sentence (words) | predlazhenie | предложение |
| sentence (prison) | prigavor | приговор |
| to separate | atdelyat'/atdelit' | отделять/отделить |
| series | seriya | серия |
| serious | ser'yozny | серьёзный |
| service (assistance) | usluga | услуга |
| service (religious) | sluzhba | служба |
| several | neskal'ka | несколько |
| to sew | shyt'/sshyt' | шить/сшить |
| sex | seks | секс |
| sexy | seksual'ny | сексуальный |
| shade/shadow | ten' | тень |

| shampoo | shampun' | шампунь |
| shape | forma | форма |
| to share (with) | delit'/padelit' (s) | делить/поделить (с) |
| to share a room | zhyt' v adnoy komnate | жить в одной комнате |
| to shave | brit'sa/pabrit'sa | бриться/пóбриться |
| she | ana | она |
| sheet (bed) | prastynya | простыня |
| sheet (of paper) | list | лист |
| shell | rakavina | раковина |
| ship | karabl' | корабль |
| to ship | gruzit'/pagruzit' | грузить/погрузить |
| shirt | rubashka | рубашка |
| shoes | tufli | туфли |
| to shoot | strelyat'/rasstrelyat' | стрелять/расстрелять |
| shop | magazin | магазин |
| to go shopping | khadit' pa magazinam | ходить по магазинам |
| short | karotkiy | короткий |
| short films | karatkametrazhniy fil'm | короткометражный фильм |
| short stories | rasskazy | рассказы |
| shortage | nedastatak | недостаток |
| shorts | shorty | шорты |
| shoulders | plechi | плечи |
| to shout | krihcat'/zakrichat' | кричать/закричать |
| a show | spektakl' | спектакль |
| to show | pakazyvat'/pakazat' | показывать/показать |

Can you show me on the map?
pakazhyte, pazhalsta, na karte
Покажите, пожалуйста, на карте.

| shower | dush | душ |
| to shut | zakryvat'/zakryt' | закрывать/закрыть |
| shy | zastenchivy | застенчивый |
| sick | bolen (m)/bal'na (f) | болен/больна |
| side | starana | сторона |
| a sign | znak | знак |
| to sign | patpisyvat'/patpisat' | подписывать/подписать |
| signature | podpis' | подпись |
| silk | sholk | шёлк |
| similar | pakhozhy | похожий |
| simple | prastoy | простой |
| sin | grekh | грех |
| since (May) | s | с |
| to sing | pet'/spet' | петь/спеть |

| | | |
|---|---|---|
| singer | pevets (m)/pevitsa (f) | певец/певица |
| single (person) | kholast (m)/ne zamuzhem (f) | холост/не замужем |
| single (unique) | edinstvenny | единственный |
| single room | adnarmesny nomer | одноместный номер |
| sister | sestra | сестра |
| to sit | sidet' | сидеть |
| size | razmer | размер |
| skates | kan'ki | коньки |
| skis | lyzhy | лыжи |
| to ski | khadit' na lyzhakh | ходить на лыжах |
| skin | kozha | кожа |
| sky | neba | небо |
| to sleep | spat' | спать |
| sleeping bag | spal'ny meshok | спальный мешок |
| sleeping car | spal'ny vagon | спальный вагон |
| sleeping pills | snatvornye tabletki | снотворный таблетке |
| sleepy | sony | сонный |
| sleigh | sani | сани |
| slide (film) | slayt | слайд |
| slow | medliny | медленный |
| small | malen'kiy | маленький |
| a smell | zapakh | запах |
| to smell | nyukhat'/panyukhat' | нюхать/понюхать |
| to smile | ulybat'sa/ ulybnut'sa | улыбаться/ улыбнуться |
| to smoke | kurit'/pakurit' | курить/покурить |
| soap | myla | мыло |
| soccer | fudbol | футбол |
| social security | satsial'nae abespechenie | социальное обеспечение |
| socialist | satsialist (m)/ satsialistka (f) | социалист/ социалистка |
| solid | tvyordy | твёрдый |
| some | neskal'ka | несколько |
| somebody/someone | kto-ta | кто-то |
| something | shto-ta | что-то |
| sometimes | inagda | иногда |
| son | syn | сын |
| song | pesnya | песня |
| soon | skora | скоро |

I'm sorry.
prastite
Простите.

| | | |
|---|---|---|
| sound | zvuk | звук |
| south | yuk | юг |

| English | Transliteration | Russian |
|---|---|---|
| souvenir | suvenir | сувенир |
| souvenir shop | suvenirny magazin | сувенирный магазин |
| Soviet | savetskiy | советский |
| space (outer) | kosmas | космос |
| to speak | gavarit' | говорить |
| special | asoby | особый |
| specialist | spetsialist | специалист |
| speed | skorast' | скорость |
| speed limit | dazvolennaya skorast' | дозволенная скорость |
| spicy (hot) | ostry | острый |
| sport | sport | спорт |
| sportsperson | spartsmen (m)/ | спортсмен/ |
| | spartsmenka (f) | спортсменка |
| a sprain | rastyazhenie svyazak | растяжение связок |
| spring (season) | vesna | весна |
| spring (coil) | pruzhyna | пружина |
| spy | shpion (m)/shpionka (f) | шпион/шпионка |
| square (shape) | kvadrat | квадрат |
| square (in town) | ploshchat' | площадь |
| stadium | stadion | стадион |
| stage | stsena | сцена |
| stairway | lesnitsa | лестница |
| stamps | marki | марки |
| standard (usual) | narmal'ny | нормальный |
| standard of living | zhyzneny uraven' | жизненный уровень |
| stars | zvyozdy | звёзды |
| to start | nachinat'/nachat' | начинать/начать |
| state (not private) | gasudarstvenny | государственный |
| station | vagzal | вокзал |
| stationers | kantselyarskie tavary | канцелярские товары |
| statue | statuya | статуя |
| to stay (somewhere) | astanavlivat'sa/ | останавливаться/ |
| | astanavit'sa | остановиться |
| to steal | krast'/ukrast' | красть/украсть |
| steam | par | пар |
| steep | krutoy | крутой |
| step | stupen' | ступень |
| stipend | stipendiya | стипендия |
| stomach | zheludak | желудок |
| stomach ache | bol' v zhelutke | боль в желудке |
| stone | kamen' | камень |
| stoned (drugged) | na kalyosakh | очищенный от |
| | | косточек |
| to stop | astanavlivat'sa/ | останавливаться/ |
| | astanavit'sa | остановиться |

| Stop! | | |
|---|---|---|
| stop! | | |
| Стоп! | | |
| storm | burya | буря |
| story | raskas | рассказ |
| stove | pech' | печь |
| straight | pryamoy | прямой |
| strange | strany | странный |
| stranger | neznakomets (m)/ neznakomka (f) | незнакомец/ незнакомка |
| stream | patok | поток |
| street | ulitsa | улица |
| strength | sila | сила |
| a strike | zabastofka | забастовка |
| string/rope | veryofka | верёвка |
| stroll/walk | pragulka | прогулка |
| strong | sil'ny | сильный |
| stubborn | upryamy | упрямый |
| student | student (m)/studentka (f) | студент/студентка |
| studio | studiya | студия |
| stupid | glupy | глупый |
| style | stil' | стиль |
| subtitles | subtitry | субтитры |
| suburb | prigarat | пригород |
| subway station | stantsiya metro | станция метро |
| success | uspekh | успех |
| to suffer | stradat' | страдать |
| sugar | sakhar | сахар |
| suitcase | chemadan | чемодан |
| summer | leta | лето |
| sun | sontse | солнце |
| sunblock | sontsezashchitny krem | солнцезащитный крем |
| sunburn | sonechny azhok | солнечный ожог |
| sunglasses | zashchitnye achki at sontsa | очки от солнца |
| sunny | solnechny | солнечный |
| sunrise | zarya | заря |
| sunset | zakat | закат |
| Sure. | | |
| kaneshna | | |
| Конечно. | | |
| surfboard | daska dlya serfinga | доска для серфинга |
| surname | familiya | фамилия |
| to survive | perezhyvat'/perezhyt' | переживать/ пережить |

| sweet | slatkiy | сладкий |
| to swim | plavat' | плавать |
| swimming | plavanie | плавание |
| swimming pool | basseyn | бассейн |
| sword | mech | меч |
| sympathetic | sachustvenny | сочувственный |
| synagogue | sinagoga | синагога |
| synthetic | sinteticheskiy | синтетический |
| syringe | shprits | шприц |

## T

| table | stol | стол |
| table tennis | nastol'ny tennis | настольный теннис |
| tail | khvost | хвост |
| to take | brat'/vzyat' | брать/взять |
| to take photographs | fatagrafiravat' | фотографировать |
| to talk | razgavarivat' | разговаривать |
| tall | vysokiy | высокий |
| tampons | tampony | тампоны |
| tasty | fkusny | вкусный |
| tax | nalok | налог |
| taxi stand | stayanka taksi | стоянка такси |
| teacher | uchitel' (m)/ | учитель/ |
| | uchitel'nitsa (f) | учительница |
| team | kamanda | команда |
| tear (crying) | sleza | слеза |
| technique | tekhnika | техника |
| teeth | zuby | зубы |
| telegram | telegrama | телеграмма |
| telephone | telifon | телефон |
| telephone book | telifonaya kniga | телефонная книга |
| to telephone | zvanit'/pazv'anit' | звонить/позвонить |
| to tell | skazat' | сказать |
| temperature/fever | likharatka | лихорадка |
| temperature (weather) | timpiratura | температура |
| tent | palatka | палатка |
| tent pegs | kolyshek dlya | колышек для |
| | palatki | палатки |
| term of office | srok polnomochy | срок полномочий |
| terrible/awful/horrible | uzhasny | ужасный |
| test | egzamen | экзамен |
| to thank | blagadarit'/ | благодарить/ |
| | pablagadarit' | поблагодарить |

T

Thank you.
spasiba
спасибо.

| theatre | teatr | театр |
|---|---|---|
| they | ani | они |
| thick | tolsty | толстый |
| thief | vor | вор |
| thin | tonkiy | тонкий |
| to think | dumat' | думать |
| this (one) | eta | это |
| thought | mysl' | мысль |
| throat | gorla | горло |
| ticket | bilet | билет |
| ticket collector | kanduktar | кондуктор |
| ticket machine | kasavy aftamat | кассовый автомат |
| ticket office | biletnaya kasa | билетная касса |
| tide (high) | prilif | прилив |
| tide (low) | atlif | отлив |
| tight | uskiy | узкий |
| time | vremya | время |
| timetable | raspisanie | расписание |
| tin (can) | banka | банка |
| tin opener | kanservny klyuch | консервный ключ |
| tip (gratuity) | chaevye | чаевые |
| tired | ustal (m)/ustala (f) | устал/устала |
| tissues | salfetki | салфетки |
| toad | zhaba | жаба |
| toast | grenka | гренка |
| tobacco | tabak | табак |
| today | sevodnya | сегодня |
| together | vmeste | вместе |
| toilet paper | tualetnaya bumaga | туалетная бумага |
| toilets | tualety | туалеты |
| tomorrow | zaftra | завтра |
| tonight | sevodnya vecheram | сегодня вечером |
| too (as well) | tozhe | тоже |
| too expensive | slishkam doraga | слишком дорого |
| too much; many | slishkam mnoga | слишком много |
| tooth | zup | зуб |
| toothache | zubnaya bol' | зубная боль |
| toothbrush | zubnaya shchyotka | зубная счётка |
| toothpaste | zubnaya pasta | зубная паста |
| Torah | tora | Тора |
| torch (flashlight) | iliktrichisky fanar' | электрический фонарь |
| to touch | trogat'/tronut' | трогать/тронуть |

DICTIONARY

248

| tour | ekskursiya | экскурсия |
|---|---|---|
| tourist | turist (m)/turistka (f) | турист |
| tourist information | turisticheskoye byuro | туристическое бюро |
| towards | k | к |
| towel | palatentse | полотенце |
| tower | bashnya | башня |
| toxic waste | taksicheskiye atkhody | токсические отходы |
| track (car-racing) | trek | трэк |
| track (footprints) | slet | след |
| track (path) | daroshka | дорожка |
| trade union | prafsayus | профсоюз |
| traffic | dvizhenie | движение |
| traffic lights | svetafor | светофор |
| train (intercity) | poezt | поезд |
| train station | vagzal | вокзал |
| tram | tramvay | трамвай |
| to translate | perevadit'/perevesti | переводить\перевести |
| to travel | puteshestvavat' | путешествовать |
| travel agency | byuro puteshestviy | бюро путешествий |
| travel/seasickness | marskaya balezn' | морская болезнь |
| travellers cheques | darozhny chek | дорожный чек |
| tree | dereva | дерево |
| trendy (person) | modny | модный |
| trip | paestka | поездка |
| trousers | bryuki | брюки |
| truck | gruzavik | грузовик |

It's true.
verna
**Верно.**

| trust | daverie | доверие |
|---|---|---|
| to trust | daveryat'/daverit' | доверять/доверить |
| truth | pravda | правда |
| to try (to taste) | probavat'/ paprobavat' | пробовать/ попробовать |
| to try (to attempt) | starat'sa/ pastarat'sa | стараться/ постараться |
| T-shirt | fudbolka | футболка |
| tune | melodiya | мелодия |
| TV | televizar | телевизор |
| twice | dvazhdy | дважды |
| twigs (for bathhouse) | venik | веник |
| twin beds | dve adnaspal'nye kravati | две односпальные кровати |
| twins | bliznetsy | близнецы |
| to type | pechyatat'na mashynke | печатать на машинке |

| typical | tipichny | типичный |
| tyres | shyny | шины |

## U

| umbrella | zontik | зонтик |
| to understand | panimat'/panyat' | понимать/понять |
| unemployment | bezrabotitsa | безработица |
| unions | prafsayuzy | профсоюзы |
| universe | fsilenaya | вселенная |
| unsafe | apasny | опасный |
| until (June) | do | до |
| unusual | neabychny | необычный |
| up | vverkh | вверх |
| uphill | v goru | в гору |
| urgent | srochny | срочный |
| useful | palezny | полезный |
| (former) USSR | (byfshy) es-es-es-er | (бывший) СССР |

## V

| vacant | vakantny | вакантный |
| vacation | kanikuly | каникулы |
| vaccination | privifka | прививка |
| valley | dalina | долина |
| valuable | tseny | ценный |
| value (price) | stoimost' | стоимость |
| van | furgon | фургон |
| vegetables | ovashchi | овощи |
| vegetarian | vegetarianskiy | вегетарианский |

I'm vegetarian.
ya vegetarianets (m)/vegetarianka (f)
Я вегетарианец/вегетарианка

| vegetation | rastitel'nast' | растительность |
| vein | vena | вена |
| venereal disease | venericheskaya balezn' | венерическая болезнь |
| very | ochen' | очень |
| video tape | videokaseta | видеокассета |
| view | vit | вид |
| village | derevnya | деревня |
| vine | vinagradnaya laza | виноградная лоза |
| vineyard | vinagradnik | виноградник |
| virus | virus | вирус |
| visa | viza | виза |
| to visit | paseshchat'/pasetit' | посещать/посетить |
| voice | golas | голос |

| vodka | votka | водка |
| volume | gromkast' | громкость |
| to vote | galasavat'/ | голосовать/ |
| | pragalasavat' | проголосовать |

## W

**Wait!**
padazhdite!
**Подождите!**

| waiter | afitsyant (m)/ | официант/ |
| | afitsyantka (f) | официантка |
| waiting room | zal azhidaniya | зал ожидания |
| to walk | gulyat'/pagulyat' | гулять/погулять |
| wall | stena | стена |
| to want | khatet'/zakhatet' | хотеть/захотеть |
| war | vayna | война |
| wardrobe | shkaf | шкаф |
| warm | tyoply | тёплый |
| to warn | preduprezhdat'/ | предупреждать/ |
| | predupredit' | предупредить |
| to wash (something) | stirat'/vystirat' | стирать/выстирать |
| to wash (oneself) | umyvat'sa/umyt'sa | умываться/умыться |
| washing machine | stiral'naya mashyna | стиральная машина |
| watch | chasy | часы |
| to watch | smatret' | смотреть |
| water | vada | вода |
| water (mineral) | mineral'naya vada | минеральная вода |
| water bottle | flyashka | фляшка |
| waterfall | vadapat | водопад |
| wave | valna | волна |
| way | daroga | дорога |

**Please tell me the way to ...**
skazhyte, kak papast' k ...?
**Скажите, как попасть к ...?**

**Which way?**
Kuda
**Куда?**

| we | my | мы |
| weak | slaby | слабый |
| wealthy | bagaty | богатый |
| to wear | nasit' | носить |
| weather | pagoda | погода |
| wedding | svad'ba | свадьба |

| week | nedelya | неделя |
| this week | na etay nideli | на этой неделе |
| weekend | uikend | уикенд |
| to weigh | vzveshyvat'/vzvesit' | взвешивать/взвесить |
| weight | ves | вес |

**Welcome!**
dabro pazhalavat'!
**Добро пожаловать!**

| welfare | satsial'nae | социальное |
| | abispichenie | обеспечение |
| well | zdarovy | здоровый |
| west | zapadny | западный |
| wet | mokry | мокрый |
| what | shto | что |

**What is he saying?**
shto on gavarit?
**Что он говорит?**

**What time is it?**
katory chas?
**Который час?**

| wheel | kaleso | колесо |
| wheelchair | invalidnae kresla | инвалидное кресло |
| when | kagda | когда |

**When does it leave?**
kagda on atpravlyaetsa?
**Когда он отправляется?**

| where | gde | где |

**Where is the bank?**
gde bank?
**Где банк?**

| white | bely | белый |
| who | kto | кто |

**Who is it?**
kto eta?
**Кто это?**
**Who are they?**
kto ani?
**Кто они?**

| whole | tsely | целый |
| why | pachimu | почему |
| wide | shyrokiy | широкий |
| wife | zhyna | жена |
| to win | vyigryvat'/ | выигрывать/ |
| | vyigrat' | выиграть |

| wind | veter | ветер |
| window | akno | окно |
| windscreen | vetravoe steklo | ветровое стекло |
| winner | pabeditel' | победитель |
| winter | zima | зима |
| wire | provalaka | проволока |
| wise | mudry | мудрый |
| to wish | zhelat'/pazhelat' | желать/пожелать |
| with | s | с |
| within | f techenii | в течение |
| without | bes | без |
| woman | zhenshchina | женщина |
| wonderful | udivitil'ny | удивительный |
| wooden | derivyany | деревянный |
| wool | sherst' | шерсть |
| word | slova | слово |
| work | rabota | работа |
| work permit | razreshenie na rabotu | разрешение на работу |
| workshop | masterskaya | мастерская |
| world | mir | мир |
| World Cup | kubak mira | Кубок мира |
| worms | glisty | глисты |
| worried | abespakoeny | обеспокоенный |
| worth | tsennast' | ценность |
| wound | ranenie | ранение |
| to write | pisat'/napisat' | писать/написать |
| writer | pisatel' (m)/ | писатель/ |
| | pisatel'nitsa (f) | писательница |
| wrong | nepravil'ny | неправильнвй |

I'm wrong. (my fault)
ya vinavat/ya vinavata
Я виноват/Я виновата.

I'm wrong. (not right)
ya ne praf (m)/prava (f)
Я не прав/права.

# Y

| year | got | год |
| this year | v etam gadu | в этом году |
| yellow | zholty | жёлтый |
| yesterday | fchera | вчера |
| yet | eshchyo | ещё |
| you (pol) | vy | Вы |

# Z

| young | maladoy | молодой |
| youth (collective) | moladast' | молодость |
| youth hostel | turbaza | турбаза |

# Z

| zodiac | zadiak | зодиак |
| zoo | zapark | зоопарк |

This Dictionary has been arranged phonetically, according to our own transliteration system, not according to Russian alphabetical order.

## A

| | | |
|---|---|---|
| abayat'sa | бояться | to be afraid of |
| abarudavanie | оборудование | equipment |
| abedenny pereryf | обеденный перерыв | lunchtime |
| abednya | обедня | mass (Orthodox) |
| abeshchanie | обещание | promise |
| abespakoeny | обеспокоенный | worried |
| abet | обед | lunch |
| | abman! | |
| | Обман! | |
| | Cheat! | |
| abmen valyuty | Обмен Валюты | exchange bureau |
| abmenny kurs | обменный курс | exchange rate |
| abnimat'/abnyat' | обнимать/обнять | to hug |
| abort | аборт | abortion |
| abratny (bilet) | обратный (билет) | return (ticket) |
| abrazavanie | образование | education |
| abshchestvenny tualet | общественный туалет | public toilet |
| abyatie | объятие | a cuddle |
| acharavatel'ny | очаровательный | charming |
| achki at solntsa | очки от солнца | sunglasses |
| adapter | адаптер | adaptor |
| adezhda | одежда | clothing |
| adin (m)/adna (f) | один/одна | alone |
| adin ras | один раз | once |
| administratsiya | администрация | administration |
| adnarmesny nomer | одноместный номер | single room |
| adres | адрес | address |
| advakat | адвокат | lawyer |
| adykhat'/adakhnut' | отдыхать/отдохнуть | to rest |
| afitsyant (m)/afitsyantka (f) | официант/официантка | waiter |
| aftastayanka | автостоянка | carpark |
| aftavagzal | автовокзал | bus station |
| aftobus | автобус | bus |
| aftsa | овца | sheep |
| agon' | огонь | fire (for heat) |
| agresivny | агрессивный | aggressive |
| aist | аист | stork |

| akean | океан | ocean |
| akno | окно | window |
| akruzhayushchaya sreda | окружающая среда | environment |
| al'pinizm | альпинизм | mountaineering |
| alen' | олень | deer |
| alergiya | аллергия | allergy |
| alimpiyskiye igry | олимпийский игры | Olympic Games |
| alkagalizm | алкоголизм | alcoholism |

allo!
**Алло!**
Hello! (answering telephone)

| ana | она | she |
| analis krovi | анализ крови | blood test |
| angliyskiy | английский | English |
| ani | они | they |
| antibiotiki | антибиотики | antibiotics |
| antikvaryat | антиквариат | antiques |
| antisepticheskae sretstva | антисептическое средство | antiseptic |
| apasny | опасный | dangerous |
| aperatar | оператор | camera operator |
| aperatsiya | операция | operation |
| aplata | оплата | payment |
| apshchestvennye nauki | общественные науки | social sciences |
| apteka | аптека | chemist/pharmacy |
| apyat' | опять | again |
| aranzhevy | оранжевый | orange (colour) |
| arendavat' | арендовать | to rent |
| arendnaya plata | арендная плата | rent |
| ariganal'ny | оригинальный | original |
| arkestr | оркестр | orchestra |
| arkhealagicheskiy | археологический | archaeological |
| armiya | армия | army |
| asamalyot | самолёт | aeroplane |
| asavet | совет | advice |
| ashybachny | ошибочный | faulty |
| ashypka | ошибка | mistake |
| asoby | особый | special |
| aspirin | аспирин | aspirin |
| astanofka | остановка | bus stop |

astarozhna!
**Осторожно!**
Careful!

| astatak | остаток | rest (what's left) |
| ataplenie | отопление | heating |

| ateist | атеист | atheist |
| atest | отъезд | departure |
| atets | отец | father |
| atdelyat'/atdelit' | отделять/отделить | to separate |
| atkazyvat'sa/atkazat'sa | отказывать/отказать | to refuse |
| atkrytie | открытие | opening |
| atkrytka | открытка | postcard |
| atkryty | открытый | open |
| atkryvalka | открывалка | bottle opener (beer) |
| atkryvat'/atkryt' | открывать/открыть | to open/discover |
| atritsat' | отрицать | to denyv |

atlichna!
**Отлично!**
**Great!**

| atlichny | отличный | excellent |
| atlif | отлив | tide (low) |
| atmasfera | атмосфера | atmosphere |
| atmenyat'/atmenit' | отменять/отменить | to cancel |
| atstafka | отставка | resignation |
| atvet | ответ | answer |
| avariya | авария | emergency |
| aviapochta | авиапочта | air mail |
| azherel'e | ожерелье | necklace |
| azonavy sloy | озоновый слой | ozone layer |

# B

| babachka | бабочка | butterfly |
| babushka | бабушка | grandmother |
| bagash | багаж | baggage/luggage |
| bagaty | богатый | rich (wealthy) |
| bagaty | богатый | wealthy |
| bal'nitsa | больница | hospital |
| bal'shinstvo | большинство | majority |
| bal'shoy | большой | big/large |
| balalaika | балалайка | balalaika |
| balel'shchiki | болельщики | fans (of a team) |
| balet | балет | ballet |
| baleutalyayushchee | болеутоляющие | painkillers |
| balezn' | болезнь | disease/sickness |
| balit | болит | painful |
| balkon | балкон | balcony |
| bank | банк | bank |
| banka | банка | can/jar |
| bankafskiy aftamat | банковский автомат | automatic teller (ATM) |

| | | |
|---|---|---|
| banya | баня | bathhouse |
| barabany | барабаны | drums |
| bashnya | башня | tower |
| basseyn | бассейн | swimming pool |
| bastavat' | бастовать | be on strike |
| batereya | батарея | battery |
| bedny | бедный | poor |
| bek | бег | race (sport) |
| bely | белый | white |
| benzin | бензин | petrol |
| berek | берег | coast |
| berek morya | берег моря | seaside |
| beremennaya | беременная | pregnant |
| beryoza | берёза | birch |
| bes | без | without |
| besplatny | бесплатный | free (of charge) |
| bessvyazny | бессвязный | delirious |
| bezapasny | безопасный | safe (adj) |
| bezapasny seks | безопасный секс | safe sex |
| bezdomny | бездомный | homeless |
| bezhat'/pabezhat' | бежать/побежать | to run |
| bezhenets (m)/bezhenka (f) | беженец/беженка | refugee |
| bezrabotitsa | безработица | unemployment |
| bibliateka | библиотека | library |
| bibliya | Библия | Bible |
| bilet | билет | ticket |
| biletnaya kassa | билетная касса | ticket office |
| binokl' | бинокль | binoculars |
| bint | бинт | bandage |
| birzha truda | биржа труда | job centre |
| biznes | бизнес | business |
| blagadarit'/ pablagadarit' | благодарить/ поблагодарить | to thank |
| blagaslavyat'/blagaslavit' | благословлять | to bless |
| blakha | блоха | flea |
| blaknot | блокнот | notebook |
| blestyashchiy | блестящий | brilliant |
| bliska ot | близко от | near |
| blizhayshaya gastinitsa | ближайшая гостиница | nearby hotel |
| bliznetsy | близнецы | twins |
| bok | Бог | God |
| boks | бокс | boxing |
| bol' | боль | a pain |
| bol' v zhelutke | боль в желудке | stomach ache |
| bol'she | больше | more |
| bolen (m)/bal'na (f) | болен/больна | ill/sick |

| brak | брак | marriage |
| brasat'/brosit' | бросать/бросить | to quit |
| brat | брат | brother |
| brat'/vzyat' | брать/взять | to take |
| brat'/vzyat' na vremya | брать/взять на время | to borrow |
| brat'/vzyat' naprakat | брать/взять напрокат | to hire |
| brit'sa/pabrit'sa | бриться/плбриться | to shave |
| britva | бритва | razor |
| bryuki | брюки | trousers |

bud'te zdarovy!
**Будьте здоровы!**
Bless you! (when sneezing)

| budil'nik | будильник | alarm clock |
| budushcheye | будущее | future |
| bufet | буфет | cupboard |
| bulachnaya | булочная | bakery |
| bumaga | бумага | paper |
| burya | буря | storm |
| bystry | быстрый | fast/quick |
| byt' | быть | to be |
| byt' za rulyom | быть за рулём | to drive |
| byurakratizm | бюрократизм | red tape |
| byuraktratiya | бюрократия | bureaucracy |
| byuro puteshestviy | бюро путешествий | travel agency |

# C

| chaevye | чаевые | tip (gratuity) |
| chashka | чашка | cup |
| chasny | частный | private |
| chast' | часть | part/piece |
| chasta | часто | often |
| chasy | часы | clock/watch |

katory chas?
**Который час?**
What time is it?

| chelavek | человек | person |
| chemadan | чемодан | suitcase |
| chempianat | чемпионат | championships |

cheres (pyat') minut
**Через (пять) минут.**
In (five) minutes.

cheres (shest') dney
**Через (шесть) дней.**
In (six) days.

| | | |
|---|---|---|
| cherez | через | across |
| chetvert' | четверть | quarter |
| chiat'/prachitat' | читать/прочитать | to read |
| chislo | число | date (time) |
| chistaya gastinitsa | чистая гостинница | clean hotel |
| chisty | чистый | clean |
| chisty | чистый | pure |
| chlen | член | member |
| chorny rynak | чёрный рынок | black market |
| chudesny | удивительный | wonderful |
| chustva | чувства | feelings |
| chustvavat' | чувствовать | to feel |
| chyorna-bely | чёрно-белый (фильм) | B&W (film) |
| chyorny | чёрный | black |

## D

da svidaniya
**До свидания.**
Goodbye.

da zaftra
**До завтра.**
See you tomorrow.

da zdrastvuyet ...!
**Да здравствует ...!**
Long live ...!

dabro pazhalavat'!
**Добро пожаловать!**
Welcome!

| | | |
|---|---|---|
| dagadyvat'sa/ | догадаться/ | to guess |
| dagadat'sa | догадываться | |

dagavarilis'!
**Договорились!**
Agreed!

| | | |
|---|---|---|
| dakumental'ny fil'm | документальный фильм | a documentary |
| dal'niy | дальний | distance/remote |
| dal'ny | дальний | long distance |
| dalina | долина | valley |
| dalyokiy | далёкий | far |
| daragoy | дорогой | expensive |
| daprashyvat'/daprasit' | допрашивать | to question |
| daroga | дорога | main road; way |
| daroshka | дорожка | trail/track |
| darozhny chek | дорожный чек | travellers cheques |

| daska dlya serfinga | доска для серфинга | surfboard |
| dastatachna | достаточно | enough |
| data razhdeniya | дата рождения | date of birth |
| davat'/dat' | давать/дать | to give |
| davat'/dat' vzyatku | давать/дать взятку | to bribe |
| daverie | доверие | trust |
| daveryat'/daverit' | доверять/доверить | to trust |
| davlenie | давление | pressure |

davol'na!
**Довольно!**
Enough!

dayte, pazhalsta ...
**Дайте, пожалста ...**
Could you give me ...?

| dazvolennaya skorast' | дозволенная скорость | speed limit |
| dedushka | дедушка | grandfather |
| defitsytny | дефицитный | hard to get |
| delat'/sdelat' ukol | делать/сделать укол | to inject |
| delit'/padelit' s | делить/поделить с | to share (with) |
| demakratiya | демократия | democracy |
| demanstratsiya | демонстрация | demonstration |
| den' razhdeniya | день рождения | birthday |

z dnyom razhdeniya!
**С днем рождения!**
Happy birthday!

| den' | день | day |
| den'gi | деньги | money |
| dereva | дерево | tree |
| derevnya | деревня | village |
| derevyanniy | деревянный | wooden |
| deshovaya gastinitsa | дешёвая гостинница | cheap hotel |
| deshovy | дешёвый | cheap |
| detal' | деталь | detail |
| deti | дети | children |
| detskae pitanie | детское питание | baby food |
| detskaya prisypka | детская присыпка | baby powder |
| detskiy sat | детский сад | kindergarten |
| devochka | девочка | girl (pre-teen) |
| devushka | девушка | girl (teenage) |
| dezodarant | дезодорант | deodorant |
| diabetik | диабетик | diabetic |
| dikoye zhivotnoye' | дикое животное | wild animal |
| direktar | директор | director |
| disident | диссидент | dissident |
| diskriminatsiya | дискриминация | discrimination |

| dizayn | дизайн | design |
| dlinny | длинный | long |
| dnevnik | дневник | diary |
| dnyom | днём | (in the) afternoon |
| do | до | before/until |

dobrae utra
**Доброе утро.**
Good morning.

dobry den'
**Добрый день.**
Good afternoon.

dobry vecher
**Добрый вечер.**
Good evening/night.

| dobry | добрый | kind |
| doch' | дочь | daughter |

dolgikh let zhyzni!
**Долгих лет жизни!**
Many happy returns!

| dom | дом | house |
| dosht' | дождь | rain |

idyot dosht'
**Идёт дождь.**
It's raining.

| draka | драка | fight |
| drama | драма | drama |
| dramaticheskiy | драматический | dramatic/exciting |
| drat'sa/padrat'sa | драться/подраться | to fight |
| drava | дрова | firewood |
| drevniy | древний | ancient |
| drugoy | другой | different |
| drugoy | другой | other |
| druk (m)/padruga (f) | друг/подруга | friend |
| duma | Дума | parliament (Russian) |
| dumat' | думать | to think |
| durak | дурак | idiot |
| dush | душ | shower |
| dvarets | дворец | palace |
| dvaynoy | двойной | double |
| dvazhdy | дважды | twice |
| dve adnaspal'nye kravati | две односпальные кровати | twin beds |
| dve nedeli | две недели | fortnight |

| dver' | дверь | door |
| dvizhenie | движение | traffic |
| dvukhspal'naya kravat' | двуспальняя кровать | double bed |
| dyshat' | дышать | to breathe |
| dyuzhyna | дюжина | dozen |
| dzhemper | джемпер | jumper (sweater) |
| dzhynsy | джинсы | jeans |
| dzhyp | джип | jeep |

## E

| eda | еда | food |
| edinstvenny | единственный | single (unique) |
| egoistichny | эгоистичный | selfish |
| egzamen | экзамен | test |
| ekanomiya | экономия | economy |
| ekhat' verkhom | ехать верхом | to ride (a horse) |
| ekran | экран | screen |
| ekskursiya | экскурсия | tour |
| ekspanometr | экспонометр | light meter |
| ekspluatatsiya | эксплуатация | exploitation |
| ekspres | экспресс | express |
| ekspres-pochta | экспресс-почта | express mail |
| el' | ель | fir |
| elektricheski fanar' | электрический фонарь | torch (flashlight) |
| elektrichestva | электричество | electricity |
| epileptik | эпилептик | epileptic |
| (byfshy) es-es-es-er | (бывший) СССР | (former) USSR |
| eshchyo | ещё | yet |
| esli | если | if |
| est'/sest' | есть/съесть | to eat |

et'te pryama!
**Едьте прямо!**
Go straight ahead. (taxi)

eta (ne) vazmozhna
**Это (не) возможно.**
It's (not) possible.

eta doraga
**Это дорого.**
It costs a lot.

| eta | это | this (one) |
| etash | этаж | floor (storey) |
| evrapeyskiy | европейский | European |
| evreyskiy | еврейский | Jewish |
| eytanaziya | эвтаназия | euthanasia |

E

| ezda na velasipede | езда на велосипеде | cycling |
| ezdit' na velasipede | ездить на велосипеде | to cycle |
| ezhednevny | ежедневный | daily |
| ezhegodny | ежегодный | annual |

## F

| f budushchem gadu | в будущем году | next year |
| f chyom dela? | | |
| В чём дело? | | |
| What's the matter? | | |
| f pradazhe | в продаже | (on) sale |
| f proshlam gadu | в прошлом году | last year |
| f proshlam mesyatse | в прошлом месяце | last month |
| f sel'skay mesnasti | в сельской местности | countryside (in the) |
| f sleduyushchem mesyatse | в следующем месяце | next month |
| f techenii chasa | в течение часа | within an hour |
| f techenii | в течение | within |
| fabrika | фабрика | factory |
| familiya | фамилия | surname |
| fanarik | фонарик | flashlight |
| fatagrafiravat' | фотографировать | to take photographs |
| fatagrafiya | фотография | photography |
| fatograf | фотограф | photographer |
| fuye | фойе | foyer |
| fchera | вчера | yesterday |
| fchera utram | вчера утром | yesterday morning |
| fchera vecheram | вчера вечером | last night |
| fekhtavanie | фехтование | fencing |
| ferma | ферма | farm |
| fermer | фермер | farmer |
| festival' | фестиваль | festival |
| fil'm | фильм | movie |
| filial | филиал | branch (bank etc) |
| fkhadit'/vayti | входить | to enter |
| fkhot (pa biletam) | вход (по билетам) | admission (by ticket) |
| fklyucheno | включено | included |
| fkusny | вкусный | tasty |
| flak | флаг | flag |
| flyashka | фляшка | water bottle |
| fokusnik | фокусник | magician |
| forma | форма | shape |
| fotaaparat | фотоаппарат | camera |
| fotomagazin | фотомагазин | camera shop |
| fperyot | вперёд | ahead |
| fpuskat'/fpustit' | впускать/впустить | to admit |

| fse | все | all |
| fsegda | всегда | always |
| fselennaya | вселенная | universe |
| fshy | вши | lice |
| fstrecha | встреча | appointment (business) |
| fstrechat'/fstrechit' | встречать/встретить | to meet |
| fstrechat'sa s | встречаться с | to date (someone) |
| fsyakiy | всякий | any |
| ftaroy | второй | second |
| fudbol | футбол | football (soccer) |
| furgon | фургон | van |
| fudbol | футбол | soccer |
| fudbolka | футболка | T-shirt |
| futurizm | футуризм | futurism |

# G

| gadalka | гадалка | fortune teller |
| galasavat'/ pragalasavat' | голосовать/ проголосовать | to vote |
| galava | голова | head |
| galavnaya bol' | головная боль | a headache |
| gallyutsianiravat' | галлюцинировать | to hallucinate |
| gara | гора | mountain |
| garash | гараж | garage |
| garderop | гардероб | cloakroom |
| garyachaya vada | горячая вода | hot water |
| gashysh | гашиш | hash |
| gasudarstvenny | государственный | state (not private) |
| gatof (m)/gatova (f) | готов/готова | ready |
| gatovit'/prigatovit' | готовить/приготовить | to cook |
| gavan' | гавань | harbour |
| gavarit'/skazat' | говорить/сказать | to say/speak |
| gazavy balon | газовый баллон | gas cartridge |
| gazeta | газета | newspaper |
| gazetny kiosk | газетный киоск | newsagency |
| gde | где | where |

gde bank?
**Где банк?**
Where's the bank?

gde mozhna kupit' (bilet)?
**Где можно купить (билет)?**
Where can I buy (a ticket)?

| gerain | героин | heroin |
| gey | гей | gay |

| | | |
|---|---|---|
| gimnastika | гимнастика | gymnastics |
| ginienicheskie salfetki | гигенические салфетки | sanitary napkins |
| giperinflyatsiya | гиперинфляция | hyperinflation |
| git | гид | guide (person) |
| gitara | гитара | guitar |
| glas | глаз | eye |
| glasnast' | гласность | glasnost |
| glavnaya daroga | главная дорога | main road |
| glisty | глисты | worms |
| glubokiy | глубокий | deep |
| glukhoy | глухой | deaf |
| glupy | глупый | stupid |
| gol | гол | goal (sport) |
| goladen (m)/galadna (f) | голоден/голодна | hungry |
| golas | голос | voice |
| gomeopatiya | гомеопатия | homeopathy |
| gomoseksualist | гомосексуалист | homosexual |
| gonachny velasipet | гоночный велосипед | racing bike |
| gorat | город | city |
| gordast' | гордость | pride |
| gorla | горло | throat |
| gornaya gryada | горная гряда | mountain range |
| gornaya izbushka | горная избушка | mountain hut |
| gornaya trapa | горная тропа | mountain path |
| gorniy velasipet | горный велосипед | mountain bike |
| got | год | year |
| grabyosh | грабёж | rip-off |
| gradus | градус | degree (measurement) |
| gram | грамм | gram |
| granitsa | граница | border |
| grazhdanin (m)/ grazhdanka (f) | гражданин/ гражданка | citizen |
| grazhdanskiye prava | гражданские права | civil rights |
| grazhdanstva | гражданство | citizenship |
| grekh | грех | sin |
| grenka | гренка | toast |
| grigarianskiy kalendar' | Григорианский календарь | Gregorian calendar |
| gromkast' | громкость | volume |
| gromkiy | громкий | loud |
| grudnaya kletka | грудная клетка | chest |
| grupa | группа | band (music) |
| grupa krovi | группа крови | blood group |
| grusny | грустный | sad |
| gruzavik | грузовик | truck |
| gruzit'/pagruzit' | грузить/погрузить | to ship |

I

| | | |
|---|---|---|
| gryazny | грязный | dirty |
| gubnaya pamada | губная помада | lipstick |
| guby | губы | lips |
| gudok | гудок | dial tone |
| gulyat'/pagulyat' | гулять/погулять | to walk |

## I

| | | |
|---|---|---|
| i | и | and |

idite pryama!
**Идите прямо!**
Go straight ahead. (on foot)

| | | |
|---|---|---|
| igla | игла | needle (sewing) |
| igra | игра | game (games) |
| igral'nye kosti | игральные кости | dice |
| igrat' f karty | играть в карты | to play cards |
| igrat' na | играть на | to play (instrument) |
| igrat' v | играть в | to play (sport) |
| ikona | икона | icon |
| ili | или | or |
| imeniny | именины | name day/Saint's day |
| immigratsiya | иммиграция | immigration |
| imya | имя | name (person) |
| inagda | иногда | sometimes |
| inastranny | иностранный | foreign |
| indus (m)/induska (f) | индус/индуска | Hindu |
| inektsiya | инъекция | injection |
| inflyatsiya | инфляция | inflation |
| ingener | инженер | engineer |
| interesny | интересный | interesting |
| interv'yu | интервью | interview |
| invalidnae kresla | инвалидное кресло | wheelchair |
| invalit | инвалид | disabled |

ischezni!
**Исчезни!**
Get lost!

| | | |
|---|---|---|
| iskat' | искать | to look for |
| isklyuchyaya | исключая | excluded |
| iskustva | искусство | art |
| ispaved' | исповедь | confession (religious) |
| istekat' krov'yu | истекать кровью | to bleed |
| itti/payti | идти/пойти | to go |
| izbiratel'ny okruk | избирательный округ | electorate |
| izdeliya iz kozhi | изделия из кожи | leathergoods |
| iznasilavanie | изнасилование | rape |

| izumitel'niy | изумительный | marvellous |

izvinite, pazhalsta
**Извините, пожалуйста.**
Excuse me.

## K

| k | к | towards |
| kaaperatif | кооператив | cooperative (business) |
| kachestva | качество | quality |
| kafkas | Кавказ | the Caucasus |
| kagda | когда | when |

kagda on atpravlyaetsa?
**Когда он отправляется?**
When does it leave?

| ka-ge-be | КГБ | KGB |
| kak | как | how |

kak dabrat'sa da ...?
**Как добраться до ...?**
How do I get to ...?

kak skazat' ...?
**Как сказать ...?**
How do you say ...?

| kakain | кокаин | cocaine |
| kal'tso | кольцо | ring (on finger) |
| kalega | коллега | colleague |
| kalena | колено | knee |
| kalendar' | календарь | calendar |
| kaleso | колесо | wheel |
| kalkhos | колхоз | collective farm |
| kaloda | колода | deck (of cards) |
| kamanda | команда | team |
| kamediya | комедия | comedy |
| kamen' | камень | stone |
| kamera khraneniya | камера хранения | left luggage |
| kamera-aftamat | камера-автомат | luggage lockers |
| kamp'yuternye igry | компьютерныеигры | computer games |
| kampaniya | компания | company |
| kamsamol | комсомол | Komsomol |
| kamunist (m)/kamunistka (f) | коммунист/коммунистка | communist |
| kamunisticheskaya partiya | коммунистическая партия | Communist Party |
| kan'ki | коньки | skates |
| kanditsianer | кондиционер | air-conditioner |
| kanduktar | кондуктор | ticket collector |

| | | |
|---|---|---|
| kaneshna | **Конечно.** | Sure. |

| | | |
|---|---|---|
| kanets | конец | end |
| kanikuly | каникулы | vacation |
| kanservativny | консервативный | conservative |
| kanservny klyuch | консервный ключ | tin opener |
| kanstitutsiya | конституция | constitution |
| kantaktnye linzy | контактные линзы | contact lenses |
| kantora | контора | office |
| kantrakt | контракт | contract |
| kantrol'ny punkt | контрольный пункт | checkpoint |
| kantsert | концерт | concert |
| kanvert | конверт | envelope |
| karabl' | корабль | ship |
| karaleva | королева | queen |
| karan | Коран | Koran |
| karandash | карандаш | pencil |
| karantin | карантин | quarantine |
| karatkametrazhniy fil'm | короткометражный фильм | short films |
| karichnevy | коричневый | brown |
| karman | карман | pocket |
| karol' | король | king |
| karopka | коробка | box |
| karotkiy | короткий | short |
| karova | корова | cow |
| karrumpiravanny | коррумпированный | corrupt |
| karta | карта | map |
| karta darog | карта дорог | road map |
| kartinnaya galereya | галлерея | art gallery |
| kartiny | картины | paintings |
| kartonka | картонка | carton |
| karty | карты | playing cards |
| karzina | корзина | basket |
| kashel' | кашель | a cough |
| kashmar | кошмар | nightmare |
| kasmetika | косметика | make-up |
| kassa | касса | cash register |
| kassavy avtamat | кассовый автомат | ticket machine |
| kasseta | кассета | cassette |
| kassier | кассир | cashier |
| katanie na kan'kakh | катание на коньках | ice skating |
| katolik (m)/katalichka (f) | католик/католичка | Catholic |
| katyonak | котёнок | kitten |
| kavyor | ковёр | rug |

| | | |
|---|---|---|
| kazhdy | каждый | each |
| kazhdy den' | каждый день | every day |
| kazyol | козел | goat |
| kemping | кемпинг | campsite |
| keramika | керамика | ceramics |
| khadit' na lyzhakh | ходить на лыжах | to ski |
| khadit' pa magazinam | ходить по магазинам | to go shopping |
| khadit' s | ходить с | to go out with |
| khadit' peshkom | ходить пешком | to hike |
| khakkey nal'du | хоккей гна льду | ice hockey |
| khaladil'nik | холодильник | refrigerator |
| khalodnaya vada | холодная вода | cold water |
| khalodny | холодный | cold (adj) |

kholodna
**Холодно.**
It's cold.

| | | |
|---|---|---|
| kharasho | хорошо | okay |
| kharoshaya gastinitsa | хорошая гостинница | good hotel |
| kharoshenkiy | хорошенький | pretty |
| khatet'/zakhatet' | хотеть/захотеть | to want |
| khitry | хитрый | crafty |
| khlep | хлеб | bread |
| khlopak | хлопок | cotton |
| kholm | холм | hill |
| khrabry | храбрый | brave |
| khranitel' | хранитель | curator |
| khristianin (m)/khristianka (f) | христианин/христианка | Christian |
| khudozhestvennaya literatura | художественная литература | fiction |
| khudozhnik | художник | painter |
| khudozhnik (m)/ khudozhnitsa (f) | художник/ художница | artist |
| khuligan | хулиган | hooligan |
| khvost | хвост | tail |
| kino | кино | cinema/movies |
| kirillitsa | кириллица | Cyrillic alphabet |
| kirka | кирка | pick/pickaxe |
| kislarot | кислород | oxygen |
| klas | класс | class |
| klasavaya sistema | классовая система | class system |

klassna!
**Классно!**
Cool! (coll)

| | | |
|---|---|---|
| klast'/palazhyt' | ласть/положить | to put |
| klaviatura | клавиатура | keyboard |

| | | |
|---|---|---|
| klient | клиент | client |
| klop | клоп | bedbug |
| kloun | клоун | clown |
| klyuch | ключ | key |
| kniga | книга | book |
| knizhny magazin | книжный магазин | bookshop |
| kolakal | колокол | bell (church) |
| kolyshek dlya palatki | колышек для палатки | tent pegs |
| komiksy | комиксы | comics |
| komnata na dvaikh | комната на двоих | double room |
| komnata | комната | room |
| konsul'stva | консульство | consulate |
| kort | корт | court (tennis) |
| koshka | кошка | cat |
| kosmas | космос | space (outer) |
| kost' | кость | bone |
| kozha | кожа | leather |
| kozha | кожа | skin |
| krasit'/pakrasit' | красить/покрасить | to paint |
| krasivy | красивый | beautiful/handsome |
| krasny | красный | red |
| krast'/abakrast' | красть/обокрасть | to rob/steal |
| kravat' | постель | bed |
| kravyanoe davlenie | кровяное давление | blood pressure |
| kreditnaya kartachka | кредитная карточка | credit card |
| kreml' | Кремль | Kremlin |
| kreshchenie | крещение | baptism |
| krest | крест | cross (religious) |
| krest'yanin (m)/krest'yanka (f) | крестьянин/крестьянка | peasant |
| krihcat'/zakrichat' | кричать/закричать | to shout |
| kriket | крикет | cricket |
| krof' | кровь | blood |
| krolik | кролик | rabbit |
| krugly | круглый | round |
| krutoy | крутой | cool (person)/steep |
| kruzheva | кружева | lace |
| kryl'ya | крылья | wings |
| krysa | крыса | rat |
| kto | кто | who |

kto ani?
**Кто они?**
Who are they?

kto eta?
**Кто это?**
Who is it?

| | | |
|---|---|---|
| kto-ta | кто-то | somebody/someone |
| kubak mira | Кубок мира | World Cup |
| kuda? | Куда? | |
| | **Куда?** | |
| | Which way? | |
| kukhnya | кухня | kitchen |
| kukly | куклы | dolls |
| kulinariya | кулинария | delicatessen |
| kupal'nik | купальник | bathing suit (for women) |
| kupal'nik | купальник | swimsuit |
| kurit'/pakurit' | курить/покурить | to smoke |
| kuritsa | курица | chicken |
| kvadrat | квадрат | square (shape) |
| kvalifikatsii | квалификации | qualifications |
| kvitantsiya | квитанция | receipt |

## L

| | | |
|---|---|---|
| ladan | ладан | incense |
| lamat'/slamat' | ломать/сломать | to break |
| lampa | лампа | a light |
| lampachka | лампочка | light bulb |
| ledarup | ледоруб | ice axe |
| legalizatsiya | легализация | legalisation |
| lekarstva | лекарство | medicine |
| lenivy | ленивый | lazy |
| les | лес | forest |
| lesnitsa | лестница | stairway |
| leta | лето | summer |
| leva | лево | left (not right) |
| levy | левый | left-wing |
| lezbianka | лесбианка | lesbian |
| lezhat' | лежать | to lie (down) |
| lezviya | лезвия | razor blades |
| lgun (m)/lgun'ya (f) | лгун/лгунья | liar |
| lichnast | личность | personality |
| likharatka | лихорадка | fever/temperature |
| liniya | линия | line |
| linza | линза | lens |
| litsenziya | лицензия | license |
| litso | лицо | face |
| list | лист | sheet (of paper) |
| loshad' | лошадь | horse |
| lotka | лодка | boat |

| luchshe | лучше | better |
| luna | луна | moon |
| lyokhkiy | лёгкий | easy |
| lyot | лёд | ice |
| lyubit' | любить | to like/love |
| lyubitel'skiy | любительский | amateur |
| lyubovnik (m)/lyubovnitsa (f) | любовник/любовница | lover |
| lyudi | люди | people |
| lyzhny sport | лыжный спорт | skiing |
| lyzhy | лыжи | skis |

## M

| magazin | магазин | shop |
| magila | могила | grave |
| mal'chik | мальчик | boy |
| mala | мало | few |
| maladoy | молодой | young |
| moladast' | молодость | youth (collective) |
| malako | молоко | milk |
| malen'kiy | маленький | little/small |
| malitva | молитва | prayer |
| malochnye pradukty | молочные продукты | dairy products |
| mama | Мама | Mum |
| manakhinya | монахиня | nun |
| manastyr' | монастырь | monastery |
| maneta | монета | coin |
| manifestatsiya | манифестация | rally |
| marki | марки | stamps |
| marozhenae | мороженое | ice cream |
| marshrut | маршрут | itinerary |
| marskaya | морская болезнь | travel sickness/ seasickness |
| mashennik | мошенник | a cheat |
| mashyna | машина | car/machine |
| masla | масло | oil (cooking) |
| massash | массаж | massage |
| mat' | мать | mother |
| matatsykl | молоцикл | motorcycle |
| match | матч | match (sport) |
| mator | мотор | engine |
| matornaya lotka | моторная лодка | motorboat |
| matrats | матрац | mattress |
| mazok | мазок | pap smear |
| mech | меч | sword |
| mechet' | мечеть | mosque |

| | | |
|---|---|---|
| medal' | медаль | medal |
| meditatsiya | медитация | meditation |
| medlenny | медленный | slow |
| medovy mesyats | медовый месяц | honeymoon |
| medsestra | медсестра | nurse |
| medved' | медведь | bear |
| mekh | мех | fur |
| mekhanik | механик | mechanic |
| melach' | мелочь | change (coins) |
| melodiya | мелодия | tune |
| men'she | меньше | less |
| menstrual'ny sindrom | менструальный синдром | period pain |
| menstruatsiya | менструация | menstruation |
| menyat'/abmenyat' | менять/обменять | to change/exchange |
| menyu | меню | menu |
| mer | мэр | mayor |
| merskiy tip | мерзкий тип | creep (col) |
| meshok | мешок | bag |
| mesny | местный | local |
| mesta | место | eat |
| mesta naznacheniya | место назначения | destination |
| mesta razhdeniya | место рождения | place of birth |
| mesta | место | place |
| mestakhazhdenie | местонахождение | location |
| mesyats | месяц | month |
| metal | метал | metal |
| meteor | метеор | meteor |
| metr | метр | metre |
| mezhdu | между | among |
| mezhdu | между | between |
| mezhdunarodny | международный | international |
| migren' | мигрень | migraine |
| militsiya | милиция | police |
| mily | милый | nice |
| mineral'naya vada | минеральная вода | mineral water |
| minuta | минута | minute |

minutku
**Минутку.**
Just a minute.

| | | |
|---|---|---|
| mir | мир | peace |
| mir | мир | world |
| misticheskiy | мистический | mystical |
| mistik | мистик | mystic |
| mnenie | мнение | opinion |
| mnoga | много | a lot/many |
| moch'/smoch' | мочь/смочь | to be able |

my mozhem zdelat' eta
**Мы можем сделать это.**
We can do it.

ya ne magu zdelat' eta
**Я не могу сделать это.**
I can't do it.

| | | |
|---|---|---|
| modem | модем | modem |
| modny | модный | trendy (person) |
| mokry | мокрый | wet |
| molat | молот | hammer |
| more | море | sea |
| most | мост | bridge |
| mozhet byt' | может быть | maybe |

mozhna (vayti)?
**Можно (войти)?**
Can I (enter)?

mozhna vas sfatagrafiravat'
**Можно вас сфотографировать?**
Can I take a photo?

| | | |
|---|---|---|
| mudry | мудрый | wise |
| muka | мука | flour |
| mukha | муха | fly |
| mul'tfil'm | мультфильм | cartoon |
| muravey | муравей | ant |
| musar | мусор | garbage/rubbish |
| mush | муж | husband |
| mushchina | мужчина | man |
| muskul | мускул | muscle |
| musul'manin (m)/ | мусульманин/ | Muslim |
| musul'manka (f) | мусульманка | |
| muzey | музей | museum |
| muzyka | музыка | music |
| muzykant | музыкант | musician |
| my | мы | we |
| myach | мяч | ball (sport) |
| myl'naya opera | мыльная опера | soap opera |
| myla | мыло | soap |
| myortvy | мёртвый | dead |
| myot | мёд | honey |
| mysh' | мышь | mouse |
| myshka | мышка | mouse (computer) |
| mysl' | мысль | thought |

# N

| na | на | on |
| na bartu | на борту | aboard |
| na dne | на дне | (at the) bottom |
| na etay nedelye | на этой неделе | this week |
| na pensii | на пенсии | retired |
| na proshlay nedele | на прошлой неделе | last week |
| na sleduyushchey nedele | на следующей неделе | next week |
| nachala | начало | kick off |
| nachinat'/nachat' | начинать/начать | to begin/start |
| nafsegda | навсегда | forever |
| naga | нога | foot/leg |
| nakazyvat'/nakazat' | наказывать/наказать | to punish |
| nakhadit'/nayti | находить/найти | to find |
| nalok | налог | tax |
| nalok na vzlyot | налог на взлет | airport tax |
| napalnyat'/napolnit' | наполнять/наполнить | to fill |
| napitak | напиток | a drink |
| naprava | направо | right (not left) |

naprimer ...
**Например ...**
For example ...

| naprotif | напротив | in front of |
| napryazhony | напряжённый | intense |
| narkodiler | нарко-диллер | drug dealer |
| narkotiki | наркотики | drugs |
| narmal'ny | нормальный | standard (usual) |
| narodnae iskustva | народное искусство | folk art |
| nasit' | носить | to wear |
| naslazhdat'sa/ | наслаждаться/ | to enjoy |
| nasladit'sa | насладиться | (oneself) |
| nasos | насос | pump |
| nastol'ny tennis | настольный теннис | table tennis |
| nat | над | above/over |
| natsianal'nast' | национальность | nationality |
| naturapat | натуропат | naturopath |
| navagodnyaya noch' | Новогодняя ночь | New Year's Eve |
| navalachka | наволочка | pillowcase |
| navisnoy zamok | нависной замок | padlock |
| nauka | наука | science |
| nazvanie | название | name (thing) |
| neabychny | необычный | unusual |
| neba | небо | sky |
| nedastatak | недостаток | shortage |
| nedavna | недавно | ago/recently |

| | | |
|---|---|---|
| nedavniy | недавний | recent |
| nedelya | неделя | week |
| nemnoga | немного | a little (amount) |
| nemoy | немой | mute |
| nepanyatny | непонятный | incomprehensible |
| nepravil'ny | неправильнвй | wrong |

ya nepraf (m)/neprava (f)
**Я не прав/неправа.**
I'm wrong. (not right)

| | | |
|---|---|---|
| neravenstva | неравенство | inequality |
| neshasny sluchay | несчастный случай | accident |
| neskal'ka | несколько | some/several |
| nesti/pdinesti | нести/понести | to carry |
| net | нет | no |

net eshchyo
**Нет еще.**
Not yet.

| | | |
|---|---|---|
| neudachnik | неудачник | loser |
| nevesta/zhenikh | невеста/жених | fiancée/fiancé |
| nevygada | невыгода | disadvantage |
| neznakomets (m)/ | незнакомец/ | stranger |
| neznakomka (f) | незнакомка | |
| nichevo | ничего | nothing |

nichevo
**Ничего.**
It's nothing.

nichevo strashnava!
**Ничего страшного!**
Forget about it!; Don't worry!

| | | |
|---|---|---|
| nikagda | никогда | never |
| nishchiy (m)/nishchaya (f) | нищий/нищая | beggar |
| niskae/vysokae | низкое/высокое | low/high blood |
| kravyanoe davlenie | кровяное давление | pressure |
| niskiy | низкий | low |
| no | но | but |
| noch' | ночь | night |
| nomer | номер | room (hotel) |
| norka | норка | mink |
| nos | нос | nose |
| nosh | нож | knife |
| novasti | новости | news |
| novy | новый | new |
| novy got | Новый год | New Year |
| nozhyk | ножик | penknife |

| nozhnitsy | ножницы | scissors |
| nuzhdat'sa v | нуждаться в | to need |
| nuzhny | нужный | necessary |
| nyanya | няня | babysitter |
| nyukhat'/panyukhat' | нюхать/понюхать | to smell |

## O

| oba (m)/obe (f) | оба/обе | bottle |
| oblachna | облачно | cloudy |
| oblaka | облако | cloud |
| ochen' | очень | very |
| ochered' | очередь | queue |
| oddykh | отдых | rest (relaxation) |
| ofsayt | офсайд | offside |
| on | он | he |
| opera | опера | opera |
| operny teatr | оперный театр | opera house |
| opshiy | общий | general |
| osen' | осень | autumn |
| osen' | осень | fall (autumn) |
| ostraf | остров | island |
| ostry | острый | spicy (hot) |
| otchestva | отчество | patronymic |
| otpusk | отпуск | holidays |
| ovashchi | овощи | vegetables |
| ozera | озеро | lake |

## P

| p'esa | пьеса | play (theatre) |
| p'yany | пьяный | drunk (sloshed) |
| pa talonam | по талонам | rationed (for coupons) |
| pabeditel' | победитель | winner |
| pachemu | почему | why |
| pachka | пачка | packet (cigarettes) |
| pachti | почти | almost |
| pachtovy indeks | почтовый индекс | post code |
| pachtovy yashchik | почтовый ящик | mailbox |
| padakhodny nalok | подоходный налог | income tax |
| padarak | подарок | gift |

padazhdite!
Подождите!
Wait!

| padguznik | подгузник | nappy |
| padlezhashchiy utilizatsii | подлежащий утилизации | recyclable |
| padnimat'/padnyat' | поднимать/поднять | to pick up |
| padnimat'sa/padnyat'sa | подниматься/подняться | to climb |
| padruga | подруга | girlfriend |
| padushka | подушка | pillow |
| padvodnae plavanie | подводное плавание | diving |
| paestka | поездка | trip |
| paeziya | поэзия | poetry |
| paftaryat'/paftarit' | повторять/повторить | to repeat |
| pagoda | погода | weather |
| pagubnaya privychka | пагубная привычка | addiction (to drugs) |

paka
**Пока.**
See you later.

| pakazatel'naya igra | показательная игра | a game show |
| pakazyvat'/pakazat' | показывать/показать | to show |

pakazhyte, pazhalsta, na karte
**Покажите, пожалуйста, на карте.**
Can you show me on the map?

| pakhot | поход | hiking |
| pakhozhy | похожий | similar |
| paklanenie | поклонение культ | worship |
| pakupat'/kupit' | покупать/купить | to buy |

ya by khatel (m)/khatela (f) kupit'…
**я бы хотел/хотела купить …**
I'd like to buy …

| pal'to | пальто | coat/overcoat |
| palatentse | полотенце | towel |
| palatka | палатка | tent |
| palavik | половик | mat (door) |
| palavina | половина | half |
| palets | палец | finger |
| palezny | полезный | useful |
| palitika | политика | politics |
| palitiki | политики | politicians |
| paluba | палуба | deck (of ship) |
| palyot | полёт | flight |
| pamagat'/pamoch' | помогать/помочь | to help |

pamagite!
**Помогите!**
Help!

| pameshchenie | помещение | accommodation |

| pamolfka | помолвка | engagement |
| pamyatnik | памятник | monument |
| panos | понос | diarrhoea |

panyatna
**Понятно.**
I see. (understand)

| papa | папа | dad |
| papirosa | папироса | cigarette (Russian style) |
| papirosnaya bumaga | папиросня бумага | cigarette papers |
| papulyarny | популярный | popular |
| paputchik (m)/paputchitsa (f) | попутчик/попутчица | companion (travelling) |
| par | пар | steam |
| para | пара | pair (a couple) |
| paralizovanny | парализованный | paraplegic |
| paren' | парень | boyfriend |
| pari | пари | a bet |
| park | парк | a park |
| parlament | парламент | parliament (foreign) |
| partiya | партия | party (politics) |
| partretny eskiz | портретный эскиз | portrait sketcher |
| paryadak | порядок | order |
| pasadachny talon | посадочный талон | boarding pass |
| pasazhyr | пассажир | passenger |
| paseshchat'/pasetit' | посещать/посетить | to visit |

pashlil
**пошли!**
Let's go.

| paskha | Пасха | Easter |
| pasledniy | последний | last |

pasmotrim!
**Посмотрим!**
We'll see!

| pasobie pa bezrabotitse | пособие по безработицу | dole |
| pasol | посол | ambassador |
| pasol'stva | посольство | embassy |
| paspart | паспорт | passport |
| pastayanny | постоянный | permanent |
| pastit'sa | поститься | to fast |
| pasylka | посылка | package |
| pasylka | посылка | parcel |
| patamu, shto | потому, что | because |
| paterya | потеря | loss |
| patok | поток | stream |

| patomak | потомок | descendant |
| patpisyvat'/patpisat' | подписывать/подписать | to sign |
| patseluy | поцелуй | kiss |
| pattverzhdat'/ | подтверждать/ | to confirm (a booking) |
| pattverdit' | подтвердить | |

pavernite naleva
**Поверните налево.**
Turn left.

pavernite naprava
**Поверните направо.**
Turn right.

| pazafchera | позавчера | day before yesterday |

Pazdravlyayu!
**Поздравляю!**
Congratulations!

| pazhar | пожар | fire (emergency) |
| pazvalyat'/pazvolit' | позволять/позволить | to allow |
| pebyonak | ребёнок | child |
| pech' | печь | stove |
| pensianer | пенсионер | pensioner |
| pepel'nitsa | пепельница | ashtray |
| peredazirovka | передозировка | overdose |
| pereryf | перерыв | intermission |
| perets | перец | pepper |
| perevadit'/perevesti | переводить/перевести | to translate |
| pervae maya | Первое Мая | May Day |
| pervy | первый | first |
| peshchera | пещера | cave |
| peshekhot | пешеход | pedestrian |
| pesok | песок | sand |
| pet'/spet' | петь/спеть | to sing |
| petitsiya | петиция | petition |
| pevets (m)/pevitsa (f) | певец/певица | singer |
| pevets i kampazitor | певец и композитор | singer/songwriter |
| pianer | пионер | pioneer |
| pil'meney | пельмени | meat dumplings |
| pik | пик | peak |
| pir | пир | feast |
| pirok | пирог | pie |
| pis'mo | письмо | letter |
| pisat'/napisat' | писать/написать | to write |
| pisatel' (m)/pisatel'nitsa (f) | писатель/писательница | writer |
| pit'/vypit' | пить/выпить | to drink |
| plafki | плавки | bathing suit (for men) |
| plakat | плакат | poster |

| plakhoy | плохой | bad |
|---|---|---|
| planeta | планета | planet |
| plastmassa | пластмасса | plastic |
| plat'e | платье | dress |
| platforma | платформа | platform |
| platit'/zaplatit' | платить/заплатить | to pay |
| plato | плато | plateau |
| plavanie | плавание | swimming |
| plavat' | плавать | to swim |
| plechi | плечи | shoulders |
| plet | плед | blanket (thin) |
| ploskiy | плоский | flat (land, etc) |
| plyash | пляж | beach |
| plyonka | плёнка | film (for camera) |
| pochta | почта | mail |
| pochta | почта | post office |
| pochva | поува | earth (soil) |
| pod | под | below |
| podpis' | подпись | signature |
| poezt | поезд | train (intercity) |
| poker | покер | poker |
| pokharany | похороны | funeral |
| pol | пол | floor |
| pol'ny | полный | full |
| polden' | полдень | noon |
| pole | поле | field |
| pol-litra | пол-литра | half a litre |
| polnach' | полночь | midnight |
| pomashch | помощь | aid (help) |
| pomnit'/fspomnit' | помнить/вспомнить | to remember |
| port | порт | port |
| posle | после | after |
| poslezaftra | послезавтра | day after tomorrow |
| pozniy | поздний | late |
| prachechnaya | прачечная | launderette |
| prafessiya | профессия | profession |
| prafsayuzy | профсоюзы | unions |
| pragulka | прогулка | stroll/walk |
| praizvadit'/praizvesti | производить | to produce |
| prakol | прокол | puncture |
| pramyshlennast' | промышленность | industry |
| prashchat'/prastit' | прощать/простить | to forgive |
| prasit'/paprasit' | просить/попросить | to ask (for something) |
| praspekt | проспект | avenue |

prastite
Простите.
I'm sorry.

| prastynya | простыня | sheet (bed) |
| prastoy | простой | plain |
| prastoy | простой | simple |
| prastuda | простуда | a cold |
| prastupak | проступок | offence |
| pratest | протест | protest |
| pratestavat' | протестовать | to protest |
| prativayaderny | противоядерный | antinuclear |
| prativazachatachnye sretstva | противозачаточные средства | contraceptives |
| pratsent | процент | percent |
| pravaslavnaya tserkaf' | православная церковь | Orthodox Church |
| pravda | правда | truth |
| praveryat'/praverit' | проверять/проверить | to check |
| pravil'ny | правильный | right (correct) |
| pravila | правила | rules |
| pravitel'stva | правительство | government |
| pravy | правый | right-wing |
| prazhektar | прожектор | projector |
| praznavat' | праздновать | to celebrate |
| praznik | праздник | holiday |
| predlazhenie | предложение | proposal |
| predlazhenie | предложение | sentence (words) |
| predpachitat'/ predpachest' | предпочитать/ предпочесть | to prefer |
| preduprezhdat'/ predupredit' | предупреждать/ предупредить | to warn |
| preimushchestva | преимущество | advantage |
| prezident | президент | president |
| pribaltika | Прибалтика | the Baltics |
| pribyl' | прибыль | profit |
| pribytie | прибытие | arrivals |
| prichina | причина | reason |
| priezhat'/priekhat' | приезжать/приехать | to arrive |
| prigarat | пригород | suburb |
| prigatavlyat'/ prigatovit' | приготавливать/ приготовить | to prepare |
| prigavor | приговор | sentence (prison) |
| prikhadit'/priyti | приходить/прийти | to come |
| prilif | прилив | tide (high) |
| primer | пример | example |
| prinimat'/prinyat' | принимать/принять | to accept |
| priroda | природа | nature |
| prismatrivat'/ prismatret' | присматривать/ присмотреть | to look after |

| | | |
|---|---|---|
| pristrastie k narkotikam | пристрастие к наркотикам | drug addiction |
| privatizasiya | приватизация | privatisation |
| privifka | прививка | vaccination |

priyatnava apetita!
**Приятного аппетита!**
Bon appétit!

| | | |
|---|---|---|
| probavat'/paprobavat' | пробовать/попробовать | to try (to taste) |
| proizvedenie iskustva | произведение искусства | artwork |
| propka | пробка | plug (bath) |
| proshlae | прошлое | past |
| protif | против | against/opposite |
| provalaka | проволока | wire |
| prozvishche | прозвище | nickname |
| pryamoy | прямой | direct/straight |
| prygat'/prygnut' | прыгать/прыгнуть | to jump |
| ptitsa | птица | bird |
| pugavitsy | пуговицы | buttons |
| pul | пулька | pool (game) |
| purpurny | пурпурный | purple |
| pustoy | пустой | empty |
| pustynya | пустыня | desert |
| puteshestvavat' | путешествовать | to travel |
| puteshestvie | путешествие | journey |
| puteshestvovat' aftastopam | путешествовать автостопом | to hitchhike |
| putevaditel' | путеводитель | guidebook |

# R

| | | |
|---|---|---|
| rabochiy (m)/rabochaya (f) | рабочий/рабочая | factory/manual worker |
| rabota pa domu | работа по дому | housework |
| rabota | работа | job/work |
| rabotadatel' | работодатель | employer |
| rabotat' | работать | to work |
| rabotat' na sebya | работать на себя | to be self-employed |
| radiatar | радиатор | radiator |
| raditeli | родители | parents |
| raman | роман | novel (book) |
| ramans | романс | romance |

rana
рано.
It's early.

| | | |
|---|---|---|
| ranenie | ранение | wound |
| ranniy | ранний | early |

**R**

| | | |
|---|---|---|
| rasa | раса | race (breed) |
| raschyoska | расчёска | comb |
| rasizm | расизм | racism |
| raspisanie | расписание | timetable |
| rasskas | рассказ | story |
| rasskazy | рассказы | short stories |
| rasslablyat'sya/ rasslabit'sya' | расслабляться/ расслабиться | to relax |
| rassmatrivat' vetriny | рассматривать ветрины | to (go) window-shopping |
| rassvet | рассвет | dawn |
| rastenie | растение | plant |
| rastitel'nast' | растительность | vegetation |
| rastroystva pishchevaveniya | растройство пищеварения | indigestion |
| rastyazhenie svyazak | растяжение связок | a sprain |
| ravnapravie | равноправие | equality |
| ravnye vazmozhnasti | равные возможности | equal opportunity |
| razgavarivat' | разговаривать | to talk |
| razhdestvo | Рождество | Christmas |
| razrushat'/razrushit' | разрушать/разрушить | to destroy |
| razmer | размер | size |
| razmyshlenie | размышление | reflection (thinking) |
| razreshenie na rabotu | разрешение на работу | work permit |
| razreshenie | разрешение | permit (piece of paper) |
| razresheno | разрешено | it's allowed |
| razvaliny | развалины | ruins |
| rebyonak | ребёнок | baby |
| redaktar | редактор | editor |
| referi | рефери | referee |
| regional'ny | региональный | regional |
| registratsiya mashyny | регистрация машины | car registration |
| registratsiya | регистрация | check-in (desk) |
| reka | река | river |
| rekamendavat' | рекомендовать | to recommend |
| rekamendatsiya | рекомендация | reference (recommendation) |
| reket | рэкет | protection racket |
| religiozny | религиозный | religious |
| religiya | религия | religion |
| remyosla | ремёсла | crafts |
| reshat'/reshyt' | решать/решить | to decide |
| respublika | республика | republic |
| restaran | ресторан | restaurant |
| retkiy | редкий | rare |
| retsenziya | рецензия | review |

**D
I
C
T
I
O
N
A
R
Y**

| revalyutsiya | революция | revolution |
| revnivy | ревнивый | jealous |
| reysavy aftobus | рейсовый автобус | local/city bus |
| rezat'/narezat' | резать/нарезать | to cut |
| rezyume | резюме | resumé |
| risk | риск | risk |
| ritm | ритм | rhythm |
| rok-gruppa | рок-группа | rock group |
| roskosh' | роскошь | luxury |
| rot | рот | mouth |
| rozavy | розовый | pink |
| rubashka | рубашка | shirt |
| ruchka | ручка | pen (ballpoint) |
| ruchnaya rabota | ручная работа | handicrafts |
| ruchnoy raboty | ручной работы | handmade |
| ruka | рука | arm |
| ruka | рука | hand |
| rukavaditel' | руководитель | leader |
| ryadam s | рядом с | beside/next to |
| ryba | рыба | fish |
| rybny magazin | рыбный магазин | fish shop |
| rynak | рынок | market |
| ryugzak | рюкзак | backpack |

## S

| s | с | since (May)/with |
| sabaka | собака | dog |
| sabor | собор | cathedral |
| sachel'nik | Сочельник | Christmas Eve |
| sachustvenny | сочувственный | sympathetic |
| sad | парк | garden |
| sadit'sa/sest' | садиться/сесть | to board (ship etc) |
| saglashat'sa/ | соглашаться/ | to agree |
| saglasit'sa | согласиться | |

ya ne saglasen (m)/saglasna (f)
**я не согласен/согласна.**
I don't agree.

| sakhar | сахар | sugar |
| salfetki | салфетки | tissues |
| samaapsluzhyvanie | самообслуживание | self-service |
| samakritika | самокритика | self-criticism |
| samalyot | самолёт | plane |
| samy luchshiy | самый лучший | best |
| sani | сани | sleigh |

# RUSSIAN – ENGLISH

| | | |
|---|---|---|
| sanitarnaya sumka | санитарная сумка | first-aid kit |
| sapagi | сапоги | boots |
| sasna | сосна | pine |
| satsial'ae abespechenie | социальное обеспечение | welfare |
| satsialist (m)/satsialistka (f) | социалист/социалистка | socialist |
| savetskiy | советский | Soviet |
| sazhalet' | сожалеть | to regret |
| seks | секс | sex |
| sel'skae khazyaystva | сельское хозяйство | agriculture |
| sem'ya | семья | family |
| semeynoye palazheniye | семейное положение | marital status |
| sennaya likharatka | сенная лихорадка | hayfever |
| serdity | сердитый | angry |
| serttse | сердце | heart |
| sery | серый | grey |
| sestra | сестра | sister |
| sever | север | north |
| sevodnya vecheram | сегодня вечером | tonight |
| sevodnya | сегодня | today |
| seychas | сейчас | now |
| seychas zhe | сейчас же | right now |
| seyf | сейф | a safe |
| shakalat | шоколад | chocolate |
| shakhmaty | шахматы | chess |

shakh i mat!
**шах и мат!**
Checkmate!

| | | |
|---|---|---|
| shampanskae | шампанское | champagne |
| shans | шанс | chance |
| shapka | шапка | fur hat |
| sharf | шарф | scarf |
| shase | шоссе | motorway (tollway) |
| shaslivy | счастливый | lucky |
| shast'e | счастье | luck |
| shchenok | щенок | puppy |
| shchyotka dlya valos | щётка для волос | hairbrush |
| sherst' | шерсть | wool |
| shitat'/pashitat' | считать/посчитать | to count |
| shkaf | шкаф | wardrobe |
| shorty | шорты | shorts |
| shpion (m)/shpionka (f) | шпион/шпионка | spy |
| shprits | шприц | needle /syringe |
| shto | что | what |

shto on gavarit?
**Что он говорит?**
What is he saying?

shto vy delaete?
**Что вы делаете?**
What are you doing?

| shtopar | штопор | bottle opener (wine) |
| shto-ta | что-то | something |
| shtraf | штраф | a fine |
| shum | шум | noise |
| shumny | шумный | noisy |
| shutit'/pashutit' | шутить/пошутить | to joke |
| shutka | шутка | joke |
| shyaslivy | счастливый | happy |

shyasliva!
**Счастливо!**
Good luck!

shyaslivava puti!
**Счастливого пути!**
Bon voyage!

| shyny | шины | tyres |
| shyolk | шёлк | silk |
| shyot | счёт | bill (account) |
| shyoty | счёты | abacus |
| shyrokiy | широкий | wide |
| shyshka | шишка | lump |
| sibir' | Сибирь | Siberia |
| sidet' | сидеть | to sit |
| sigareta | сигарета (Western style) | cigarette |
| sigarety s fil'tram | сигареты с фильтром | filtered (cigarettes) |
| sil'ny | сильный | strong |
| sila | сила | strength |
| sinagoga | синагога | synagogue |
| kholast (m)/ ne zamuzhem (f) | холост/ не замужем | single (person) |
| sinniy | синий | blue (dark) |
| sinteicheskiy | синтетический | synthetic |
| sinyak | синяк | bruise |

skol'ka stoit paestka v ...?
**Сколько стоит поездка в ...?**
How much does it cost to go to ...?

| skalalazanie | скалолазание | rock climbing |
| skavarada | сковорода | pan |
| skazat' | сказать | to tell |

skazhyte, kak papast' k ...?
**Скажите, как попасть к ...?**
Please tell me the way to ...

| skitka | скидка | discount |
|---|---|---|
| skushny | скучный | boring |
| slabitel'nae | слабительное | laxatives |
| slaby | слабый | weak |
| slatkiy | сладкий | sweet |
| slavar' | словарь | dictionary |
| slayt | слайд | slide (film) |
| sledavat'/pasledavat' | следовать/последовать | to follow |
| sleduyushchiy | следующий | next |
| slepoy | слепой | blind |
| slet | след | track (footprints) |
| sleza | слеза | tear (crying) |
| slishkam doraga | слишком дорого | too expensive |
| slishkam mnoga | слишком много | too much; many |
| slomanny | сломанный | broken (doesn't work) |
| slova | слово | word |
| slukhavoy apparat | слуховой аппарат | hearing aid |
| slushat' | слушать | to listen |
| sluzhayshchiy (m)/ | служащий/ | employee |
| sluzhayshchaya (f) | служащая | |
| sluzhayshchiy | служащий | office worker |
| sluzhba | служба | service (religious) |
| slyakat' | слякоть | mud |
| slyshat'/uslyshat' | слышать | to hear |
| smatret' | смотреть | to watch |
| smatret'/pasmatret' | смотреть/посмотреть | to look |
| smekh | смех | laugh |
| smeshyvat'/smeshat' | смешивать/смешать | to mix |
| smushchyony | смущённый | embarrassed |
| snadvornye tabletki | снотворный таблетки | sleeping pills |
| snaruzhy | снаружи | outside |
| snimak | снимок | photo |
| sok | сок | juice |
| sol' | соль | salt |
| solnechny azhog | солнечный ожог | sunburn |
| solnechny | солнечный | sunny |
| solntse | солнце | sun |
| solntsezashchitny krem | солнцезащитный крем | sunblock |
| sonny | сонный | sleepy |
| soska | соска | dummy/pacifier |
| sotaviy telefon | сотовый телефон | mobile phone |
| spal'nya | спальня | bedroom |
| spal'ny meshok | спальный мешок | sleeping bag |
| spal'ny vagon | спальный вагон | sleeping car |
| spartsmen (m)/spartsmenka (f) | спортсмен/спортсменка | player (sports) |
| spasat'/spasti | спасать/спасти | to save |

spasiba
**спасибо.**
Thank you.

| | | |
|---|---|---|
| spat' | спать | to sleep |
| spektakl' | спектакль | performance/show |
| speshyt' | спешить | to be in a hurry |
| spesnya | песня | ong |
| spetsialist pa travam | специалист по травам | herbalist |
| spetsialist | специалист | specialist |
| spichki | спички | matches |
| spina | спина | back (body) |
| spit | СПИД | AIDS |
| sploshchat' | площадь | square (in town) |
| spolki | полки | shelves |
| sporit' | спорить | to argue |
| sport | спорт | game (sport) |
| sportzal | спортзал | gym |
| sprashivat'/sprasit' | спрашивать/спросить | to ask (a question) |
| spravedlivast' | справедливость | justice |
| spruzhyna | пружина | pring (coil) |
| srakavina | раковина | hell |
| srazumny | разумный | ensible |
| srednyaya aziya | Средняя Азия | Central Asia |
| srednyaya shkola | средняя школа | high school |
| sremen' | ремень | seatbelt |
| srochny | срочный | urgent |
| srok polnomochy | срок полномочий | term of office |
| satsial'nae abespechenie | социальное обеспечение | social security |
| sekretarsha | секретарь | secretary |
| seksual'ny | сексуальный | sexy |
| sekunda | секунда | second (n) |
| ser'yozny | серьёзный | serious |
| seriya | серия | series |
| shampun' | шампунь | shampoo |
| shkola | школа | school |
| skora | скоро | soon |
| skorast' | скорость | speed |
| skul'ptura | скульптура | sculpture |
| sora | ссора | quarrel |
| spartsmen (m)/spartsmenka (f) | спортсмен/спортсменка | sportsperson |
| stadion | стадион | stadium |
| statuya | статуя | statue |
| stsena | сцена | stage |
| suvenirny magazin | сувенирный магазин | souvenir shop |
| stakan | стакан | glass |
| stantsiya metro | станция метро | subway station |

# RUSSIAN – ENGLISH

**S**

| | | |
|---|---|---|
| starana | сторона | side |
| starat'sa/pastarat'sa | стараться/постараться | to try (to attempt) |
| stary | старый | old |
| stary gorat | старый город | old city |
| stavit'/pastavit' mashynu | ставить/поставить машину | to park |
| stayanka taksi | стоянка такси | taxi stand |
| stena | стена | wall |
| stepen' | степень | degree (academic) |
| stil' | стиль | style |
| stipendiya | стипендия | stipend |
| stiral'naya mashyna | стиральная машина | washing machine |
| stirat'/vystirat' | стирать/выстирать | to wash (something) |
| sto | сто | a hundred |
| stoimost' | стоимость | value (price) |
| stoit' | стоить | to cost |
| stol | стол | table |

**stop!**
**Стоп!**
**Stop!**

| | | |
|---|---|---|
| stoyka vydachi bagazha | стойка выдачи багажа | baggage claim |
| straitel'nye raboty | строительные работы | construction work |
| strakh | страх | fear |
| strakhavanie | страхование | insurance |
| strana | страна | country (nation) |
| stranitsa | страница | page |
| stranny | странный | strange |
| stroit'/pastroit' | строить | to build |
| stsenicheskoye iskustva | сценическое искусство | performance art |
| student (m)/studentka (f) | студент/студентка | student |
| studiya | студия | studio |
| stul | стул | chair |
| stupen' | ступень | step |
| subota | суббота | Saturday |
| subtitry | субтитры | subtitles |
| sud'ya | судья | judge |
| sumachka | сумочка | handbag |
| sumashedshiy | сумасшедший | crazy/mad |
| sushyt'/vysushyt' | сушить/высушить | to dry (clothes) |
| sut | суд | court (legal) |
| suvenir | сувенир | souvenir |
| svabodny | свободный | free (not bound) |
| svad'ba | свадьба | wedding |
| svadebny padarak | свадебный подарок | wedding present |
| svecha | свеча | candle |

**DICTIONARY**

291

| | | |
|---|---|---|
| svekrof' | свекровь | mother-in-law (husband's mother) |
| svet | свет | light (sun/lamp) |
| svetafor | светофор | traffic lights |
| svetly | светлый | light (adj) |
| svezhemarozhennye pradukty | свежемороженые продукты | frozen foods |
| svidanie | свидание | date (with someone) |
| svidetel'stva | свидетельство | certificate |
| svidetel'stva a razhdenii | свидетельство о рождении | birth certificate |
| svin'ya | свинья | pig |
| svyashchennik | священник | priest |
| svyataya nedelya | Святая Неделя | Holy Week |
| svyatoy | святой | saint |
| svyaz' | связь | relationship |
| svyokar | свёкор | father-in-law (husband's) |
| syn | сын | son |
| syp' | сыпь | a rash |
| syr | сыр | cheese (hard) |
| syroy | сырой | raw |
| syurpris | сюрприз | a surprise |

# T

| | | |
|---|---|---|
| t'yurma | тюрьма | jail |
| tabak | табак | tobacco |
| tabachny kiosk | табачный киоск | tobacco kiosk |
| tabletka | таблетка | pill |
| tablo | табло | scoreboard |
| taksicheskiye atkhody | токсические отходы | toxic waste |
| talkat'/talknut' | толкать/толкнуть | to push |
| talon | талон | coupon |
| tamozhnya | таможня | customs |
| tampony | тампоны | tampons |
| (palchasa) tamu nazat | (пол-часа) тому назад | (half an hour) ago |
| tantsy | танцы | dancing |
| taryelka | тарелка | plate |
| tashnata | тошнота | nausea |
| taskavat' pa | тосковать по | to miss (feel absence) |
| teatr | театр | theatre |

| | | |
|---|---|---|
| tekhnicheskiy paspart | технический паспорт | car owner's title |
| tekhnika | техника | technique |
| tekhnikum | техникум | college |
| tela | тело | body |
| telefon | телефон | telephone |
| telefonnaya butka | телефонная будка | phone box |
| telefonnaya kartachka | телефонная карточка | phonecard |
| telefonnaya kniga | телефонная книга | phone book |

   ya vam pazvanyu
   **Я вам позвоню.**
   I'll give you a call.

| | | |
|---|---|---|
| telegrama | телеграмма | telegram |
| teleskop | телескоп | telescope |
| televizar | телевизор | TV |
| temperatura | температура | temperature (weather) |
| ten' | тень | shade/shadow |
| tennis | теннис | tennis |
| tennisny kort | теннисный корт | tennis court |
| terpelivy | терпеливый | patient (adj) |
| teryat'/pateryat' | терять/потерять | to lose |
| test' | тесть | father-in-law (wife's) |
| tikhiy | тихий | quiet |
| tol'ka | только | only |
| tolsty | толстый | fat/thick |
| tonkiy | тонкий | thin |
| tora | Тора | Torah |
| tot zhe (m)/ta zhe (f) | тот же/та же | same |
| tozhe | тоже | also |
| tozhe | тоже | too (as well) |
| tramvay | трамвай | tram |
| trapinka | тропинка | path |
| tratuar | тротуар | footpath |
| trava | трава | grass |
| travma | травма | injury |
| trovy | травы | herbs |
| trek | трэк | track (car-racing) |
| trogat'/tronut' | трогать/тронуть | to touch |
| truba | труба | pipe |
| trudavoy lager' | трудовой лагерь | labour camp |
| trudny | трудный | difficult |
| trudny | трудный | hard (difficult) |
| tselavat'/patselavat' | целовать/поцеловать | to kiss |
| tsely | целый | whole |
| tsena | цена | price |

| | | |
|---|---|---|
| tsennast' | ценность | worth |
| tsenny | ценный | valuable |
| tsentr gorada | центр города | city centre |
| tsentral'naya ploshchat' | центральная площадь | main square |
| tserkaf' | церковь | church |
| tsvet | цвет | colour |
| tsvetok | цветок | flower |
| tsyfry | цифры | figures |
| tsyrk | цирк | circus |
| tantsevat' | танцевать | to dance |
| tipichny | типичный | typical |
| tualetnaya bumaga | туалетная бумага | toilet paper |
| tualety | туалеты | toilets |
| tufli | туфли | shoes |

tumana
**Туманно.**
It's foggy.

| | | |
|---|---|---|
| tundra | тундра | tundra |
| turbaza | турбаза | youth hostel |
| turist (m)/turistka (f) | турист | tourist |
| turisticheskiye batinki | туристические ботинки | hiking boots |
| turisticheskiye marshruty | туристические маршруты | hiking routes |
| turisticheskoye byuro | туристическое бюро | tourist information |
| tvyordy | твёрдый | solid |
| tyanut'/patyanut' | тянуть/потянуть | to pull |
| tyazholy | тяжёлый | heavy |
| tyomny | тёмный | dark |
| tyoply | тёплый | warm |
| tyoshcha | тёща | mother-in-law (wife's mother) |
| tyotya | тётя | aunt |
| tyur'ma | тюрьма | prison |

## U

| | | |
|---|---|---|
| u (possessor) est' | у (possessor) есть | to have |

u menya est' ...
**У меня есть ...**
I have ...

u menya kruzhytsa galava

**У меня кружится голова.**

I feel dizzy.

u vas est' ...?

**У Вас есть ...?**

Do you have ...?

| | | |
|---|---|---|
| ubaltivat'/ubaltat' | убалтывать/уболтать | to chat up |
| ubivat'/ubit' | убивать/убить | to kill |
| uchit'/vyuchit' | учить/выучить | to learn |
| uchitel' (m)/uchitel'nitsa (f) | учителью/учительница | teacher |
| uchyony (m)/uchyonaya (f) | учёный/учёная | scientist |
| udaryat'/udarit' nagoy | ударятв/ударитв ногой | kick |
| udastavereniye lichnosti | удостоверение личности | identification card |
| ugal | угол | corner |
| uikend | уикенд | weekend |
| ukazatel' | указатель | indicator |
| ukazyvat'/ukazat' | указывать/указать | to point |
| ukha | ухо | ear |
| ukhazhyvat' (za) | ухаживать (за) | to care (for) |
| ukus | укус | bite (dog, insect) |
| ulichny muzykant | уличный музыкант | busker |
| ulitsa | улица | street |
| ulybat'sa/ulybnut'sa | улыбаться/улыбнуться | to smile |
| um | ум | mind |
| umeret' | умереть | to die |
| umyvat'sa/umyt'sa | умываться/умыться | to wash (oneself) |
| univermak | универмаг | department store |
| universitet | университет | university |
| upryamy | упрямый | stubborn |
| upryash' | упряжь | harness |
| urazhay | урожай | harvest |
| ushchimleniye praf | ущемление прав | harassment |
| ushy | уши | ears |
| uskiy | узкий | tight |
| usluga | услуга | service (assistance) |
| usny | устный | oral |
| uspekh | успех | success |
| ustal (m)/ustala (f) | устал/устала | tired |
| ustanavleniye lichnosti | установление личности | identification |
| utilizatsiya | утилизация | recycling |
| utra | утро | morning (6am-1pm) |

| utyos | утёс | cliff |
| uval'nenie | увольнение | dismissal |
| uvazhenie | уважение | respect |
| uvlazhnyaushchiy krem | увлажняющий крем | moisturising cream |
| uyutny | уютный | comfortable |
| uzhasny | ужасный | awful/horrible/terrible |
| uzhe | уже | already |
| uzhyn | ужин | dinner (evening meal) |
| uznavat'/uznat' | узнавать/узнать | to recognise |

## V

| v etam gadu | в этом году | this year |
| v etam mesyatse | в этом месяце | this month |
| v goru | в гору | uphill |
| vaaruzhenie | вооружение | armaments |
| vada | вода | water |
| vadapat | водопад | waterfall |
| vaditel'skie prava | водительские права | driver's licence |
| vaennaya sluzhba | военная служба | military service |
| vaenny | военный | military |
| vagon-restaran | вагон-ресторан | dining car |
| vagzal | вокзал | railway station |
| vakantny | вакантный | vacant |
| valna | волна | wave |
| vanna | ванна | bath |
| vannaya | ванная | bathroom |
| vapros | вопрос | question |
| varota | ворота | gate |

vashe zdarov'e!
Ваше здоровье!
Good health!; Cheers!

| vastok | восток | east |
| vayna i mir | Война и Мир | War and Peace |
| vayna | война | war |
| vazhny | важный | important |

vazhna
Важно.
It's important.

ne vazhna
Не важно.
It's not important.

# RUSSIAN – ENGLISH

**V**

| vazmozhny | возможный | possible |
| vazvrashchat'sa/<br>vernut'sa | возвращаться/<br>вернуться | to return |
| vazvrashchenie denek | возвращение денег | refund |
| vecher | вечер | evening |
| vecherinka | вечеринка | party (fiesta) |
| vechnaya merzlata | вечная мерзлота | permafrost |
| vedro | ведро | bucket |
| vedushchiy | ведущий | presenter (TV, etc) |
| vegetarianskiy | вегетарианский | vegetarian |

ya vegetarianets (m)/vegetarianka (f)
**Я вегетарианец/вегетарианка.**
I'm vegetarian.

| velasipedist | велосипедист | cyclist |
| velasipet | велосипед | bicycle |
| velikiy | великий | great |
| velikiy post | Великий Пост | Lent |
| vena | вена | vein |
| venericheskaya balezn' | венерическая болезнь | venereal disease |
| venik | веник | twigs (for bathhouse) |
| ventilyatar | вентилятор | fan (machine) |
| verkhavaya ezda | верховая езда | horse riding |

verna
**Верно.**
It's true.

| verny | верный | loyal |
| veryofka | верёвка | rope/string |
| ves | вес | weight |

vesela
**весело**
It's fun.

| veselit'sa | веселиться | to have fun |
| vesna | весна | spring (season) |
| vetchina | ветчина | ham |
| veter | ветер | wind |
| vetravoe steklo | ветровое стекло | windscreen |
| vich infetsiravany | ВИЧ инфицированный | HIV positive |
| videokaseta | видеокассета | video tape |
| videt' son | видеть сон | to dream |
| vilka | вилка | plug (electricity) |

**DICTIONARY**

297

| vina | вина | fault (someone's) |
|---|---|---|
| vinadel'nya | винодельня | winery |
| vinagradnaya laza | виноградная лоза | vine |
| vinagradnik | виноградник | vineyard |
| vinagrat | виноград | grapes |
| vino | вино | wine |
| virus | вирус | virus |
| vit | вид | view |
| vitaminy | витамины | vitamins |
| viza | виза | visa |
| vizit | визит | appointment (doctor) |
| vladelets | владелец | owner |
| vlast' | власть | power |
| vmeste | вместе | together |
| vnuk (m)/vnuchka (f) | внук/внучка | grandchild |
| vnutri | внутри | inside |
| volasy | волосы | hair |
| vor | вор | thief |
| votka | водка | vodka |
| vovremya | вовремя | on time |
| vozdukh | воздух | air |
| vozrast | возраст | age |
| vrach | врач | doctor |
| vratar' | вратарь | goalkeeper |
| vremya | время | time |
| vverkh | вверх | up |
| vy | Вы | you (pol) |

vy mozhete (pamoch' mne)?
Вы можете (помочь мне)?
Can you (help me)?

vy pravy
Вы правы.
You're right.

| vybary | выборы | elections |
|---|---|---|
| vybirat'/vybrat' | выбирать/выбрать | to choose |
| vyigryvat'/vyigrat' | выигрывать/выиграть | to win |
| vykhadit'/ | выходить\ | to marry |
| vyti zamush | выйти замуж | (take a husband) |
| vykhat | Выход | exit/way out |
| vykidysh | выкидыш | miscarriage |
| vyrupka lesa | вырубка леса | deforestation |
| vysata | высота | altitude |

| vysmeivat' | высмеивать | to make fun of |
| vysokiy | высокий | high |
| vysokiy | высокий | tall |
| vystafka | выставка | exhibition |
| vystup | выступ | ledge |
| vzbirat'sa/ vzabrat'sa na | взбираться/ взбираться на | to scale/climb |
| vzrosly (m)/vzroslaya (f) | взрослый/взрослая | adult |
| vzveshyvat'/vzvesit' | взвешивать/взвесить | to weigh |

## Y

| ya | я | I |

ya vinavat/vinavata
**Я виноват/Я виновата.**
I'm wrong. (my fault)

| yadernaya energiya | ядерная энергия | nuclear energy |
| yagady | ягоды | berries |
| yantar' | янтарь | amber |
| yasli | ясли | childminding |
| yazyk | язык | language |
| yuk | юг | south |
| yuvelirnye izdeliya | ювелирные изделия | jewellery |

## Z

| z bia-dabafkami | с био-добавками | biodegradable |
| za | за | behind |
| za granitsey | за границей | abroad |
| zabastofka | забастовка | a strike |
| zabavny | забавный | entertaining |
| zabor | забор | fence |
| zabotit'sa (o) | заботиться (о) | to care (about) |
| zabotlivy | заботливый | caring |
| zabyvat'/zabyt' | забывать/забыть | to forget |

ya zabyl (m)/ya zabyla (f)
**Я забыл/забыла.**
I forget.

| zadershka | задержка | delay |
| zadiak | зодиак | zodiac |
| zaftra | завтра | tomorrow |
| zaftrak | завтрак | breakfast |

| zakanchivat'sa/ zakonchit'sa | заканчиваться/ закончиться | to end |
|---|---|---|
| zakat | закат | sunset |
| zakaznoe pis'mo | заказное письмо | registered mail |
| zakazyvat'/zakazat' | заказывать/заказать | to book/order/reserve |
| zakon | закон | law |
| zakonadate'stva | законодательство | legislation |
| zakryta | закрыто | closed |
| zakryvat'/zakryt' | закрывать/закрыть | to shut |
| zakryvat'/zakryt' | закрывать/закрыть | to close |
| zal azhydaniya | зал лжидания | waiting room |
| zal azhydaniya | зал ожидания | transit lounge |
| zamok | замок | lock |
| zanuda | зануда | pain in the neck (person) |
| zanyat (m)/zanyata (f) | занят/занята | busy |
| zapadny | западный | west |
| zapakh | запах | a smell |
| zapark | зоопарк | zoo |
| zapavednik | заповедник | national park |
| zapavednik | заповедник | protected forest |
| zapirat'/zaperet' | запирать | to lock |
| zapis' | запись | recording |
| zapiska | записка | message |
| zapor | запор | constipation |

zapreshcheno
**запрещено.**
It's not allowed.

| zarplata | зарплата | salary |
|---|---|---|
| zarya | заря | sunrise |
| zashchishchat'/zashchitit' | защищать/защитить | to protect |
| zastenchivy | застенчивый | shy |
| zavisit at geraina | зависит от героина | heroin addict |
| zazhygalka | зажигалка | lighter |
| zbor fruktaf | сбор фруктов | fruit picking |
| zdanie | здание | building |
| zdarov'e | здоровье | health |
| zdarovy | здоровый | well |
| zdelany iz | сделанный из | made (of) |
| zdes' | здесь | here |

zdrastvuyte!
**Здравствуйте!**
Hello.

| zelyony | зелёный | green |
| zemletryasenie | землетрясение | earthquake |
| zemlya | земля | Earth/land |
| zerkala | зеркало | mirror |
| zhaba | жаба | toad |
| zhakey | жокей | jockey |
| zhara | жара | heat |
| zharkiy | жаркий | hot (weather) |

zharka
**жарко.**
It's hot.

mne zharka
**Мне жарко.**
I'm hot.

| zhelat'/pazhelat' | желать/пожелать | to wish |
| zheleznaya daroga | железная дорога | railroad |
| zheludak | желудок | stomach |
| zhena | жена | wife |
| zhenit'sa | жениться | to marry (take a wife) |
| zhenshchina | женщина | woman |
| zhevatel'naya rezinka | жевательная резинка | chewing gum |
| zholty | жёлтый | yellow |
| zhuk | жук | bug |
| zhurnal | журнал | magazine |
| zhurnalist (m)/ | журналист/ | journalist |
| zhurnalistka (f) | журналистка | |
| zhyrny | жирный | rich (food) |
| zhyt' | жить | to live (somewhere) |
| zhyt' v adnoy komnate | жить в одной комнате | to share a room |
| zhyvapis' | живопись | painting (the art) |
| zhyzneny uraven' | жизненный уровень | standard of living |
| zhyvotnye | животные | animals |
| zhyzn' | жизнь | life |
| zima | зима | winter |
| zimnee adeyala | зимнее одеяло | blanket (thick) |
| znak | знак | a sign |
| znamenity | знаменитый | famous |
| znat' | знать | to know |

ya ne znayu
**Я не знаю.**
I don't know.

| zontik | зонтик | umbrella |
| zubnaya bol' | зубная боль | toothache |
| zubnaya pasta | зубная паста | toothpaste |

| | | |
|---|---|---|
| zubnaya shchyotka | зубная счётка | toothbrush |
| zubnoy vrach | зубной врач | dentist |
| zuby | зубы | teeth |
| zup | зуб | tooth |
| zut | зуд | itch |
| zvanit'/pazv'anit' | звонить/позвонить | to telephone |
| zvanok | звонок | bell (alarm) |
| zvuk | звук | sound |
| zvyozdy | звёзды | stars |
| zzadi | сзади | at the back (behind) |

# INDEX

# RUSSIAN FINDER

F
I
N
D
E
R

F
I
N
D
E
R

F
I
N
D
E
R

NOTES

NOTES

# Phrasebooks

**L** onely Planet phrasebooks are packed with essential words and phrases to help travellers communicate with the locals. With colour tabs for quick reference, an extensive vocabulary and use of script, these handy pocket-sized language guides cover day-to-day travel situations.

- handy pocket-sized books
- easy to understand Pronunciation chapter
- clear & comprehensive Grammar chapter
- romanisation alongside script to allow ease of pronunciation
- script throughout so users can point to phrases for every situation
- full of cultural information and tips for the traveller

'... vital for a real DIY spirit and attitude in language learning'
*– Backpacker*

'the phrasebooks have good cultural backgrounders and offer solid advice for challenging situations in remote locations'
*– San Francisco Examiner*

Australian *(Australian English, Aboriginal & Torres Strait languages)* • Baltic *(Estonian, Latvian, Lithuanian)* • Bengali • Brazilian • British *(English, dialects, Scottish Gaelic, Welsh)* • Burmese • Cantonese • Central Asia *(Kazakh, Kyrgyz, Pashto, Tajik, Tashkorghani, Turkmen, Uyghur, Uzbek & others)* • Central Europe *(Czech, German, Hungarian, Polish, Slovak, Slovene)* • Costa Rica Spanish • Czech • Eastern Europe *(Albanian, Bulgarian, Croatian, Czech, Hungarian, Macedonian, Polish, Romanian, Serbian, Slovak, Slovene)* • East Timor *(Tetun, Portuguese)* • Egyptian Arabic • Ethiopian *(Amharic)* • Europe *(Basque, Catalan, Dutch, French, German, Greek, Irish, Italian, Maltese, Portuguese, Scottish Gaelic, Spanish, Turkish, Welsh)* • Farsi *(Persian)* • Fijian • French • German • Greek • Hebrew • Hill Tribes *(Lahu, Akha, Lisu, Mong, Mien & others)* • Hindi & Urdu • Indonesian • Italian • Japanese • Korean • Lao • Latin American Spanish • Malay • Mandarin • Mongolian • Moroccan Arabic • Nepali • Pidgin • Pilipino *(Tagalog)* • Polish • Portuguese • Quechua • Russian • Scandinavian *(Danish, Faroese, Finnish, Icelandic, Norwegian, Swedish)* • South-East Asia *(Burmese, Indonesian, Khmer, Lao, Malay, Pilipino (Tagalog), Thai, Vietnamese)* • South Pacific *(Fijian, Hawaiian, Kanak languages, Maori, Niuean, Rapanui, Rarotongan Maori, Samoan, Tahitian, Tongan & others)* • Spanish *(Castilian, also includes Catalan, Galician & Basque)* • Sinhala • Swahili • Thai • Tibetan • Turkish • Ukrainian • USA *(US English, vernacular, Native American, Hawaiian)* • Vietnamese

**Also available;** Journeys travel literature, illustrated pictorials, calendars, diaries, Lonely Planet maps and videos. For more information on these series and for the complete range of Lonely Planet products and services, visit our website at **www.lonelyplanet.com**.